CHANGING SEX

AND

BENDING GENDER

SOCIAL IDENTITIES

General Editors: Shirley Ardener, Tamara Dragadze and Jonathan Webber

Based on a prominent Oxford University seminar founded over two decades ago by the social anthropologist Edwin Ardener, this series focuses on the ethnic, historical, religious, and other elements of culture that give rise to a social sense of belonging, enabling individuals and groups to find meaning both in their own social identities and in what differentiates them from others. Each volume is based on one specific theme that brings together contemporary material from a variety of cultures.

CHANGING SEX
AND
BENDING GENDER

Edited by
Alison Shaw and Shirley Ardener

Berghahn Books
New York • Oxford

First published in 2005 by
Berghahn Books
www.berghahnbooks.com

Library of Congress Cataloging-in-Publication Data

Changing sex and bending gender / edited by Alison Shaw and Shirley Ardener.
    p.cm. -- (Social identities ; v. 1)
Includes index.
ISBN 1-84545-053-1 (hardback) -- ISBN 1-84545-099-X (pbk.)
1. Gender identity. 2. Sex role. 3. Body, Human--Social aspects. I. Shaw,
Alison, 1957- II. Ardener, Shirley. III. Series.

HQ1075.C523 2005
305.3--dc22

                                                              2005041084

British Library Cataloguing in Publication Data

A catalogue record for this book is available from the British Library

Printed in the United States on acid-free paper

ISBN 1-84545-053-1 hardback

Widow Twankey from Aladdin. (Courtesy St Joseph's Players, Leigh, Lancaster.)

CONTENTS

LIST OF ILLUSTRATIONS

PREFACE

Shirley Ardener

The theme of this book has emerged as part of a long-standing dialogue focussing around questions of identity and ethnicity, in their various aspects, at a seminar founded by Edwin Ardener. After his death I have carried it on, together with Jonathan Webber and Tamara Dragadze, latterly with Ian Fowler, Lydia Sciama and Elisabeth Hsu, at the Institute of Social and Cultural Anthropology in the University of Oxford. Berg has issued nine books based on the presentations at the seminar.

This volume, which initiates a new cross-cultural series ('Social Identities') being published by Berghahn Books, is also based on papers delivered at the seminar. It could also be seen as a companion to the many books, issued over the years, by the International Gender Studies Centre (first known as the Centre for Cross-Cultural Research on Women) at Queen Elizabeth House, the University of Oxford.

Alison Shaw opens the book with an excellent overview of the field implied by its title, drawing attention to comparative material which could not be explored in detail within its confines, thus providing a context within which to place the contributions which follow.

Suffice to say here that the rest of the volume falls into three main, but overlapping parts. The first three chapters (by Shaw, Dembour and Tougher) deal with the different ways in which humans treat the physical properties of the body which do not conform to socially recognised norms and, or, seek to change their sexual ascription by law. These studies are followed by two contributions (by Littlewood and Young and by Johnson) which illustrate how some women assume new, enduring gender constructions without resort to manipulation of the physical body. Finally we look at three studies (by Moore, Powell and myself) illustrating how, temporarily and publicly, people can imaginatively embody alternative gender roles.

The studies combine to show that 'sex' and 'gender' are not fixed concepts, but can carry a plurality of messages. These can vary over space and time, and from person to person. The stories in the chapters below demonstrate the creativity of persons within their, often confining, social systems. Anomalies and ambiguities inevitably arise as humans seek to create and maintain these systems. Some chapters below tell of the consequent human tragedies and how people struggle to overcome them and make successful lives. Others illustrate how the ambiguities and absurdities of social constructs can be exploited in high art and low comedy, through the imaginative explorations of writers and artists.

Together these texts should increase our understanding of variation in sex and gender identities, the constraints within which people construct these identities, and the impact that socially constructed norms, including those within which doctors and lawyers operate, may have on the lives of others.

1

CHANGING SEX AND BENDING GENDER: AN INTRODUCTION

Alison Shaw

An Indian folk-tale tells the story of two Rajas who agree that if one of them has a son and the other a daughter, their children will marry. When they both have daughters, one Raja disguises his daughter as a boy and raises her as his son. This does not solve the problem of her biological sex, however, and at her marriage the deceit is discovered and the boy's father declares revenge. Desperate, the girl attempts suicide by throwing herself into the river Juma, but instead emerges from it transformed into a male. Her grateful father builds temples on the river bank in gratitude (Penzer 1927: 229–230). In this story, gender is manipulated through disguise and a sex change is effected by supernatural means, for it would have been impossible to achieve, at that time and place, through human efforts alone. In many other myths and legends, a transformation of biological sex is itself the source of the changed person's supernatural powers. For example, the Greek myth of Kaineus tells the story of a young, vulnerable woman who is miraculously transformed into an aggressive and superhuman warrior king. In one version, the transformation of Kainis-the-girl to Kaineus-the-man seems to be a form of revenge, for it occurs after Kainis has been raped by Poseidon, while in another version her sex change happens in time for her to outwit the sea god and avoid the rape (Forbes-Irving 1990: 155–62).

Stories of 'changing sex and bending gender' in folk tales and ancient mythology can thus be regarded as representations of the power of human imagination, as fantastic transformations that could not possibly happen in real life (Forbes-Irving 1990, Warner 2002). In fact, however, the anthropological record shows that changes of sex and transformations of gender occur in a wide range of social contexts and have probably taken place in all known human societies. These changes and transformations take a variety of different forms, ranging from the temporary or intermittent donning of an alternative gender identity, such as in instances of cross-dressing in the theatre, to permanent transformations of biological sex, such as those resulting from modern medical gender reassignment surgery. As we shall see, while some forms of sex change and gender transformation are voluntary, others are enforced, and although some are relatively informal, others are quite elaborately institutionalised. The case studies in this book explore some of these possibilities for changing sex and bending gender. This introduction offers an overview of the forms that sex change and gender transformation have taken, thus providing a context in which the individual contributions to this volume can be considered.

Alterations and transformations of sex and gender occur, by definition, at the boundaries of what a society defines as male or female, boy or girl, and man or woman, usually according to a dual system of classification. For this reason they constitute implicit challenges to conventional sex and gender classifications. Sex changes and gender transformations are often associated with supernatural power, with magic and with danger *precisely* because they occur at boundaries and thus challenge conventional categorisations (Douglas 1966). As we shall see, changes to conventional allocations to sex and gender categories are in some contexts condemned outright as unnatural, while in others they are associated with extraordinary spiritual powers, echoing the magical features of sex change and gender transformation found in folk-tale and myth. They may also be viewed simultaneously as a source of spiritual power and a danger to established conventions and, as such, as phenomena to be contained and controlled and sometimes exploited.

A society's responses to sex change and gender transformation reflects the ways in which it perceives and maintains sex and gender distinctions, including whether two or more sex and gender categories are recognised and what is regarded as 'possible, proper and perverse' in gender-linked behaviour (Ramet 1996: 2). To focus on situations of ambiguous or changed sex and on transformed gender roles and categories, as we do in this book, can illuminate cultural perceptions of what constitute 'normal' sex differences and appropriate expressions of gender, and therefore enrich our insights into different symbolic and social constructions of gender. First, however, some definitions of terms are in order: what do we mean by 'sex' and 'gender'?

Defining sex and gender

The comparative and ethnographic literature is fraught with problems of definition, not least because the relationship between 'sex' and 'gender', and thus between what it means to be male or female, a boy or girl, a man or woman, varies in different cultural contexts. Moreover, some scholars use the term gender synonymously with sex, or else in a way that includes biological sex in order to emphasise that sex too is socially perceived (Kessler and McKenna 1978). However, for the purposes of this introduction, it seems crucial to be able to distinguish the social status of persons as women or men, or occupying alternative or intermediate genders, and their anatomical or genetic status. The term 'sex', as I use it here, refers to the biological characteristics located in anatomical features and physiological processes that people use, in ways that are socially and culturally mediated and not always dichotomous or fixed, to define maleness or femaleness. In this usage, 'sex' is analytically distinguishable from both 'sexuality', which refers to sexual desire and behaviour, and 'gender'. I use 'gender', a term derived from the Latin 'genus' meaning 'kind', 'sort' or 'class', to refer to social categorisations of persons, usually as women or men, boys or girls, in ways that encompass at least some distinct patterns of social and cultural difference and often draw on perceptions of sex (Roscoe 1994: 341). Gender classification is usually dichotomous, but 'third gender' traditions (Herdt 1994) have also been identified, as I discuss below. Sex and gender are not always either mutually exclusive or corresponding categories because ideas about the nature and significance of anatomical and physiological sex differences vary and can influence the rigidity or flexibility of gender categories and, conversely, the social significance of gender in any given context may in turn influence the ways in which biological differences are perceived.

In Western discourses of sex and gender, gender is usually regarded as grounded in, or as an elaboration of, the 'objective reality' of 'natural facts' of sex difference as these are located in anatomy and physiology. Further, sex differences are usually perceived dichotomously as 'male' and 'female'. In this view, nature gives us two sexes and it follows logically that there are therefore two genders. This view of dichotomous sex difference as a natural given is so deeply rooted in Western discourses that it can bias practical research into the nature of variation in human physiology or behaviour. The routine dividing of research subjects into male and female categories, for example, can prejudice the results of research by positing a sex-typed difference at the outset (Kessler and McKenna 1978: 72, Devor 1989: 1–3). The choice of descriptive terminology in research reporting sex differences frequently reflects prior assumptions about the nature of men and women in society, revealing more about gender than about sex (Martin 1991) while negative evidence of sex difference is frequently unreported (Fausto-Sterling 1985). In fact, careful scrutiny of the Western scientific evidence on sex differences suggests that what makes a person male or female, thus determining their biological sex, and what is involved in the construction of gender, in becoming a (culturally defined) boy or girl, man or a woman, is a complex interplay of genetic instruction, hormones, culture and socialisation. Towards understanding these processes, 'the biological sciences, at best, provide only strong suggestions about why human females and males act the way they do' because 'human sex differences can only be described in terms of averages, tendencies and percentages, rather than clear-cut absolutes' (Devor 1989: l).

People in other societies do not necessarily give the same degree of salience to biological difference in their understandings of gender as it is accorded in the West and gender may be, in comparison, relatively independent of biology. In fact, Western understandings of anatomical sex have not been historically consistent, but have changed over time in ways that reflect historical, political and social concerns. Laqueur (1990) argues that the Western 'two sex model' of male and female as incommensurably separate, and a consequence of natural differences grounded in the body, has in fact dominated only since the Enlightenment. For thousands of years previously a 'one sex model' of the genitals prevailed and male and female bodies were seen as mutable, the boundaries between them being 'of degree and not of kind' (Laqueur 1990: 25). Laqueur argues that although gender was an important marker of social status and cultural role before the rise of science and the social and political transformations of the late eighteenth century onwards, it was nevertheless regarded as logically prior to and thus independent of bodily sex.

Human understandings of the body, bodily substance and procreative processes define 'male' and 'female' in socially and culturally specific ways. One example, offered here as illustration, shows how sexual difference may be a matter of degree, or of the relative strength of male and female substances that all bodies contain. The Hua people of the New Guinea highlands, like most other peoples, assign an infant to the male or female sex on the basis of genital configuration at birth. However, a person can become 'more' male or 'more' female according to how much contact they have with female bodily substances. Men absorb female substances by eating food prepared by reproductively active women, through sexual intercourse with women and through casual contact (Meigs 1990). In this example, the substance determining maleness is fluid and sex is thus seen as mutable. Elsewhere, sex differences may be seen as fixed but may still be treated as independent of gender to a significant degree, as we shall see below from examples of females and males in long-term gender-transformed roles.

Some societies have acknowledged that there may be more than two sexes, by recognising an additional sex, or sexes, that combine the features of the other two, and to which persons of ambiguous sex or who have some of the characteristics of both sexes may belong. 'Third sex' categories, as I show in Chapter 2, may also be culturally elaborated as alternative or 'third' genders to which persons who are unambiguously male or female may also choose to belong. The remaining sections of this introduction describe the main forms that sex changes and gender transformations have taken, noting some of their functions and limits. For heuristic purposes, three broad categories can be identified: alterations to the physical body; long-term gender transformations without corresponding sex changes; and, thirdly, temporary or short-term manipulations of gender identity, although, as we shall see, there is often some overlap between these categories.

Changing bodily sex

Alterations to the physical body that can result in a new sex or gender assignation are sometimes performed as surgical procedures in response to the birth of infants with ambiguous genitalia, as I show in Chapter 2. Births of infants with genitalia that cannot be defined as clearly male or female from external observation have occurred in all human societies and are more common than is generally known, probably accounting for almost 2 percent of all live births (Fausto-Sterling 2000:

51). These 'intersex' conditions show that the attributes of biological sex, such as chromosome configuration, internal reproductive structure, external genital morphology and hormonal functions, exist as a continuum of variation, rather than as two discrete categories, but from a social viewpoint they make sex assignment problematic, at birth, in childhood or in later life.

In Chapter 2, I outline some of the cultural responses to this ambiguity. Between the most extreme cultural reactions of horror or of reverence, infants with ambiguous genitalia may also be raised gender-ambiguously, in ways that enable some individuals to become men, others to become women, and yet others to remain ambiguously gendered as adults, as they choose. Thus, infants born with ambiguous genitalia and reared with an ambiguous or, as yet, undetermined gender identity do not, *necessarily*, suffer socially or psychologically in later life, as is assumed in the dominant Western biomedical approach to intersex births. Even so, since the twentieth century the predominant Western medical assumption that unambiguous sex assignment at birth, *combined with* sex-appropriate gender socialisation and sex-appropriate hormonal changes at puberty, is critical for the formation of gender identity has justified many surgical and medical 'corrections' of genital ambiguity in infants.

Another challenge to the dominant biomedical approach to the formation of gender identity comes from people with unambiguous genitalia who grow up identifying strongly with the sex *opposite* to that which they were assigned at birth on the basis of their genital appearance. In some cultures, individuals may identify with at least some characteristics of the 'opposite' sex in a number of culturally recognised ways, including as members of alternative or third gender categories. In contemporary Europe and the United States, some individuals choose to alter their anatomical sex by surgical and hormonal means, not in order to participate in alternative or third gender categories but to achieve physical conformity with the gender with which they identify psychologically.

The term 'transsexual' usually defines both the pre- and post-operative state of individuals who feel they were born mistakenly into the body of the 'wrong' sex, and who therefore present 'a formidable challenge to the assumption that sex-based biological factors determine gender' (Devor 1989: 20).[1] Until recently, in Western Europe and the United States, transsexuals could opt only for surgery and hormonal treatment or for being identified as transvestites or 'cross-dressers' (persons whose gender and sex correspond, but who temporarily dress and act to correspond with the opposite sex and gender). However, recent trans-genderist movements, which seek to challenge the rigidity of the two-gender culture of Western societies, may have made it easier for some individuals to live as 'transgendered' persons without opting for surgery or being categorised as transvestites. Nevertheless, many transsexuals do opt for medical treatment and surgery, 'taking whatever steps they can to alter their sexual status to conform to their gender' (Devor 1989: 20 and 1997).

'Corrective' surgery, however, does not necessarily remove all of the discordance that transsexuals experience between their sex and their gender identity. As

Dembour demonstrates in Chapter 3, the remaining inconsistencies lie within
society rather than in biology. The post-operative transsexual's sexual morphology
may now be regarded as consistent with their gender identity but remain at odds
with their sex as assigned and legally registered at birth. Dembour presents
poignant cases that illustrate the far-reaching implications of this discontinuity.
Dembour's examination of the slowness of the European Court of Human Rights
in responding to individual suffering caused by this discontinuity suggests that a
person's sex, as assigned at birth or defined by their chromosomes, is frequently
still accorded primacy.

Tougher's discussion in Chapter 4 offers another perspective on the consequences of alterations to anatomical sex, this time through castration, from the
historical example of eunuchs in Byzantium. A 'true' eunuch is a male who has
been castrated, usually deliberately and before puberty, often in order to qualify
for specialist roles (such as slaves, courtiers, administrators, musicians, singers and
religious specialists). Early castration lessens the effect of the hormone androgen
at puberty and produces the eunuch's characteristic high-pitched voice, lack of
facial hair and 'female' distribution of body fat (as famously illustrated by the
European *castrati*, men castrated before puberty in order to retain their soprano
or alto voices). Castration was often enforced, as in the case of imported slaves
who were portrayed with ambivalence and hostility in the late antique texts that
Tougher analyses. Paradoxically, such men sometimes gained economically and in
power and reputation, and Tougher suggests that by the early twelfth century,
social perceptions of eunuchs had changed. Eunuchs were more likely to be
recruited from within Byzantium: parents would castrate their own sons to give
them opportunities for court careers, while some men chose to become religious
eunuchs whose self-imposed chastity was thought to enable them to reach a
higher state of purity than was attainable without castration. Tougher's discussion
of this shift in the social circumstances of eunuchs is suggestive of how cultural
perceptions of sex and gender are often inconsistent at any one time, and liable
to alter in response to socio-economic and political change. My chapter, likewise,
draws attention to the dynamics of cultural responses to intersex births and accidental mutilations.

Long-term gender transformations

While genital surgery, or being born with ambiguous genitalia, can result in either
enforced or voluntary gender transformations (with varying degrees of success),
gender transformation is also possible *without* changing sex, in this case usually
requiring some form of ritual marking and modifications to secondary sexual
characteristics such as bodily hair. Such gender transformations are often discussed as 'cross-dressing' because they are always effected and expressed, at least
in part, through clothing – a universal symbol of gender difference. Long-term or
permanent gender alterations are discussed here as: transformations to a culturally
recognised 'alternative' gender; disguise as someone of the 'opposite' gender; and

adoption of gender identities and roles that 'blend' aspects of both genders but lack formal cultural recognition as alternative genders. Historically and cross-culturally, it has been far more common for biological females to adopt aspects of the social identity, role and gender attributes of men on a long-term or permanent basis, than for men to dress, live and work as women. While the definition of 'female subordination' and the assumption of its universality is problematic (Sanday and Goodenough 1990), the general explanation for this lies with the limitations of socially acceptable roles for women, with the exceptions proving, on close scrutiny, to prove the rule.

Women in transformed gender roles

In some strongly gender-differentiated societies, history, demography, custom and tradition combine to allow women to adopt at least some aspects of men's roles. One example comes from a remote region of the Himalayan foothills (Phillimore 1991). As elsewhere in South Asian society, it is extremely unusual for a woman to remain unmarried, for an unmarried woman is a burden and potential liability to her natal family. In the Himalayan foothills, however, some women choose to become female saints, called *sadhin*. A *sadhin* can take on many of a man's social roles and behavioural attributes, can wear men's clothes and can cut her hair short like a man. Becoming a *sadhin* is regarded as a respectable alternative to marriage for a female. Her status as a saint or ascetic, however, is not directly equivalent to that of a male renouncer. A man can become an ascetic, renouncing worldly responsibilities, at any time in his life, regardless of financial or family commitments, but a girl becomes a *sadhin* specifically at puberty as an alternative to marriage and remains living 'in the world', at home (Phillimore 1991: 332). In effect, she exchanges the status and reproductive potential of married womanhood for aspects of male religious privilege. Becoming a *sadhin* transforms her not into a man but into a celibate woman, who retains her female name with the suffix Devi. A further limit to her gender transformation is revealed in the ambiguity that surrounds her participation at cremations for, conventionally, Hindu cremations can only be attended by men.

A second example, discussed by Littlewood and Young in Chapter 5, comes from Northern Albania. Northern Albanian society is rigidly patriarchal, gender roles are firmly demarcated and women are expected to marry and have children. However, a Southern Balkan tradition, reported from Albania, Serbia, Kosova, Bosnia, Montenegro and Macedonia, allows a woman access to male status and privilege by becoming a 'sworn virgin', known in Serb as *muskobanja* or 'man-like woman'. A girl, at puberty, may make a ritually marked vow to remain a virgin and thus to remain unmarried. She may take a masculine name, dress as a man, take a man's social role, with its corresponding social autonomy and physical freedoms, and be treated with deference by the women of her household. This institution is particularly important for households lacking a son because, although not entitled to inherit property herself, a 'sworn virgin' holds rights in property as a conduit for her closest male descendants.[2] While particular women may have felt compelled to become sworn virgins because of family circumstance, Littlewood and Young's contemporary case material suggests that women may become 'sworn virgins' for the perceived advantages of the role.

This section would be incomplete without mention of the *berdache* or 'two spirit' traditions of the less strongly gender-differentiated societies of many Native American tribes, which sometimes included gender-transformed females (Blackwood 1984). 'Two spirits' were persons with qualities of both men and women, whose attire combined aspects of both, and whose spiritual knowledge and specialist skills were highly valued. Most 'two spirits' were gender-transformed males, but in perhaps ten to fifty percent of all the tribes with 'two spirits', female 'two spirits' were also recognised, sometimes by a distinct term, for instance, as *hwame* as distinct from *alyha* (male 'two spirits') among the Mohaves of the Colorado River area (Callender and Kochems 1983, Roscoe 1994). Female 'two spirits' participated in men's ceremonials including their sweat baths in which men seemed not to notice a female two-spirit's anatomical sex (Blackwood 1984: 32).

Women disguised as men

Gender transformation for females has also been effected through a tradition of disguise. The European historical record documents some striking instances of female-to-male gender transformation in the many cases of women who disguised themselves as men in order to take up careers closed to women and thus to escape the restrictions of life as women. In the Middle Ages, certain women, some of whom became legendary, chose to live as men, 'in order to preserve their virginity and become closer to god', some eventually being canonised as saints (Bullough and Bullough 1993: 57, 51–6). The famous example of Joan of Arc (who wore male clothes, rallied French troops to victory against the English in the mid-fifteenth century and reversed the fortunes of Dauphin, Charles of France) actually departs from the tradition of full disguise as a man, for Joan did not conceal the fact that she was female. Nevertheless, her refusal to wear women's clothes became one of the excuses given for her execution (Bullough and Bullough 1993: 57); her canonisation only took place in 1920. The power of Joan's story, over the centuries, lies in the fact that Joan 'placed herself...on borders' (Warner 1981: 23), not just national boundaries, but the boundaries of sex and gender. Joan was viewed as an ambiguous female, who did not menstruate, had not been transformed to womanhood by marriage, and had remained in the liminal state of virginity that is often associated with power and danger (Hastrup 1978).

Over and over again, the theme of rebellion against the restrictions of women's lives occurs in historical accounts of women who disguised themselves as men, to become adventurers, sailors or soldiers (Wheelwright 1989, Bullough and Bullough 1993). One famous sixteenth century example, recorded in autobiography, drama and a portrait, is of a Spanish woman, Catalina de Erauso, who escaped from a convent dressed as a man and then joined a galleon crew, sailed to South America, and enlisted in the Spanish army where she was promoted to the rank of ensign. When her sex was revealed, she became known as the 'nun-ensign' and on her return to Spain she was authorised by the Pope to continue wearing men's clothing (Bullough and Bullough 1993: 96, 111).

The late sixteenth to nineteenth centuries were the 'golden age' of female cross-dressing in Europe (Dekker and van de Pol 1988). Dutch records show that in the seventeenth and early eighteenth centuries, one hundred and nineteen women set out for the Dutch East Indies disguised as men, in most cases not to follow lovers or husbands, as popular songs and stories would have it, but to escape their lot as women, to seek adventure and, most importantly, a better life (Dekker and van de Pol 1988, Bullough and Bullough 1993: 97–100). Wearing men's clothes and sometimes false beards and moustaches, some women even took to the seas as pirates. In 1720, two women, Mary Read and Anne Boney, were sentenced to death for their piracy (Bullough and Bullough 1993: 134). One Irish-born woman, Christian Davis, enlisted in the army disguised as a man and her sex was only discovered some years later when she was seriously wounded. She continued to serve in her regiment, with pay, until she died in 1775 in Dublin, where she 'was buried among the old pensioners with military honors' (Bullough and Bullough 1993: 101–3). One woman who cross-dressed to attend an Edinburgh medical school and become an army surgeon was discovered to be female only on her death in 1865 (Rae 1958).

Women dressed as men also served on both sides of the American Civil War, some of them subsequently writing about their experiences; many of them escaped detection until after their deaths (Bullough and Bullough 1993: 157–8). A detailed account of Russian army life during the Napoleonic Wars was written by a woman who, for ten years, was successfully disguised as a soldier (Durova 1988). Hundreds of Russian women disguised as men are reported to have fought in the First World War, their sex only being discovered if they were killed or wounded (Yurlova 1934, Botchkareva 1919, Wheelwright 1989: 33). In some of these cases at least, it is likely that the sex of the women was known to their comrades, who, being peasants, were well aware that women were 'as physically capable of enduring the privations of war as they were of other hardships' (Wheelwright 1989: 33). Women have also, of course, dressed in men's clothing in order to avoid the restrictions imposed by conventional female attire without attempting to 'pass' as men: in Europe and the United States from the late nineteenth century, their wearing of trousers provided a symbol of female liberation and confidence, as is famously illustrated by the example of the French novelist George Sand.

Women with 'manly' attributes, and the issue of sexuality

A third form of gender transformation for women is the 'gender bending' that occurs when self-identified women are regarded by others as having at least some of the behavioural attributes of men. Some sixty years ago, Oscar Lewis reported 'a unique type of female personality', the 'manly hearted woman' or *ninau-poskitzipxpe*, among the North Piegan tribe of the Canadian Blackfoot Indians. Particular women were called 'manly hearted', for they behaved like stereotypical men rather than women, being generally aggressive and known for their sexual assertiveness (Lewis 1941). Neither homosexual, nor masculine in appearance, the 'manly hearted women' were always older, married or formerly married, women who had achieved their status as a result of their individual efforts, skills, wealth, reputed sexual assertiveness and aggressive personalities. The North Peigan were adamant that a young woman could not be 'manly hearted', although they thought it 'nowadays' easier for a young woman to be 'bold' than before. Lewis suggests that the status of 'manly hearted' women represents 'a form of female protest in a man's culture' (1941: 184). The categorisation seems similar to the Polynesian *vehine mako* or 'shark woman', which is based on assertive sexuality rather than occupation (Kirkpatrick 1983: 177–8).

In contemporary Western Europe and North America, assertive or 'boyish' characteristics in girls, such as the cropped hair and trousers of the stereotypic 'tomboy', are now, in some contexts at least, viewed positively and certainly as less problematic than 'sissy' behaviour in a boy. The clothing styles of contemporary youth cultures are also more 'unisex' than previously. Nevertheless, subtle markers of gender remain, and individuals whose dress or attributes lack these markers may be regarded ambivalently or mistaken for the 'opposite' sex. Devor's (1997) study of sixteen American women frequently mistaken for men shows how social acceptance remains problematic for women with 'blended' gender characteristics, perhaps especially so for heterosexual 'gender blended' women in comparison with those in homosexual relationships, presumably because the gender identity and sexuality of the latter conform to the Western cultural expectation that women who display 'masculine' gender characteristics are necessarily lesbian.[3]

The historical and ethnographic record reveals no simple or necessary link between a female-bodied woman's sexuality, her gender role and her personal attributes. Despite academic and journalistic speculation about possible lesbian tendencies, the role of the Albanian virgin, like that of the Himalayan *sadhin*, is effectively an asexual one (Young 2000), while heterosexuality was a feature of being 'manly hearted' among the North Piegan (Lewis 1941). The recorded European history of females dressed as men indicates a range of sexualities. Some had been married to men before 'passing' as men themselves, or married men after their sex was revealed. Many, however, who 'passed' as men, including those who married women, remained celibate, while others had (clandestine) sexual relationships with women. In the Native American 'two-spirit' traditions, marriage was permissible with someone of the opposite gender and not with another 'two-spirit' person; the relationship was thus not regarded as a homosexual relationship in the Euro-American sense (Blackwood 1984).

Johnson in Chapter 6 discusses a case of female homosexuality in relation to a transformed gender identity for women in the Southern Philippines. The *tomboi* of the Southern Philippines are adult women who are 'like men' in their dress, demeanour, in the importance they accord to their occupations and in having sexual relationships with women. The category *tomboi* has a quite distinct local meaning, even though the Western term 'tomboy' has been incorporated into local discourse, in the Southern Philippines as across many parts of South East Asia.

Here, because heterosexual reproduction is central to women's identity, the *tomboi* are seen as deviant, for the dissociation between female sexuality and reproduction that they embody challenges the 'natural' pattern of gender and sexuality. Their non-productive and thus 'abnormal' female sexuality renders them vulnerable to abuse and violence from men, so that rather than 'coming out' as some lesbians in the West do, or as male 'gays' in the Southern Philippines (Johnson 1997), the *tomboi* constitute a muted gender category and must be circumspect in their behaviour to avoid drawing attention to themselves.

Men in transformed gender roles

Long-term gender transformations for men include roles based on or originating in genital alteration or birth ambiguity, as well as roles that are independent of anatomical sex. Transformed or variant genders for males have usually been discussed in terms of institutionalised male 'cross-dressing' and homosexuality, in ways that often reflect observers' assumptions about 'abnormality' and 'inversion' more than they inform about indigenous perceptions of sex, gender and sexuality (Jacobs 1994, Herdt 1994).

The North American 'two spirit' traditions were first documented by European travellers from the seventeenth century onwards. One account of 'these Hermaphrodites', distinguishable from men and women by the colours of their headdress, stresses their servile status as effeminate men 'strongly inclined to sodomy' (Francisco Coreal 1722, quoted in Roscoe 1994: 329). It now seems that, far from being a servile position, the part-shamanistic status of the 'two spirit' offered a good career option for persons with special aptitudes for cross-gendered tasks and for youths who had seen visions that were signs of their special calling (Whitehead 1981: 100). In a society marked by relative equality and where gender roles were only rigorously enforced in relation to childrearing (Whitehead 1981: 105), rather than indicating 'downward mobility', the role was one of a variety of avenues for achieving individual status. Further, homosexual activity was not the leading motivation, as opportunities existed for this without becoming a 'two spirit' (Whitehead 1981: 96–7).

Other 'alternative genders' for men are more clearly associated with homosexuality. In Polynesia, where again gender disparity is not strongly marked, boys inclined to feminine tasks may be trained to specialise in women's occupations as adults. The Polynesian terms for these roles, reported by western explorers and observers since the nineteenth century, include the Tahitian and Hawaiian term *mahu* (Kirkpatrick 1983: 177–8) and the Samoan term *fa'afafine* (Besnier 1994). Levy (1973: 74) considers the *mahu* 'a substitute female', Kirkpatrick (1983: 177) describes the category as a 'variant' gender role for men, while Besnier (1994) understands the *mahu* as a 'liminal' gender that draws attention, through contrast, to local definitions of masculinity. Undoubtedly, these categories have changed over time. In contemporary Polynesian contexts, gender-liminal men associate with tourists and expatriates, work as prostitutes, performers, or in domestic service, and borrow many aspects of Western 'gay' culture in their creation of modern gender-variant identities (Besnier 1994: 328; Bolin 1996: 29)

The homosexual element (described by Wikan 1977) is a defining part of an alternative gender role for men in the strongly gender-differentiated Muslim society of Oman. The term *xanith*, the Arabic for 'effeminate', 'soft' or 'impotent', denotes a category of men with characteristics of both men and women. They have masculine names, earn a living, own property, attend mosques and mix socially with men (which women, who observe *purdah*, cannot). Their clothing is distinctly intermediate: they wear ankle-length tunics as men do, with a tight waist like women, made from unpatterned but coloured cloth distinct from both the white cloth used for men's clothes and the patterned cloth for women. They do housework like women and their appearance is judged by standards of female beauty: fair skin, round cheeks, large eyes and shiny, heavily oiled hair, combed in women's styles. Particularly striking, in this strictly gender-segregated society, is that *xanith* also mix freely with women, singing with them at weddings and working alongside them as domestic servants.

The *xanith*'s distinct gender identity, Wikan argues, arises not from their anatomical sex but from Omani notions of the male role in sexual intercourse. In addition to their other activities, *xanith* are male homosexual prostitutes (in this gender-differentiated society, female prostitutes are difficult to find). The defining feature of maleness in Omani society is the ability to have penetrative sex with a woman, and what defines a *xanith* is that he is female in his role as a recipient. After some years, a *xanith* may choose to return to being a man, marry and have a family; proof that penetrative sex has occurred, as displayed by a bloodstained handkerchief after the wedding night, clinches this re-transformation. Wikan argues that the *xanith* role, occupied by approximately one in fifty men, provides economic opportunities for men in times of hardship and a sexual outlet, particularly for single men, which preserves the sexual modesty of women.[4]

Temporary gender transformations

Temporary gender transformation through disguise may be a device to outwit an enemy, fool the gods, or avert evil spirits (Modi 1925). In Egypt, dressing a male child as a girl is said to protect him from the evil eye (Bullough 1969). Gender transformations are also common features of many rites of passage in which, sometimes, male initiates are dressed as girls, while girls are dressed as boys. An uninitiated girl or boy, not yet a fully social man or woman, is in a liminal state, having characteristics of both genders. In some male rites of passage, symbols associated with female qualities such as menstruation or lactation emphasise the boy's pre-adult status, when he associated with women, which he is now leaving behind (Turner 1967).

Short-term or intermittent gender transformations also feature in religious ritual in emulation or celebration of deities with cross-gendered identities. In ancient myth, the Sumerian goddess Inanna represented the 'non-domesticated woman, ... who does not behave in socially approved ways'; her devotees would wear the clothes of the opposite gender in rituals celebrating her power (Frymer-Kensky 1992: 25, 29). Sometimes, a gender-transformed individual achieves divinity, or gains spiritual powers, through possession by a deity or spirit. Unlike the gender transformations associated with becoming saints or ascetics discussed above (with respect to female saints in Christian Europe and the Himalayan foothills and the spiritual eunuchs of Byzantium), the gender alteration is temporary, although the change in religious status may be long-term.

Male possession in rural South India provides an intriguing example of bias existing 'against women in the religious sphere, in all castes' (Kapadia 1995: 125), effected through short-term gender transformation in institutionalised possession by a female deity. In order to become possessed, the devotee must allow himself to become symbolically female. The devotee permits his body to be pierced with spears, spikes, skewers and hooks, in an expression of the qualities of submission, obedience, sacrifice and suffering valued in women. By making himself vulnerable like a woman and temporarily relinquishing a man's power to control, the devotee enables the deity to possess him. This instance of gender reversal has a broader significance for gender and power, because the freedom to 'become' male, even temporarily in ritual, is not open to women. Moreover, because men can 'become' women renders women 'ideologically irrelevant' to religious ritual, reinforcing the ideological superiority of men and inferiority of women, a process which, Kapadia suggests, 'occurs very widely in men's possession events throughout India' (1995: 140–1, 157–60).

This example illustrates a common function of ritual gender reversals, that they serve to support the status quo through social and symbolic means. They may allow the expression of frustrations with an existing social order, without permanently disrupting the system (Turner 1967). On the other hand, ritual acts containing elements of gender reversal can also constitute challenges to an existing hierarchy, albeit temporarily (Ardener 1975). These themes of supporting and

sometimes challenging gender stereotypes and social hierarchies recur in the gender reversals of carnival and burlesque, and in comic and serious theatrical performances. In early European history, gender reversals in local festivals may have
challenged, not merely reinforced, the social order. In early modern France, the
dominant image of women as inferior to men, and disorderly because of their
reproductive physiology, was challenged in comic theatrical performances, in
which women dominated or made fools of men, and in ritual performances at
local carnivals and festivals where women took men's roles and men became
unruly cavorting women. In the urban uprisings of the transition to modern society, temporary gender reversals constituted a politically significant challenge to
the social order. Women could 'get away with' politically subversive acts that men
could not, because the fact that they were considered unruly made them less
answerable for their actions (Zemon-Davis 1965).

Women playing men on the stage

In both comic and serious theatre, in Europe and elsewhere up to the present day,
there has, on the whole, been a less developed tradition of women playing men
than of men playing women. It is well known from Shakespeare's plays that
women's parts in Elizabethan England had to be played by boys or men because
social restrictions prevented women from taking up acting careers. Women
entered the stage at the English Restoration and following the Revolution in
France, where several plays featured women going to war dressed as men. In the
nineteenth century, with gender divisions in society becoming increasingly formal, 'gender impersonation became a staple on the stage' and by the end of the
century, female impersonators of men outnumbered men playing female roles
(Bullough and Bullough 1993: 226).

The role of the 'Principle Boy', discussed by Ardener in this volume (Chapter
8) as a star part of popular contemporary English pantomime, originated in the
English theatre of the Victorian era. Ardener notes that actresses playing the
'breeches role' of Principle Boys always retained some clearly feminine attributes,
such as a swelling bust, fat thighs, or small hands and feet, and this characteristic
of Principle Boys was particularly approved by (male) critics of the time. Perhaps
this was because it showed that the Boys were not seeking to deceive their audiences by 'passing' as men. Playing such roles may have provided women with
opportunities for adventure denied them in ordinary life, by vicariously killing
dragons, braving demons, outwitting enemies, and rescuing maidens, but if there
was a symbolic challenge to gender conventions, it was not, usually, viewed as
threatening. Various actresses became famous for their breeches parts, including
Marie Wilton, who astonished Charles Dickens with the impudence of a performance that was 'so stupendously like a boy … yet perfectly free from offence'
(Baker 1968: 138), and Vesta Tilley, whose soprano voice always betrayed her sex,
though it did not protect her from offending Queen Mary at a 1912 performance

(Baker 1968: 209). English music halls and American variety shows also gave women opportunities for more boisterous impersonations of men.

Some nineteenth-century actresses took male parts in serious theatre, for instance playing 'the boy who never grew up' in stage versions of the story of Peter Pan and playing men's roles in Shakespeare's plays, to extend their experience and display their acting skills. Sarah Bernhardt was one of the most well known of the fifty or so actresses who played Hamlet in the nineteenth century. Actresses may have particularly coveted roles such as Hamlet because they gave actresses opportunities to demonstrate their skills and extend their experience in ways denied by the more restricted parts written for women.

A genre of Japanese theatre called Takarazuka discussed by Powell in this volume (Chapter 9) offers an interesting contrast with the European history of female actors playing men's roles, for this Japanese genre is performed entirely by professionally trained women, whose skills include the impersonation of men. The Takarazuka theatre company, founded in 1914, had many of the functions of a finishing school for girls, the genre appealing particularly to teenage girls and their families. Powell shows how, although the ban on women appearing on the Japanese stage had been lifted in 1888, it took time for women actresses to be taken seriously as people who could act.

Men playing women on the stage

In Japan, a tradition of men acting female roles in the highly stylised manner of *kabuki* developed in the seventeenth century when women were barred from the stage. For over two hundred years, Powell writes, playwrights wrote female parts knowing that male *kabuki* actors would play them. Actors specialised in female parts, honing the art of female impersonation in ways that, in the case of a famous early *kabuki* actor, included dressing and behaving like a woman off-stage as well. Female impersonation in the *kabuki* style enabled actors to demonstrate their skill *as actors*; indeed, one prominent present-day *kabuki* actor is also famous for acting female parts in non-*kabuki* genres, as Shakespeare's Lady Macbeth, for example. Within the *kabuki* tradition, however, the representation of women became so highly stylised that when women took to the *kabuki* stage from 1888, actresses playing women's parts continued to imitate the *kabuki* style.

In Europe, the tradition of men playing women in mainstream theatre declined from the seventeenth century when women were allowed on stage. Since the nineteenth century, in Europe and the United States, men have played women in the music hall tradition, particularly in 'drag performance', which Moore in this volume (Chapter 7) defines as men wearing women's clothes in an 'exaggerated burlesque'. Unlike the *kabuki* actors whose skills lie in accurate, if stylised, portrayals of women, drag performers, including the Dames of the English tradition of Christmas pantomime discussed by Ardener (Chapter 8), are quite clearly men dressed as women. Indeed, the comedy lies in this bending of gender. A pantomime dame is an ugly and somewhat absurd woman whose banter is assertive and sexually explicit, a style usually associated with men. Ackroyd (1979: 104) suggests that by evoking a sexually aggressive woman and making fun of her, the Dame role elicits and then disperses the audience's fears of female sexuality and male homosexuality. In the United States, female impersonation featured in nineteenth century minstrel shows, in which, besides blackening their faces as minstrels, white men dressed as mulatto women or 'plantation yellow girls'. Toll (1974: 63) suggests that here the comedy served to assure the white man of his superiority.

Moore (Chapter 7) in this volume offers a challenge to the many recent studies of 'drag' performance through her analysis of drag performances in the 'gay village' of Ontario, Canada. Moore suggests that gay drag performances are best viewed, not as a means of asserting female inferiority, or as playing with transgressing gender boundaries, but as a means through which tensions and contradictions in definitions of masculinity are symbolically expressed. These tensions vary for different categories of participants and observers, but for gay men, Moore suggests, the drag performance, with its expressions of an underlying 'machismo', is a means of defining masculinity.

Conclusion

Although gender identity is commonly regarded as 'fixed' and rooted in biology, changes to anatomical sex and gender identity have taken many forms, with different functions and meanings in a range of historical and cultural contexts. This introduction has attempted to provide an overview of the diversity of forms that such transformations have taken across cultures and throughout history. These range from changes to bodily sex, to long-term gender transformations, to short-term gender reversals.

In the recent Western medical tradition, where it is possible surgically to 'correct' genital ambiguity and change an adult's anatomical sex, we see the continuing influence of a two-gender model that is rooted in assumptions about the salience of sex-difference, as it is defined by chromosomes or legally assigned at birth. Departures from the two-sex model continue to challenge our sense of order, predictability and 'proper' sexuality. Gender and sex categories have also been challenged through long-term gender transformations, made in response to the restrictions of women's roles, in times of social upheaval, to fulfill culturally sanctioned alternative social or spiritual roles, and in some instances also linked with homosexuality. Such transformations are often ultimately restricted, in subtle ways, by aspects of the continuing salience accorded to biological sex. Finally, short-term gender reversals in ritual, carnival and theatre may provide symbolic challenges to conventional categories, but cross-gender impersonation is often highly stereotypical, usually serving to reinforce, for the audience, local ideas of femininity or masculinity as much as they challenge them.

The individual case studies presented in the following chapters explore in further details some of these transformations, their forms, functions and meanings, in the specific contexts in which they occur. We turn, first, to discussions of the context and consequences of changes to bodily sex in contemporary Europe and America.

Notes

1. For a discussion of attempts to identify biological causes of transsexualism see Devor 1989: 20–22 and 1997.
2. A similar result may ensue, occasionally, among the Nuer of Southern Sudan, when a widow brings her children to live with her natal kin and, over time, becomes viewed as constituting a patrilineal link between her son and her father, and thus as having 'become a man' (Evans-Pritchard 1951: 16). The Nuer offer another example of a woman taking on aspects of a man's social role in the institution of 'woman-woman' marriage. A Nuer girl becomes a woman at marriage, but is not fully a wife until she bears children. If she is barren, she can instead follow the rituals of conventional (male-female) marriage, take a wife and become a husband. Any children her wife bears are then legally hers. A barren woman married in this way 'counts in some respects as a man', for she is entitled to acquire cattle through inheritance, and is treated deferentially by her wives and children, but the extent to which female-husbands changed their dress and demeanour is not clear from Evans-Pritchard's account (1951: 108–109).
3. For a discussion of the relationship between childhood cross-gender identity, adult homosexuality, cross-dressing and transsexuality see Bullough and Bullough 1993: 30–1.
4. For evidence of roles for men who wish to resemble women elsewhere in the Islamic world, see Bullough and Bullough 1993: 12–14.

References

Ackroyd, R. 1979. *Dressing Up: Transvestism and Drag: the History of an Obsession.* New York: Simon and Schuster.

Ardener, S. 1975. 'Sexual Insult and Female Militancy'. In *Perceiving Women,* Ardener, S. (ed.). London: Dent, 29–53.

Baker, R. 1968. *Drag: A History of Female Impersonation on the Stage.* London: Triton.

Besnier, N. 1994. 'Polynesian Gender Liminality through Time and Space'. In *Third sex, third gender: beyond sexual dimorphism in culture and history,* Herdt, G. (ed.) New York: Zone books, 285–328.

Blackwood, E. 1984. 'Sexuality and Gender in Certain American Indian Tribes: the Case of Cross-gender Females'. *Signs: the Journal of Women in Culture and Society,* 10, 1.

Botchkareva, M. 1919. *Yashka: My Life as a Peasant, Exile and Soldier, as Set Down by Issac Don Levine.* London: Constable and Company.

Bolin, A. 1996. 'Traversing Gender: Cultural Context and Gender Practices'. In *Gender Reversals and Gender cultures,* Ramet, S.P. (ed.). London: Routledge, 22–51.

Bullough, B. 1969. 'Malnutrition among Egyptian infants'. *Nursing Research,* 18, 172–3.

Bullough, V.L. and B. Bullough, 1993. *Cross Dressing, Sex, and Gender.* Philadelphia: University of Pennsylvania Press.

Callender, C. and L.M. Kochems. 1983. 'The North American Berdache'. *Current Anthropology,* 24, 4.

Dekker, R. and L. van de Pol. 1988. *The Tradition of Female Transvestism in Early Modern Europe*. London: Macmillan.

Devor, H. 1989. *Gender Blending: Confronting the Limits of Duality*. Bloomington: Indiana University Press.

———— 1997. *FTM: Female-to-Male Transsexuals in Society*. Bloomington: Indiana University Press.

Douglas, M. 1966. *Purity and Danger*. London: Routledge and Kegan Paul.

Durova, N. translated by M.F. Zirin, 1988. *The Cavalry Maiden: Journals of a Russian Officer in the Napoleonic Wars*. London: Angel Books.

Evans-Pritchard, E.E. 1951. *Kinship and Marriage among the Nuer*. Oxford: Clarendon Press.

Fausto-Sterling, A. 1985. *Myths of Gender: Biological Theories about Women and Men*. New York: Basic Books.

———— 2000. *Sexing the Body: Gender Politics and the Construction of Sexuality*. New York: Basic Books.

Forbes-Irving, P.M.C. 1990. *Metamorphosis in Greek Myths*. Oxford: Clarendon Press.

Frymer-Kensky, T. 1992. *In the Wake of the Goddesses: Women, Culture, and the Biblical Transformation of Pagan Myth*. New York: Free Press.

Hastrup, K. 1978. 'The Semantics of Biology: Virginity'. In *Defining Females*, Ardener, S. (ed.). London: Croom Helm, 49–65.

Herdt, G. (ed.) 1994. *Third Sex, Third Gender: Beyond Sexual Dimorphism in Culture and History*. New York: Zone Books.

Jacobs, S.E. 1994. 'Native American Two Spirits'. *Anthropology Newsletter*, 35(8), 7.

Johnson, M. 1997. *Beauty and Power: Transgender and Cultural Transformation in the Southern Philippines*. Oxford: Berg.

Kapadia, K. 1995. *Siva and Her Sisters: Gender, Caste, and Class in Rural South India*. Boulder: West View Press.

Kessler, S.J. and W. McKenna. 1978. *Gender: An Ethnomethodological Approach*. New York: John Wiley & Sons.

Kirkpatrick, J. 1983. *The Marquesan Notion of the Person*. Epping, England: Bowker Publishing Company.

Laqueur, T. 1990. *Making Sex: Body and Gender from the Greeks to Freud*. Cambridge Massachusetts: Harvard University Press.

Lewis, O. 1941. 'Manly hearted women among the North Piegan'. *American Anthropologist*, 43, 173–87.

Levy, R.I. 1973. *Tahitians: Mind and Experience in the Society Islands*. Chicago: University of Chicago Press.

Martin, E., 1991. 'The Egg and the Sperm: How Science has Constructed a Romance Based on Stereotypical Male-female Roles'. *Signs: Journal of Women in Culture and Society*, 16, 3, 485–501.

Meigs, A. 1990. 'Multiple Gender Ideologies and Statuses'. In *Beyond the Second Sex: New Directions in the Anthropology of Gender*. Sanday, P.R. and R.G. Goodenough (eds). Philadelphia: University of Pennsylvania Press, 99–112.

Modi, J. 1925. 'A Note On the Custom of the Interchange of Dress between Males and Females'. *Man in India*, 5, 115–117.

Penzer, N.M. 1926. *The Ocean of Story, Vol. VII*. Delhi: Moltilal Banarsidass.

Phillimore, P. 1991. 'Unmarried Women of the Dhaula Dhar: Celibacy and Social Control in Northwest India'. *Journal of Anthropological Research*, 47, 331–350.

Rae, I. 1958. *The Strange Story of Dr. James Barry*. London: Longman.

Ramet, S.P. (ed.) 1996. *Gender Reversals and Gender Cultures: Anthropological and Historical Perspectives.* London and New York: Routledge.

Roscoe, W. 1994. 'How to Become a Berdache: Toward a Unified Analysis of Gender Diversity'. In *Third Sex, Third Gender: Beyond Sexual Dimorphism in Culture and History.* Herdt, G. (ed.). New York: Zone Books, 329–372.

Sanday, P.R. and R.G. Goodenough. 1990. *Beyond the Second Sex: New Directions in the Anthropology of Gender.* Philadelphia: University of Pennysylvania Press.

Toll, R.C. 1974. *Blacking Up: The Minstrel Show in Nineteenth-Century America.* New York: Oxford University Press.

Turner, V. 1967. *The Forest of Symbols.* Ithaca and London: Cornell University Press.

Warner, M. 1981. *Joan of Arc: The Image of female Heroism.* London: Vintage.

_____ 2002. *Fantastic Metamorphoses. Other Words: Ways of Telling the Self.* Oxford: Oxford University Press.

Wheelwright, J. 1989. *Amazons and Military Maids: Women Who Dressed as Men in Pursuit of Life, Liberty and Happiness.* London: Pandora Press.

Whitehead, H. 1981. 'The Bow and the Burdenstrap: A New Look at Institutionalised Homosexuality in Native North America'. In *Sexual Meanings: The Cultural Construction of Gender and Sexuality,* Ortner, S.B. and H. Whitehead (eds). Cambridge: Cambridge University Press, 80–115.

Wikan, U. 1977. 'Man Becomes Woman: Transsexualism in Oman as a Key to gender Roles'. *Man* n.s., 12, 304–19.

Young, A. 2000. *Women Who Become Men.* Oxford: Berg publishers.

Zemon-Davis, N. 1965. *Society and Culture in Early Modern France.* Cambridge: Polity Press.

2

IS IT A BOY, OR A GIRL? THE CHALLENGES OF GENITAL AMBIGUITY

Alison Shaw

In contemporary Europe and the United States, an infant's sex is often ascertained before birth through amniocentesis or ultrasound scan and, if not, it is one of the first things to be examined at birth. Almost universally, the first statement made about a newborn baby is its sex. 'What have you got?' the midwives persistently asked me, when I had just given birth to a healthy baby. It took me some minutes to realise what they were asking for; I had not thought to look at the baby's genitals.

We would expect this focus in societies where gender has considerable social, political, legal or economic significance. In parts of India, Pakistan, the Middle East or North Africa, for example, where, broadly speaking, sons are regarded as an economic asset and daughters as a liability, the birth of a son is cause for more celebration than the birth of a daughter (Tillion 1983; Donnan 1988). However, sex-assignment at birth, which may also establish an initial gender identity such as a name, is performed even in societies such as those of island South East Asia in which, while gender matters politically, it is less economically or socially significant (Atkinson 1990). In contemporary Europe and the United States too, where gender is, in principle at least, of comparatively less socio-economic or political significance – although it affects the legal right to marry and may matter for military service – a mother must, by law, register a baby as male or female within the first six weeks.

In fact, in Europe and the United States, sex and gender, terms which are often used synonymously in official discourse, continue to be important markers of individual identity during childhood and adulthood. People are asked to identify the sex or gender to which they belong by ticking the appropriate box on medical records, nursery and school entry applications, job and visa applications, research questionnaires, census questions, and so on. Beyond the assignation of biological sex, gender is continuously indicated in style of dress and hair, adornment and demeanour. It is still generally assumed that a particular sex determines a particular gender identity and that this in turn determines a person's sexuality. Yet some individuals, who are now usually referred to as transsexuals, grow up with a strong sense of a gender identity inconsistent with their sex and sometimes, also, with their sexuality. Such persons may not legally marry someone of the 'same' sex; indeed, for a person to claim a sex other than that with which they are registered at birth can have far-reaching social and legal implications (see Dembour, Chapter 3). Processes of sex-assignment at birth can profoundly shape and sometimes severely constrain the options and choices of childhood, adolescence and adult life.

A 'common sense' explanation for the assignment of sex in a newborn might be that its sex is one of the few things – perhaps the only thing, apart from who the birth mother is – that can be known about the baby on sight (Astuti 1998). However, ascertaining a newborn's sex is not always so straightforward, because an estimated 1.7 percent of all live-born infants are born with ambiguous genitalia (Fausto-Sterling 2000: 51). In this chapter, I wish to consider, from a cross-cultural perspective, what happens when a baby is born with genitalia that are neither clearly male nor clearly female, but exhibit characteristics of both sexes and to explore how sex-assignment at birth, in whichever direction it is made, affects later life choices. In this light, I then review contemporary Euro-American practices of sex-assignment at birth and the debate over the importance of early sex-assignment for the development of gender identity and gender role in later life.

Intersex conditions

In medical and legal terminology, infants born with genital ambiguity are now usually known as having intersex conditions. The medical and legal term 'intersex' or 'intersexual' in fact encompasses a number of different intersex conditions which are characterised by ambiguities in the external sex organs and internal reproductive structures and caused by genetic and hormonal irregularities. The category includes conditions in which a 'female' infant has an enlarged, penis-sized clitoris and fused labia that resemble a scrotum, and a 'male' infant has a small penis, undescended testes and a split scrotum resembling a vagina. Some scholars (such as Geertz 1983) and clinicians use the terms 'hermaphrodite' or 'hermaphroditism' to describe intersex conditions; these terms suggest the infant has both male and female anatomical features, like the mythical Greek god Hermaphroditos, without differentiating the different forms of genital ambiguity. Some clinicians distinguish the very rare 'true' hermaphrodite forms from the more common 'pseudo' hermaphrodites, a formulation that assumes – in keeping with recent medical practice for managing intersex conditions – that such individuals are 'really' either male or female (Fausto-Sterling 2000: 49–51). In fact, nature gives us a spectrum of bodies with a mixture of male and female characteristics. One way of categorising gradations along this continuum is to identify five sexes: male, female, so-called true hermaphrodites (who have one testis and one ovary), and male and female 'pseudohermaphrodites' (respectively, persons with one testis and some female genitalia but no ovaries, and persons with ovaries, some male-like genitalia but no testes) (Fausto-Sterling 1993, see also Fausto-Sterling 2000: 277 n.15)

The frequency of intersex births worldwide varies somewhat from population to population, in relation to both genetic and environmental factors. Genetic causes include departures from the 'normal' number of sex chromosomes associated with being male or female, which are two X chromosomes for a female (XX) and an X and a Y chromosome for a male (XY). Females who have only one X chromosome (Turner Syndrome, chromosomally XO) have undeveloped ovaries and a lack of secondary sexual characteristics, while males with an extra X chromosome (Klinefelter Syndrome, XXY) are often infertile and experience breast enlargement after puberty. Genetic causes also include mutations in a particular gene, or genes, within chromosomes. The genitals of XX (chromosomally female) children may be 'masculinised' at birth, in childhood or in puberty as the result of a mutation in a gene associated with the production of steroid hormones (a condition known as Congenital Adrenal Hyperplasia [CAH]). A mutation inhibiting production of testosterone can produce 'feminised genitalia' in XY (chromosomally male) infants at birth, and these children may develop breasts and a 'female' body shape at puberty (a condition known as Androgen Insensitivity Syndrome [AIS]). A different mutation, associated with a hormone involved in the masculinisation of the genitals, can produce genital ambiguity in XY males at birth and 'virilisation' at puberty (called 5 Alpha Reductase hermaphrodism). For a chart of some common types of intersex conditions, see Fausto-Sterling (2000: 52)

Since the frequency of particular genes varies from population to population, particular intersex conditions are more common in some populations and less common or very rare in others. Congenital Adrenal Hyperplasia is a relatively common recessively inherited condition that affects about 1.5 per thousand females. Affected females may be 'tomboys' as children, behave in 'masculine' ways as adults, and be sexually attracted to women, although they nearly always feel that they are women. The gene occurs at relatively high frequencies in Yupik Eskimos, affecting 3.5 per thousand, but at low frequencies at 0.005 per thousand in New Zealanders (Fausto-Sterling 2000: 53). Rare recessively inherited intersex conditions may cluster in local populations, particularly if there has been intermarriage over some generations. The recessive condition 5 Alpha Reductase hermaphrodism, associated with ambiguous genitalia in XY infants at birth and virilisation at puberty, has been noted in a particular area of the Dominican Republic and in parts of New Guinea, sometimes also occurring in the United States and in Europe, and has been subject to considerable medical and ethnographic debate over the relationship between sex-assignment at birth, gender identity and gender role, as will be discussed below. Individuals with what is medically defined as a 'true hermaphrodite' condition, being born with both an ovary and a testis, are in fact very rare (0.00012 per thousand) (Fausto-Sterling 2000: 53).

Reactions to intersex births

In hospitals in Europe and the United States, if a child is born with ambiguous genitalia – when it is not clear whether the infant has an enlarged clitoris or a penis, and enlarged labia or testes – one or more of a variety of tests might be performed to ascertain other aspects of what is more often thought of as the 'true' sex of the child. These include chromosome examination (by microscope) to ascertain the presence or absence of a Y chromosome and the number of X chromosomes; mutation analysis to assist particular genetic diagnosis; ultrasound scanning to locate the position, number and form of the gonads and the internal urino-genital configuration; and tests for indications of likely hormone function at puberty. Parents will then be advised on how to register the sex of the infant on its birth certificate (the relevant box on the birth certificate is in practice sometimes left blank in the case of intersex infants, despite the legal requirement) and on whether to raise the child as a girl or a boy.

A barrage of technology may thus be drawn upon to help ascertain the 'true' sex of the child and enable diagnosis and management. How, then, in the absence of such technology, are intersex births managed? More generally, how do people in other societies allocate infants to gender categories, especially where this allocation depends on the inspection of the body by sight and touch, unmediated by the use of such technologies as chromosome analysis, mutation analysis and ultrasound scanning? It seems intuitively correct to say that all societies recognise two sexes. The very idea of there being two sexes, grounded in clear-cut biological differences, is so very deeply rooted in Western 'common sense' that it is hard to imagine a society that does not classify people as male and female in the same way that we do. However, a closer look at the ethnographic record suggests some slightly different possibilities when people are faced with the 'cultural challenge' (Geertz 1983: 80) of intersex infants.

Botched pots, unnatural horrors and supernatural blessings

An infant with ambiguous genitalia born into a family and community in which male children are strongly preferred, such as rural Pakistan, is very likely to be categorised as male, though not without some anxiety, as we shall see. The same child born in a Western hospital is likely to be diagnosed as having an intersex condition. In this case, however, the diagnosis and medical recommendations, which might include the 'corrective' surgical removal of the 'false' penis in the case of chromosomally female infants with masculinised genitalia, will not always or necessarily be culturally acceptable to the parents. Parents of XX infants with masculinised genitalia (in the case of Congenital Adrenal Hyperplasia) or of XY infants with feminised genitalia (Androgen Insensitivity Syndrome) are usually advised to raise the infants as girls, sometimes, in the case of Androgen Insensitivity Syndrome, after testing for indications of likely hormone activity at puberty.

It is reported that Saudi parents of XX infants with Congenital Adrenal Hyperplasia have strongly resisted the recommendations of their European trained Saudi doctors, and rejected the offer of corrective surgery (Fausto-Sterling 2000: 58–9). Similarly, British Pakistani parents of XY infants with Androgen Insensitivity Syndrome have sometimes rejected the medical recommendation to raise these children as girls. This lies, in part, in a strong cultural preference for male children and indicates that responses to genital ambiguity are culturally mediated.

Responses to intersex births have varied over time and place and also, to some extent, according to type of intersex condition. On the basis of the ethnographic record, Clifford Geertz (1983) identifies three distinct cultural responses to genital ambiguity at birth. These are the theory of the 'botched pot'; the tragedy of 'unnatural horror'; and the story of 'supernatural blessing'. Each 'theory' of cultural response is ethnographically associated with specific ethnic groups, but it is not necessarily restricted to them. Each theory also has implications for how intersex infants born into these cultural contexts are treated and for their later life choices.

According to the 'botched pot' theory, intersex infants are freaks of nature, or God's mistakes. They are cast aside or killed, along with microcephalic infants (infants with very small heads) and those with major developmental defects such as missing limbs. The Romans regarded the birth of intersex babies as 'expressions of divine anger and portents of national calamity' and introduced laws under which such infants were put to death (Cawadias 1943: 59). The African Ibo tradition was to destroy anomalous births of animals and humans (Shirley Ardener, personal communication). The Pokot of Kenya, Africa, regarded infants with incomplete genital development as God's mistakes. Sometimes they killed them, despite government laws against infanticide and sometimes they allowed them to live, but as socially liminal persons. The infant would be cast aside like a badly fashioned pot and it would either die or survive; either way, it was treated in an off-hand way, like a useless object. The Pokot term for intersex infants, and for the adults that survive this indifferent treatment, is *sererr*. An intersex Pokot could not 'pass' as a male or female through disguise, because traditional attire, for men and women, did not conceal the genitals and male genitals were continually exposed. Adult *sererr* occupied an in-between, genderless status in Pokot society, where circumcision and reproduction are the marks of proper adult male and adult female status. *Sererrs* could be neither circumcised, on account of their underdeveloped genitals, nor assume normal reproductive roles. 'A *sererr* cannot be a real person', one Pokot told Edgerton (1964: 1295). Another admitted, 'I only sleep and eat and work. What else can I do? God made a mistake', and a third commented, 'God made me this way. There was nothing I could do … I was no real Pokot' (Edgerton 1964: 1295, 1293).

The second cultural narrative, that of 'unnatural horror', Geertz associates with the United States. He quotes Edgerton on the American view of intersexuals as presenting:

a moral and legal enigma ... Can such a person marry? Is military service relevant? How is the sex on a birth certificate to be made out? Can it properly be changed? Is it psychologically advisable, or even possible, for someone raised as a girl, suddenly to become a boy? And so on. The practical problems are also immense. How can an inter-sexed person behave in school shower rooms, in public bathrooms, in dating activities? (Edgerton, 1964: 1289)

The American reaction to this 'horror' is to assign the infant to the male or female sex and the associated, subsequent gender role. Sometimes this is achieved by 'passing' as one or the other sex, but in contemporary American society, once the individual's 'true' sex has been established, more often medical treatment and sur-gery is deemed necessary. The assumption behind such practice is that essentially a person must be 'really' one or the other sex and that biology must therefore be altered, and socialisation and psychological development shaped, in order to align properly these different elements of a person's sex and gender identity. In short, in the American view, 'if the facts don't measure up to your expectations, change the facts, or, if that's not feasible, disguise them' (Geertz 1983: 82). This Ameri-can response to 'unnatural horror' could also describe the dominant Euro-Amer-ican medical model for the management of intersex births. What distinguishes this response from the 'botched pot' model, in which intersex infants (if not put to death) are regarded as useless and essentially left to fend for themselves, is that the Euro-American medical model demands that something is done to 'correct' the mistake. An intersex person must fit one or other sex and gender category, either by disguise, or, as is more common, by 'appropriate' medical treatment and management, from birth onwards. The implications of this practice for a person's choices in later life, especially where sex-assignment at birth contradicts a devel-oping gender identity, are discussed later in this chapter.

A third cultural response to intersex infants is to regard them not with indif-ference or horror, but as 'supernatural blessings' and the bearers of good fortune. The Greeks were generally 'reasonable and humane' in their attitudes to the birth of intersex infants and to adults with hermaphroditic characteristics (Cawadias 1943: 59), as the mythical status of the god Hermaphroditos would suggest. Another favourable response was shown by the Native American Navaho, who considered that intersex infants brought good fortune, assuring the success and wealth of the family into which they were born. The Navaho accorded intersex adults a distinct cultural categorisation, as *nadle*, which means 'transformed'. These 'transformed' individuals dressed in gender-intermediate styles, were greatly respected for being able to do the work of both men and women and often became custodians of wealth. The role is clearly described in Navaho origin-myths, teaching the skills of farming, pottery-making and basketry that are dis-tinctive in Navaho culture (Williams 1986). Hill, who studied the Navaho 'hermaphrodites' in 1935, quotes informants who described the *nadle* as 'sacred and holy' and as 'leaders, just like President Roosevelt', bringing good fortune and wealth that were regarded central to the continuation of the Navaho presence and identity. One informant connected the *nadle* role and Navaho identity by saying, 'I think when all the [intersexuals] are gone, that it will be the end of the Navaho' (Hill 1935: 274).

Though the Navaho viewed the birth of anatomically intersex infants as auspicious, this view must also be set in the context of their less rigid perceptions of both sex and gender. Roscoe (1994: 356) notes that the term *nádleehé* (*nadle*) translates literally as 'one who changes continuously' and suggests that the role represents a conception of persons as having an 'inner' and one or more 'outer' forms, the 'outer' forms existing as processes that may fluctuate between male and female. Moreover, the Navaho category of *nadle* included gender-transformed individuals who were not in every case biologically intersex persons. The category was thus more than simply a response to the anatomical intersex condition, and while it may have done so, it did not necessarily originate specifically to accommodate the intersex person (Whitehead 1981: 86). The Navaho recognised that persons could be men, women and *nadle* and they differentiated 'real' *nadle* from *nadle* 'pretenders' who could be biologically male or, less commonly, female. In other words, they recognised a 'third sex' category and this recognition may have been elaborated into, or may have evolved alongside, a third gender, in which gender identity enjoyed a degree of independence from the dictates of anatomical sex. Moreover, the positive cultural recognition accorded to biological intersex persons and to gender variant roles for both men and women was not limited to the Navaho, but has been noted for many North American tribes, of which the Navaho are but one example. These North American 'third gender' or 'two spirit' traditions were very often positively sanctioned in myth (see Chapter 1).

A cultural typology of ideological possibilities in response to intersex births, such as Geertz's, while informative, tells us little about the socio-economic contexts in which these cultural beliefs are located. Nor does it consider how differently situated actors, even within the same society and broad cultural framework, may have alternative, and sometimes competing, reactions to intersex births. There is very little good 'clinical ethnography' of intersex conditions (Herdt 1994). However, Edgerton's case histories include a telling description of the different reactions of a mother and a father to the birth of their intersex baby. This infant was to grow into a person who dressed as a woman, who had well-developed breasts and a normal-looking vagina, but who never menstruated, and who had a normal sized penis, but rudimentary testes. Recalling the birth, the father said '… it could never marry and what would I get in return? It could never bring me bridewealth. So I thought it would be better to kill this *sererr*. But the mother said "no, no – do not kill it. It is a child like any other – it can help me with my work and I will feed it". So I did not kill the *sererr* – I did not want to annoy my wife so I let her have this child' (Edgerton 1964: 1292).

It is also often difficult, in many contexts, to isolate 'indigenous' ideas from the Euro-American model because the latter increasingly influences thinking about sex, gender and the management of intersex births. This is perhaps most poignantly illustrated by the effects of pressures exerted by American and Canadian government agents and missions to persuade male 'two spirits' living on reservations to wear men's clothing, and cut their hair short. While some men changed their ways, others chose, instead, to hang themselves; reports indicate that there are now far fewer 'two spirit' persons in Native American tribes (Williams 1986).

A closer contextual and historical examination of cultural responses to genital ambiguity thus reveals how perceptions of, and responses to, intersex persons not only vary between differently placed individuals within the same society, but also that these perceptions change over time. Other sets of cultural categorisations of individuals with ambiguous genitalia that illustrate this point include the eunuch in antiquity, discussed by Tougher (Chapter 3, this volume), and the *hijras*, or religious eunuchs, of India. Like the Byzantine eunuch, the category *hijra* includes persons born with ambiguous genitalia, some of whom were evidently raised with an ambivalent gender identity and only became recognised as *hijras* in youth or adulthood. Becoming a *hijra*, like becoming a eunuch, is not, however, restricted to those born with ambiguous genitalia: boys or men with unambiguous male genitalia may be made *hijras* by genital mutilation, for an uncastrated *hijra* is expected eventually to undergo an emasculation operation, called *nirvan*, which means rebirth (Nanda 1994: 383). Occasionally, women who fail to menstruate also become *hijras*.

The *hijras* have existed in the Indian subcontinent for over a thousand years and in many respects they would seem to provide an example of the theory of genital ambiguity as a 'supernatural blessing'. In Hindu ideology, *hijras* are thought of as heterosexually impotent men who become vehicles of divine power, particularly as it relates to male and female sexual potency in fertility and reproduction, through their renunciation of conventional male sexuality. According to a Hindu myth, the ascetic god Siva castrated himself, and it was this denial of sexuality that, paradoxically, gave him power over fertility (Nanda 1994). The category of *hijra* seems, thus, to have originated, in part at least, within Hinduism, in that Hindu mythology provides a religious justification for its existence.

In contemporary South Asian society, in Pakistan as well as India, attitudes to *hijras* are, however, ambivalent. *Hijras* belong to separate *hijra* communities, usually located in urban centres. One of their main economic activities involves their dressing as women to dance and to play the ritual clown at both Muslim and Hindu weddings, where they challenge conventional boundaries of sex, gender and hierarchy (Nanda 1994). Their presence at weddings and at births is believed to be both auspicious and threatening, for while they bring fertility and good fortune to the newly weds, to offend or turn *hijras* away, or refuse their demands for money, will bring misfortune. When a child is born, *hijras* traditionally inspect the infant's genitalia, and may claim an intersex infant as one of them. Ambivalence towards *hijras* and more explicit reactions of disgust and hostility are also increasingly linked to their diminished religious status in contemporary society. Moreover, this loss of status is also associated with their increasing dependence on prostitution for a livelihood – in response to broader social change – and to the fact that *hijras* reportedly draw recruits to their community from among poor or orphaned youth. Rather than celebrating the birth of an intersex infant (as the theory of supernatural blessing would imply), parents in South Asia, or of South Asian origin in Europe and the United States, may react with dismay and shame, not only because of the implications of genital ambiguity for marriage, fertility and reproduction, which are of central importance in South Asian society, but because of the cultural association with a stigmatised community.

During my fieldwork[1] exploring British Pakistani responses to the diagnosis of genetic disorders, one mother described the particular shock of discovering that her stillborn child had, among many other problems, ambiguous genitalia:

> We called the baby [a boy's name] because the hospital doctor said, when we went to register the death, that we could choose. They did a post-mortem to find out the sex but could not. It was not clear that the organs were male or female. It was that which really got to me, they could not tell us. Only my husband and I know that the baby had no sex. I did not tell my parents, because they would have taken it very badly. It is not that we're ashamed, my husband and I, but my in-laws had already taken it badly when they heard about the baby and my father-in-law got really ill when he heard the baby was born dead. To hear also that it had no sex – that would have been too much for him. (Interview, 11th June 2002)

Another woman described the shock of indeterminate sex, when her sister's child was born:

> It was not obvious whether the girl thing was a penis or not. Everywhere else she looked like a girl, but the clitoris was really stumpy like a boy's penis – a girl with a boy's penis. The doctor said he would check the genes before they could say definitely if she is a girl. It took a week before they could tell us. That was a shock, not knowing if the child was a boy or girl straight away. It is usually the first thing you know about a baby. (Interview, 15th October 2002)

This child's mother was so afraid that her family and community would gossip about her 'abnormal' baby that she had only told two sisters about the infant's condition, and allowed only one of them to help with nappy-changing. She had not even told her mother, and would not agree to take the child to visit relatives in Pakistan, despite her grandmother's pleading, 'because there the aunties would want to look after her and give her a bath. But, if it was to come out, my daughter would have this label, abnormal'. Doctors tried to reassure her that the child's penis-sized clitoris will 'grow in', but the mother did not want her daughter to 'feel different' and wanted her to have the operation 'so people don't stare, so that she can be as normal as possible'. The child's mother's sister added that such people are known in Pakistan as *khusra* (the Panjabi for *hijra*) or 'a person who is half man and half woman'.

What these examples suggest is that we need to look beyond one cultural interpretation to understand the social and cultural significance of gender categories, especially in structurally complex contexts. In focusing on reactions to genital ambiguity in the newborn, and later in life, it is worth remembering also (as we saw in Chapter 1) that, even for those with unambiguously male or female genitalia, sex-assignment at birth does not *necessarily* confine that person to the corresponding sex or gender category in later life. This is also true in relatively gender-undifferentiated societies, as illustrated by the 'two spirit' traditions. Alternative gender choices have existed even in strongly patriarchal and gender-differentiated societies, as illustrated by the 'sworn virgins' of northern Albania (see Littlewood and Young, Chapter 5), and the *sadhin* of the Himalayan foothills (Phillimore 1991). Among the Vezo of Madagascar, some men may voluntarily 'become' women, by participating in female activities and adopting a distinctively female demeanour (Astuti 1998). The Vezo call such people *sarin'ampela*, or 'men who are images of women'. Long-term gender transformations of this sort generally occur under distinctive social circumstances (see Shaw, Chapter 1) and tend to be limited ultimately by certain attributes of biological sex: for instance, the Himalayan *sadhin* may not attend cremations, which are only attended by men, and the Vezo *sarin'ampela* cannot be treated as women at death (Phillimore 1991, Astuti 1998). Nevertheless, the ethnographic observation is that genitalia, in themselves, do not *necessarily* limit a person's gender identity and role, and sex-assignment at birth is, *in itself*, not a *necessary* pre-requisite for subsequent gender identity; the social and cultural context in which sex-assignment occurs (as well as, sometimes, other aspects of biological sex) may play crucial mediating roles.

'Correcting' intersex infants

Contemporary Euro-American medical practice with regard to intersex births dates from about the 1960s. Somewhat anachronistically, in a society in which birth-assigned sex has relatively little legal significance (but see Dembour, Chapter 3) and where gender dichotomies have become blurred in many aspects of social life, intersex infants do indeed seem to be generally regarded with 'what can only be called horror' (Geertz 1983: 81). Moreover, it is seen as a horror that necessitates corrective action. According to a 1981 medical article on intersexuality, 'ambiguous sex in the newborn infant is a medical emergency' (quoted in Fausto-Sterling 2000: 276).

Yet it seems that this was not true in the first part of the twentieth century. A case described in 1937 in a book on intersex conditions concerns a young 'hermaphrodite' called Emma, raised as female, who could have sexual relationships with both men and women. Married more than once, she also had girlfriends on the side, and sometimes thought she would prefer to be a man. However, when her doctor suggested surgery to remove the vagina, she said she would rather not, '… that's my meal ticket. If you did that, I would have to quit my husband and go to work. So I think I'll keep it and stay as I am'. The doctor was happy to leave it at that (quoted in Fausto-Sterling 2000: 43).

Today, it is unlikely that Emma would have become a young 'uncorrected' woman. Contemporary American medical practice usually 'corrects' intersex infants through surgery and through hormonal treatment in the early neonatal period and subsequently, as appropriate, backing this up with psychological treatment. A recent study estimates that between one and two live births per thousand require corrective genital surgery as a result of intersex conditions (Blackless et al. 2000).

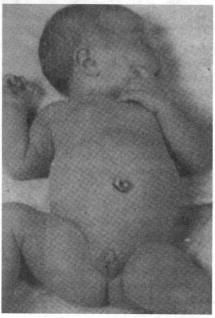

2.1 A six-day old XX infant with masculinized external genitalia. (Original photograph courtesy of Dr. Lawson Wilkins in W.C. Young (ed.) *Sex and Internal Secretions*, 1961 [figure 23.1, p.1405], the Williams & Wilkins Co.; reprinted with permission, Lippincott Williams & Wilkins).

One surgeon aims to assign gender within twenty four hours of birth, in order to 'send the child out as a sex' (quoted in Fausto-Sterling 2000: 276). Parents, under these circumstances, have little time to consult other paediatricians or patient support groups for advice about the wisdom of surgery. In 1998, two surgeons wrote that 'one of the more devastating problems that can befall new parents is the finding that their child has ambiguous genitalia. This is truly an emergency necessitating a team approach by the neonatologist, endocrinologist, geneticist, and pediatric urologist' (Rink and Adams 1998: 212, quoted in Fausto-Sterling 2000: 276). A textbook on intersexual disorders published in 1969 opens with the photograph of an infant with ambiguous genitalia (Figure 2.1) accompanied by the following tale of tragedy:

One can only attempt to imagine the anguish of the parents. That a newborn should have a deformity … [affecting] so fundamental an issue as the very sex of the child …

it is a tragic event which immediately conjures up visions of a hopeless psychological misfit doomed to live always as a sexual freak in loneliness and frustration (quoted in Fausto-Sterling 2000: 47).

In this case, the baby had two X chromosomes, so was chromosomally female. We learn that the baby's parents were told that the baby was 'really' a female, whose genitalia had been masculinised by high levels of androgen during foetal development. She was 'corrected' by surgery that opened the vaginal passage and shortened the clitoris.

In Europe and the United States, parents of chromosomally female (XX) infants with CAH are usually advised to raise the children as girls, and have the child's ambiguous genitalia surgically corrected (Fausto-Sterling 2000: 58). The surgical aspects of the therapy depend on a cultural definition of male and female genitalia that is sometimes based on actual measurements of the phallus imposed upon the continuum of sexual bodies that nature gives us. A United States Intersexual Rights, Movement campaigning against infant genital surgery produced a drawing of a 'phallometer' in order to represent the medical definitions of a 'normal' clitoris and a 'normal' penis. (Figure 2.2). A 'normal' clitoris is one that measures between 0.2 and 0.85 centimetres. One that is 'too big', measuring more than 0.8 centimetres, such as occurs in the case of XX infants with Congenital Adrenal Hyperplasia, may then be reduced surgically to within the 'normal' range. Surgical shortening is surgically easier than lengthening of the phallus. The practice of clitoral reduction, sometimes combined with surgical vaginal expansion, has mostly replaced the complete clitorodectomy that was practiced in the 1950s. However, shortening the clitoris remains damaging to sexual function, as evidenced by the practice of clitorodectomy that originated from parts of Africa. Phallic measurement and clinical judgment inform decisions about sex-reassignment surgery (Fausto-Sterling 2000: 59–63).

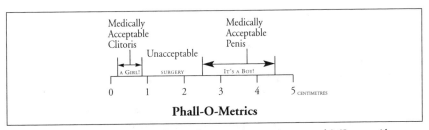

2.2 Phall-0-metrics. The ruler numbers indicate centimeters (not to scale) (Source: Alyce Santoro, for Anne Fausto-Sterling, *Sexing the Body: Gender Politics and the Construction of Sexuality*, 2000, Basic Books [figure 3.4, p.59]; reprinted by permission of Basic Books, a member of the Perseus Books group).

Prenatal hormonal therapy can also be offered for one of the more common types of intersex conditions. Congenital Adrenal Hyperplasia is a recessively inherited genetic disorder, one that arises from inheriting two copies of the relevant mutation, one from each parent. The genetic mutation in this case involves an alteration in the function of between one and six enzymes that are involved in making steroid hormones. Infants who are chromosomally female (XX) with Congenital Adrenal Hyperplasia are born with masculinised genitalia and may develop masculine secondary characteristics at puberty. Generally, XY (chromosomally male) infants with Congenital Adrenal Hyperplasia cause less clinical anxiety; as Ann Fausto-Sterling puts it, 'you can never, apparently be *too* masculine' (2000: 55).

If both parents are carriers of the mutation for Congenital Adrenal Hyperplasia, their risk of having a child affected with Congenital Adrenal Hyperplasia is one in four, and their risk of having an XX (chromosomally female) affected child is one in eight. A woman in this situation can have a prenatal diagnostic test from the ninth week of pregnancy. However, the prenatal hormonal treatment has to begin in the fourth week. Thus, 'for every eight fetuses treated for CAH, only one will actually turn out to be an XX child with masculinized genitals' (Fausto-Sterling 2000: 55). The safety of the prenatal treatment has not been established, and its use is the topic of considerable debate. Even if it becomes established as safe, it is certainly unlikely to be acceptable in communities in which parents are unwilling to raise, as a girl, a baby originally identified at birth as a boy. If the infant has been originally identified as a male in a society where male children are strongly preferred, parents may resist the medical advice. However, the very possibilities of prenatal treatment, as well as the practices of surgical, medical and psychological 'correction', underline the considerable importance that is attached, in contemporary medical practice, to correcting biological ambiguity from infancy.

Much of the contemporary Euro-American psychological and medical treatment offered for intersex conditions depends on the belief that intersex individuals are 'really' either male or female. As noted above, in medical classification of intersex conditions, 'true' hermaphrodites comprise a very rare minority. Therapy is offered to enable a less ambiguous fit to one or the other category. The well-intentioned assumption, of clinicians and often of parents too, is that with 'correct management', intersex infants can lead the sexual and reproductive life of 'normal' men and women, since 'normal' psychosexual development is regarded as being dependent upon fitting a conventional gender category. These practices are founded on the belief that early treatment, before birth, at birth, and shortly afterwards, enables this transition to occur most effectively, with the least psychosocial harm to the individual.

However, evidence based on accounts from individuals who have undergone such treatments, and on the recommendations of patient support groups, is now beginning to challenge the assumptions about the development of 'normal' gender identity that have for over forty years informed the medical management model. The most famous case is that of a boy, named Bruce Reimer at birth, one of a pair of unambiguously male identical twins, who lost his penis during a circumcision operation that went wrong in 1966 when he was seven months old. On the advice of Dr John Money, a psychologist/paediatrician at the Johns Hopkins medical school in Baltimore, the parents agreed to have their son surgically castrated at twenty two months of age in 1967, and to raise him as a girl, renaming him Brenda. For John Money, this case confirmed the theory he was championing, in his development of protocols for the management of intersex births, that environment, including clinical management and therapy, prevails in the formation of gender identity. In this dramatic 'natural experiment', Brenda's uncastrated twin brother provided the control case. Money advised Brenda's parents to conceal the truth of Brenda's birth, the circumcision accident and the sex-reassignment, to raise her unambiguously as a girl and to bring her to him for annual counselling. By 1972, Money's celebrated case of successful sex reassignment had not only established his reputation, but justified a procedure in relation to intersex births that 'today is performed in virtually every major country', at a rate of perhaps one thousand per year (Colapinto 2000a: 11).

However, Brenda's sex reassignment, far from being an unqualified success, had been problematic from the beginning, for he/she was unhappy as a girl. As a teenager, Brenda reluctantly took oestrogen pills for breast development, but stubbornly opposed surgery for vaginal construction. Her parents eventually told her the truth, Brenda immediately renamed herself David, and undertook treatment 'to complete her metamorphosis back from girl to boy' (Colapinto 2000a). The family lost contact with John Money, and twenty-five years passed before a psychologist and psychiatrist were to report that this case actually proved the opposite thesis, that, as a result of pre-natal hormonal influences, infants are *not* psychosexually neutral at birth (Diamond and Sigmundson 1997a). First written up under pseudonyms as the 'John/Joan' case (Diamond and Sigmundson 1997a), David, then married, and living 'as nature made him', eventually told his full story to a journalist (Colapinto 2000b).[2]

Deeply held beliefs about the 'naturalness' of gender roles and about 'normal' male and female sexuality and 'normal' psychosexual development continue to underpin the Euro-American medical management of intersex conditions, but cases such as that of David Reimer are beginning to challenge at least some aspects of clinical practice. The case for or against gender reassignment surgery, such as the early removal of testes in children with Androgen Insensitivity Syndrome (Diamond and Sigmundson 1997b) is not proven, partly because it is very difficult to obtain long-term follow-up data. There has, however, been a resurgence of professional debate in clinical meetings and journals in Europe and the United States. Specific practices of clinical management continue to vary from practitioner to practitioner, from medical centre to medical centre, and for different intersex conditions.

Lessons from the Dominican Republic

An example from the Dominican Republic has gained a central place in debates over biology versus upbringing in the creation of gender identity and gender roles. It illustrates the complex and not necessarily predictable relationship between various aspects of biological sex (chromosomes, genes, hormones and genital configuration) and a person's subsequent gender identity. The test here is whether individuals *feel* they are male or female, and whether they take on a female or male gender role.

In 1974, a medical team headed by Dr Imperato-McGinley identified an instance where infants assigned to the female sex at birth, and raised as girls, changed to a male gender identity as they approached puberty, without any medical intervention. The researchers described this as 'an experiment of nature', which supported the view that the hormone androgen was critical to the formation of male gender identity, in utero and at puberty, overriding the effects of upbringing in determining male gender identity (Imperato-McGinley et al. 1979: 1236).

The story concerns a condition called '5-Alpha Reductase Hermaphrodism', which arises from a rare, recessively inherited autosomal mutation that alters the enzyme involved in the metabolism of testosterone, involved in the masculinisation of the genitals. The condition only affects male infants (chromosomally XY), and produces ambiguous genitalia at birth. The scrotum is 'bifid' or labia-like in appearance; the penis is absent or more like a clitoris; and the testes are undescended (Imperato-McGinley et al. 1974: 1213). As a result, affected infants are sometimes assigned to the male sex and raised as boys, and sometimes defined as females and raised as girls. Then at puberty the youngsters 'virilise' as a result of naturally produced testosterone: their voices deepen, their muscles develop, their penises grow, and their testes descend. Erections occur and sexual intromission is possible but without insemination because of the position of the urethra (Imperato-McGinley et al. 1979: 1233).

The Dominican Republic research identified thirty eight cases, in three villages, from twenty-three extended families, going back four generations. Of these thirty-eight cases, nineteen had supposedly been raised 'unambiguously' as girls, and research on eighteen of these 'girls' said that seventeen had successfully changed, from around the age of twelve, towards a male gender identity and, from the age of sixteen, had adopted male gender roles. Furthermore, they had common-law marriages with women, and had become farmers and woodsmen rather than housewives. The researchers concluded that – even when 'the sex of rearing is contrary to the testosterone-mediated biological sex, the biological sex prevails if the normal testosterone-induced activation of puberty is permitted to occur'- biology thus overrides gender socialisation (Imperato-McGinley et al.1974: 1235).

This report challenged the theory that sex-assignment at birth, plus rearing, made the most important contribution to gender identity. This theory, dating from 1955, was, as we have seen above in relation to the story of David Reimer, associated in particular with the psychologist and paediatrician John Money and his colleagues at Johns Hopkins medical school in Baltimore in the 1960s. As noted above, by the 1970s, this theory was guiding the clinical management of infants with ambiguous genitalia both in the United States, *and beyond*, particularly in Europe. According to this principle, sex-assignment before the age of two-and-a-half was the best predictor of unproblematic gender development (Money and Ehrhardt 1972). This appears, then, as a straightforward 'nature versus nurture' debate, with Imperato-McGinley and colleagues claiming that biology prevails, and Money and his associates arguing that upbringing prevails. It is worth stressing that 'upbringing', in this theory, refers to an 'unambiguous' sex-assignment at (or soon after) birth and child-rearing that includes, and indeed justifies, practices of genital surgery and psychological 'fixing' (through counselling of the child and especially the parents), as being in the child's best interests.

Money and his colleagues challenged the Imperato-McGinley study, not least because it raised questions about standard clinical hospital practice (Money 1976, see also Herdt 1990: 436). Of the many questions raised about the original study (such as whether the youngsters who 'became' men at puberty were really sexually attracted to women), a central one concerns their upbringing: were these children *really* reared unambiguously as females? Local knowledge suggests otherwise. For it seems, in fact, that the villagers were well aware of the existence of this condition, known to occur in just three villages in one area, going back four generations. What is more, there was a local name for it: *guevedoche*, meaning 'penis at twelve'. In other words, it was locally known that a phallus would become obvious at around the age of twelve, and develop into a functional penis. There was also another local name, with which such persons were ridiculed: *machihembra*, or 'first woman, then man'. This indicates that, in the local system for sex-assignment and gender socialisation, a third category was recognised, one described quite precisely in local terminology. As Herdt (1994: 428) puts it, 'the village ontology includes a third sex category – neither male nor female, but *guevedoche*'. How does this challenge the biological answers to the developmental questions?

If a local culture recognises a third sex category of 'penis at twelve', the story is not that of a 'natural experiment', because the very fact that the youngsters are called *guevedoche* suggests they are *unlikely* to have been raised *unambiguously* as girls. Given the fact that males have more status and socio-economic power than females in these villages, it is not surprising that the *guevedoche* should aspire to be male as adults, for there are good socially and culturally induced reasons for this. In this case 'anatomically ambiguous and stigmatised hermaphrodites have much to gain and little to lose by "switching" sex roles' (Herdt 1994: 249).

Gilbert Herdt (1990, 1994) offers another example of the same condition among New Guinea Sambian people. Such infants, who would most likely be operated on at birth in the United States and in Europe, are recognised among the Sambian people as *kwolu-aatmwol,* which means transformation 'into a male thing'. In this dichotomously gendered society, a male-identified *kwolu-aatmwol* is reared somewhat ambiguously as a boy, because he does not partake in all of the rites of passage associated with social transformation to an adult man, while *kwolu-aatmwols* who happen sometimes to have been raised as girls do not always make a successful transition to the status of adult woman. However, that the transformation eventually takes the direction of the male role is not simply a reflection of the greater power and freedom of men in Sambian society, as in the Dominican Republic case, or of the influence of testosterone at puberty. *Kwolu-*

aatmwok defined as females at birth, and raised as girls, generally transformed ambiguously to men only after failing as women, on account of their sexual anatomy and inability to reproduce. This observation points to the power of gender socialisation in a society that, while recognising three sexes, recognises two genders (Herdt and Davidson 1988, Herdt 1990, 1994).

There is little detailed ethnographic case material from which we might be able to ascertain the important features of gender-identity development for individuals born with this condition, by comparing life-histories from different cultural contexts. It is also unlikely that such material will emerge, because the Western medical model now prevails in the management of such conditions: in the Dominican Republic today, infants diagnosed with 5-Alpha Reductase Hermaphrodism are being raised as boys and the local 'third-sex' category is ignored (Herdt 1994). A person's gender identity is constructed through biology, culture and upbringing. Anatomical sex and hormonal processes can importantly influence the outcome of a person's life, but local perceptions and meanings of sex and gender combined with patterns of gender socialisation are also profoundly important in shaping individual life choices and desires.

Conclusions and implications

Nature offers us variation in bodily form, but while some societies recognise *three* categories of sex, most societies have two relatively fixed gender categories. Departures from 'normal' biological variation are interpreted positively or negatively in ways that reflect aspects of the social significance of sex and gender in particular contexts. Sex and gender transformations, including those that involve surgical, hormonal and psychological treatment, tend to be ritually managed (or else to represent ritual forms of challenge to the status quo), and are seen as ultimately limited by biology. Contemporary Euro-American concern with assigning sex at birth, as part of the legal requirement for birth-registration at six weeks (though sometimes 'sex' is left blank in practice in the case of intersex infants), is linked to assumptions regarding how 'correct' psychosexual development proceeds, and is in turn linked with fears about homosexuality.

Nevertheless, in recent years, established medical practice and legal treatment of intersex persons has been challenged. Today the law rarely has to pronounce upon whether someone is male or female, except in the case of the marriage of intersexual persons, or of post-operative transsexuals (Dembour, Chapter 3). This calls into question the current legal insistence that every person must be either male or female. A recent review of legal decision making in intersex cases suggests that there is a strong case for a person's right to choose their own sex, at least where the medical answer is inconclusive, and that a wider range of categories of sex should be recognised. The review concludes with a comment on the consequences this would have for medical practice regarding intersex infants. At present, corrective surgery is still done to ensure that an infant has one, consistent, sexual appearance, but:

> It can be argued that doctors should only perform medical procedures necessary for clinical reasons (for example, to repair any defects in the genito-urinary system so that physiological functions can be carried out normally), but otherwise wait until the child is old enough to decide what, if any, surgery is wanted to change the appearance of the sexual organs. (Herring and Chau 2001: 5)

It will be difficult, not just for clinicians with established medical protocols, but for many parents of newborn intersex infants to follow such advice, given the force of social and medical tradition, and the stigma that parents may encounter when confronting their wider families and community with the fact of genital ambiguity, and their inability to say 'definitively' that their child is a boy or a girl. However, the legal challenge is also reflected in the views of some patient support groups, the accumulating testimonies of patients (usually, rather than parents), and in the recommendations of clinicians who also caution against hasty surgical procedures. The present situation is thus one of debate, challenge and change in contemporary gender systems and in the understanding of biological sex.

Notes

1. My research is supported by a project grant from the Wellcome Trust, U.K.
2. See also Andrew Cohen, 2000, 'The boy who turned into a girl', A BBC/WGBH Boston production for Horizon. David Reimer committed suicide on May 4, 2004, aged 38 (www.cshink.com/space/death_by_ theory.htm).

References

Astuti, R. 1998. '"It's a Boy", "It's a Girl"! Reflections on Sex and Gender in Madagascar and Beyond'. In *Bodies and Persons: Comparative Perspectives from Africa and Melanesia*, Lambek, M. and A. Strathern (eds). Cambridge: Cambridge University Press, 29–52.

Atkinson, J.M. 1990. 'How Gender makes a Difference in Wana Society'. In *Power and Difference: Gender in Island Southeast Asia*, Atkinson, J.M and S. Errington (eds). California: Stanford University Press, 59–93.

Blackless, M., A. Charuvastra, A. Derryck, A.Fausto-Sterling, K. Lauzanne and E. Lee. 2000. 'How Sexually Dimorphic Are We?' Review Article. *American Journal of Human Biology*, 12, 2, 151–66.

Cawadias, A.P. 1943. *Hermaphroditos: The Human Intersex*. London: Heinemann medical books.

Colapinto, J. 2000a. 'The Boy They Made into a Girl: A True Story of Surgical Catastrophe and Medical High-handedness'. *The Independent on Sunday*, 6th February, 8–13.

———— 2000b. *As Nature Made Him: The Boy Who was Raised as a Girl*. London: Quartet Books.

Diamond, M. and H.K. Sigmundson. 1997a. 'Sex-reassignment at Birth: Long-term Review and Clinical Implications'. *Archives of Pediatrics and Adolescent Medicine*, 151, 298–304.

_____ 1997b. 'Management of Intersexuality: Guidelines for Dealing with Persons of Ambiguous Genitalia'. *Archives of Pediatrics and Adolescent Medicine*, 151, 1046–50.

Donnan, H. 1988. *Marriage among Muslims: Preference and Choice in Northern Pakistan*. Leiden: E.J. Brill.

Edgerton, R.B. 1964. 'Pokot Intersexuality: An East African Example of the Resolution of Sexual Incongruity'. *American Anthropologist*, 66: 1288–99.

Fausto-Sterling, A. 1993. 'The Five Sexes: Why Male and Female are Not Enough'. *The Sciences*, March/April, 20–25.

_____ 2000. *Sexing the Body: Gender Politics and the Construction of Sexuality*. New York: Basic Books.

Geertz, C. 1983. 'Common Sense as a Cultural System'. In *Local Knowledge*. New York, Basic Books, 73–93.

Herdt, G. 1990. 'Mistaken Gender: 5-Alpha Reductase Hermaphroditism and Biological Reductionism in Sexual Identity Reconsidered'. *American Anthropologist*, 92, 433–446.

Herdt, G. (ed.) 1994. *Third Sex, Third Gender: Beyond Sexual Dimorphism in Culture and History*. New York: Zone Books.

Herdt, G. and J. Davidson. 1988. 'The Sambia "Turnim-man": Sociocultural and Clinical Aspects of Gender Formation in Male Pseudohermaphrodites with 5-Alpha Reductase Deficiency in Papua New Guinea'. *Archives of Sexual Behaviour*, 17, 1, 33–56.

Herring, J. and P.L. Chau. 2001. 'Assigning Sex and Intersexuals'. *Family Law*, 762, 1–5.

Hill, W.W. 1935. 'The Status of the Hermaphrodite and Transvestite in Navaho Culture'. *American Anthropologist*, 37, 273–279.

Imperato-McGinley, J., L. Guerrero, T. Gautier and R.E. Peterson. 1974. 'Steroid 5-Alpha Reductase Deficiency in Man: An Inherited Form of Male Pseudohermaphroditism'. *Science*, 186, 1213–15.

Imperato-McGinley, J., R.E. Petersen, T. Gautier and E. Sturla. 1979. 'Androgens and the Evolution of Male-gender Identity among Male Pseudohermaphrodites with 5-Alpha Reductase Deficiency'. *New England Journal of Medicine*, 300, 1233–37.

Money, J. 1976. 'Gender Identity and Hermaphroditism: Letter'. *Science*, 191, 872.

Money, J. and A.A. Erhardt. 1972. *Man & Woman, Boy & Girl: The Differentiation and Dimorphism of Gender Identity from Conception to Maturity*. Baltimore: Johns Hopkins University Press.

Nanda, S. 1994. 'Hijras: An Alternative Sex and Gender Role in India'. In *Third sex, third gender*, Herdt, G. (ed.). New York: Zone Books, 373–417.

Phillimore, P. 1991. 'Unmarried Women of the Dahaula Dhar: Celibacy and Social Control in Northwest India'. *Journal of Anthropological Research*, 47, 331–350.

Rink, R.C. and M.C. Adams. 1998. 'Feminizing Genitoplasty: State of the Art'. *World Journal of Urology*, 16, 3, 212–18.

Roscoe, W. 1994. 'How to become a Berdache: Toward a Unified Analysis of Gender Diversity'. In *Third Sex, Third Gender: Beyond Sexual Dimorphism in Culture and History*, Herdt, G. (ed.). New York: Zone Books, 329–72.

Tillion, G. 1983. *The Republic of Cousins: Women's Oppression in Mediterranean Society*. London: Al Saqi Books.

Whitehead, H. 1981. 'The Bow and the Burdenstrap: A New Look at Institutionalised Homosexuality in Native North America'. In *Sexual Meanings: The Cultural Construction of Gender and Sexuality*. Ortner, S.B. and H. Whitehead (eds). Cambridge: Cambridge University Press, 80–115.

Williams, W.L. 1986. *The spirit and the flesh: sexual diversity in American Indian culture*. Boston, Massachusetts: Beacon Press.

3

WHY SHOULD BIOLOGICAL SEX BE DECISIVE? TRANSSEXUALISM BEFORE THE EUROPEAN COURT OF HUMAN RIGHTS

Marie-Bénédicte Dembour

Introduction

Some individuals grow up with a feeling of certainty, developed from an early age, that they belong to the sex *opposite* to that which they were assigned at birth on anatomical grounds (see Shaw's contribution in this volume). Severe depression is a typical outcome of the split between physical appearance and personal sense of gender identity. This condition is now medically recognised and known as 'transsexualism' – which can be a move either from male-to-female or, less commonly, female-to-male (British Medical Association 1995: 1011, but see Reid 1995: 38–9).

If the condition is diagnosed and therapy is sought, hormonal treatment is available to help alleviate the split between sexual appearance and deep-felt identity. This treatment suppresses or encourages the development of so-called secondary sexual features, related to body and facial hair, breasts and voice tone. Some transsexuals seek an even greater reconciliation between their two contradictory identities and subject themselves to what is today referred to as 'gender reassignment surgery'. The surgery consists of a series of operations which lead to the removal of existing sexual organs and, at its most extreme, the construction of either a vagina-like cavity or of a phallus-like organ.

After successful hormonal treatment, the transsexual now feels she appears more or less as the person she always felt she was. (As the male-to-female move is more common than its reverse, I hereafter use the feminine form to refer to the 'generic' transsexual.) Surgery more completely reconciles external appearance and inner sense of gender identity, though chromosomes remain unchanged, and therefore of the 'wrong' sex. While surgery generally leads to improved mental well-being, it does not necessarily signal the end of all the transsexual's social problems (Whittle 2002). In particular, her legal identity may lag behind in a past that she felt was never hers. The state administration may refuse to correct the mention of her sex on her birth certificate or other identity documents; to allow her to marry a person of the 'opposite' sex; and, in the case of a female-to-male transsexual, to recognise him as the legal father of the child to whom his partner had given birth following artificial insemination.

These are the three main sets of issues regarding transsexualism that the European Court of Human Rights ('the Court') has had to face so far. Put simply, in any one case, either the Court can accept the plea of the transsexual or it can reject it. At first sight, there are convincing reasons to reject it. The sexual categorisation as male or female is fundamental; social chaos ensues if an aberrant individual appears so coherent in his 'delusion' that society is ready to follow him (Wachsmann and Marienburg-Wachsmann 2003). Notwithstanding, the plight of the transsexual cannot leave one indifferent. How can we refuse to alleviate her suffering? Compassion, or simply respect, demands that her plea be accepted.

Human beings make sense of their lives through categories which, however natural they appear, can only but produce some misfits. The transsexual is such a misfit. One would expect law, which works through categories, to have difficulty dealing with the misfit that the transsexual represents. By contrast, one would expect human rights, which puts the emphasis on the individual as individual rather than the embodiment of a particular type of person, to offer recognition to the transsexual. In its case law on transsexualism, the European Court of Human Rights has proved to be a legal institution before being a human right instrument. To simplify a slightly more complicated history, transsexual applicants have kept losing before the Court for twenty years, before finally winning in 2002.

This article traces how the Court has gradually changed its position regarding transsexualism (see also Niveau et al. 1999). By the time the Court found the United Kingdom in violation of the European Convention of Human Rights (the Convention) in 2002, the great majority of the over forty states then belonging to the Council of Europe (the Council) had adapted their national legal systems to accommodate the transsexual condition. Even the United Kingdom had woken up to the need to undertake reform. It is this double evolution, taking place at *national* level,[1] which eventually led the Court, after repeated complaints, to take a stand against one of the few states that persisted in its refusal to accommodate transsexualism. The 2002 Court's ruling is anything but a manifestation of judicial engineering aimed at fostering more understanding for the transsexual. The Court *followed* social change, rather than anticipated or precipitated it.

The Court is called the European Court of Human Rights. The reference to human rights seems to imply that the institution is committed to realising grand ideals, and thus, one would hope, is progressive and proactive. The reality is different. The actual task of the Court is rather mundane, namely it has to enforce the law contained in the Convention – nothing else. Its task is not to bring about a form of justice informed by an ethical or utopian vision of what human rights might entail. Rather, the grounding of the Court as a 'purely' judicial institution, albeit at the pinnacle of the judicial hierarchy, ensures that it is conservative.

It is 'conservative' in its 'tendency to preserve or keep intact and unchanged' (*Shorter Oxford English Dictionary 1973*). The Court is reluctant to force changes in the Council's member states' national laws. Its conservatism happens to go hand-in-hand with political conservatism. Its policy to resist change is deliberate. This caution can be open to criticism, and I personally regret that it took so long for the Court to support the transsexuals in their plight for recognition. At the same time, I suspect that a proactive European institution could be equally, if not more, dangerous – although I do not develop this view, informed by issues which go beyond transsexualism, in the present article.

The Convention

The European Convention on Human Rights, signed in 1950 and in force since 1953, is the work of the Council of Europe, whose institutions sit in Strasbourg. It provides for a number of civil and political rights, including the right to life, freedom from torture, freedom of expression and, most importantly for our purposes, the right to private and family life and the right to marry. Revolutionarily at the time of its adoption, the Convention also provided an institutional framework for its enforcement, enabling individuals to complain that they had suffered a violation of the Convention at the hand of any state that was party to the Convention. Such a right of individual petition, though conditional, was a first in international law (van Dijk and van Hoof 1998: Chapter 1).

Originally two institutions, the European Commission of Human Rights ('the Commission') and the Court, were established to examine complaints that a state, party to the Convention, had violated one or more of its provisions. Grounds for refusing a hearing included the applicant's failure to have 'exhausted national remedies', and a claim being 'manifestly ill-founded'. If declared admissible, the Commission generally reported on whether or not it thought the state government against which the petition was addressed had violated the Convention.[2] The report was non-binding. Within three months of its issue, the Commission or the relevant state government could bring the case before the Court. In most such cases, the Court's judgment was based on 'the merits' of the case. (The Court could also declare the case inadmissible, strike it off the list, or register a friendly settlement made between the parties.) The judgment by the Court was final (van Dijk and van Hoof 1998: Chapters 3 and 4).

By the late 1980s, due to a backlog, it was taking five or six years for the Court to deliver its judgment upon petitions which had been allowed to proceed. The delay was partly due to the growth in the number of individual petitions reaching Strasbourg. Through Protocol 11, which entered into force in November 1998, the institutional arrangements originally set up in the Convention were amended, and a new – permanent – Court was created. This also signalled the demise of the Commission (after a transitional period of one year). The new Court now assumed the functions of the old Court plus those of the Commission (Leach 2001).[3]

The cases

The applicants in the transsexual cases reviewed here all claimed that, under their national governments, they had suffered from a violation of Article 8 of the Convention, which reads:

1. Everyone has the right to respect for his private and family life, his home and his correspondence.

2. There shall be no interference by a public authority with the exercise of this right except such as is in accordance with the law and is necessary in a democratic society ... for the protection of health or morals, or for the protection of the rights and freedoms of others.

In the reviewed cases, the Court always accepted that there had indeed been an interference with the private (and sometimes the family) life of the applicant. In other words, Article 8 *did* apply. Having established this, the Court had to decide whether the interference by the government in question had nevertheless met the three conditions outlined in paragraph 2 of Article 8, because, if so, no violation of the first paragraph could be said to have occurred.

Central to the case law of the Court on paragraph 2 of Article 8 is the so-called doctrine of the 'margin of appreciation', through which the Court accepts that state authorities may be better placed than itself to assess whether an 'interference' with a right provided for in the Convention is justified. The doctrine has been widely criticised, not least because it allows the Court to abdicate control over participating state governments. Until the 2002 decision, with one exception, the Court had repeatedly decided in transsexual cases that the state government had remained within its 'margin of appreciation' when it interfered with the right of private/family life of the applicant. (The Commission generally held a different opinion, although this was hardly a consolation for the applicants as the Commission's reports were not binding.)

Another provision that has often been pleaded by transsexual applicants is Article 12 of the Convention ('Article 12'), which reads:

Men and women of marriageable age have the right to marry and to found a family, according to the national laws governing the exercise of this right.

For a long time the Court persistently refused to find a violation of Article 12. (By contrast, the Commission had thought a violation of this provision had occurred in the first three cases that came before the Court.)[4] The Court eventually found a violation of Article 12 in 2002.[5]

The personal history of each of the applicants in the transsexual cases brought before the Court indicates a similar awareness, from an early age, that something is wrong with their 'sex'; and similar experiences of distress and depression, and a similar commitment to sex-reassignment operations. Table 3.1 lists the full range of cases that have come before the Commission and the Court. The next sections consider in some detail the eight cases that have come before the Court.[6]

Table 3.1: Strasbourg transsexual case law

DATE*	CASE: & object of complaint	COMMISSION	COURT
[4.10.80]	*Van Oosterwijck (Mr)* v. *Belgium* Certificate of civil status	V of 8 (unanimous) V of 12 (7 v. 3)	Inadmissible (13 v. 4)
25.09.86	*Rees (Mr)* v. *UK* Birth certificate. Cannot marry.	V of 8 (unanimous) V of 12 (unanimous?)	No V of 8 (12 v. 3) No V of 12 (unanimous)
29.08.90	*Cossey (Ms)* v. *UK* Birth certificate. Cannot marry.	No V of 8 (10 v. 6) V of 12 (10 v. 6)	No V of 8 (10 v. 8) No V of 12 (14 v. 4)
[9.11.89]	*Eriksson (Ms) & Goldschmidt* v. *Sweden* Cannot marry someone of opposite sex but same gender.	Inadmissible	
24.01.92	*B. (Ms)* v. *France* Wishes to marry. Civil status, docs & name cause daily embarrassment.	V of 8 (17 v. 1) No V of 3 (15 v. 3) 12 inadmissible	V of 8 (15 v. 6) 3 unnecessary (unanimous)
20.03.97	*X, Y, Z (Mr)* v. *UK* Fatherhood after AID.	V of 8 (13 v. 5) 14 unnecessary (17 v. 1) 12 inadmissible	No V of 8 (14 v. 6) 14 unnecessary (17 v. 3)
[2.07.97]	*LF (Ms)* v. *Ireland* Right to visit her children.	Inadmissible	
[23.10.97]	*Roetzheim* v. *Germany* Birth certificate of non-operated applicant.	Inadmissible	
25.06.98	*Sheffield (Ms) & Horsham (Ms)* v. *UK* Birth certificate and legal sex causes embarrassment on various occasions.	V of 8 (15 v. 1) 12 unnecessary (9 v. 7)/(10 v. 6) 14 unnecessary (unanimous) No V of 13 (unanimous)	No V of 8 (11 v. 9) No V of 12 (18 v. 2) No V of 14 (unanimous) 13 unnecessary (unanimous)
11.07.02	*Goodwin (Ms)* v. *UK* [*I.(Ms)* v. *UK*] Birth certificate, NI file, harassment at work, age of retirement.	N/A (post Protocol 11)	V of 8 (unanimous) V of 12 (unanimous) 14 unnecessary (unanimous) No V of 13 (unanimous)
12.06.03	*Van Kück* v. *Germany* Refunding of medical expenses	N/A (post Protocol 11)	V of 6 (4 v. 3) V of 8 (4 v. 3)

Key:

* Date of judgement on merits OR, if none, date of decision of inadmissibility in brackets.

V of 8:　　Verdict of violation of Article 8　　　　(7 v. 3): Decision adopted by 7 votes against 3
No V of 8: Verdict of non-violation of Article 8

Art. 3:	inhuman treatment	Art. 12:	right to marry
Art. 6:	fair trial	Art. 13:	national remedy
Art. 8:	private and family life	Art. 14:	non-discrimination

Van Oosterwijck v. *Belgium* (1980): Typical facts

Danielle Van Oosterwijck lodged the first transsexual case to come before the
Court. For this case, I shall go through the facts, as reported in the judgment, in
some detail. Van Oosterwijck was born in Belgium in 1944 with all the physical
and biological characteristics of the female sex. He recalled being conscious of having a dual personality from around age five. In 1962, aged sixteen, he attempted
suicide. In 1963, he started to work, as a female, in the Secretariat of the Commission of the European Communities. From 1966 he sought to solve his problems by having what was then called a 'sex-change' operation. In 1969 he
undertook hormonal therapy and started to develop male secondary characteristics. In 1970 he underwent two operations of sexual conversion, namely a bilateral
mammectomy and a hysterectomy-bilateral ovariectomy. Subsequently a phallo-
plasty was carried out in ten stages from October 1971 to October 1973 in London. While this is not the case for all applicants, Mr Van Oosterwijck did not
encounter difficulties at work during this period. His employer supported him by
bearing some of the costs of treatment and by issuing him a new employment card
in the name of Mr D. Van Oosterwijck.[7] (*Van Oosterwijck*, paragraphs 7–11)[8]

In October 1973, the applicant filed a petition to rectify his 'certificate of civil
state'. However, his petition failed to convince the Belgian administrative and
judicial authorities. The Attorney-General's department before the Brussels Court
of Appeal argued that:

> From the point of view of public policy … the petition prompted the most serious
> reservation: its acceptance might provoke numerous other petitions and it would be
> dangerous to encourage indirectly by this means the proliferation of treatment whose
> effects, being irreversible, might subsequently be regretted by the patients themselves.
> [Furthermore], the perpetual calling in question of certain situations, particularly in
> the realm of personal status, conflicted with the requirements of a rational organisation
> of the community: it would tend to an increase in personal problems and engender a
> climate of insecurity and instability in family and social relationships (paragraph 13).

Mr Van Oosterwijck lodged a petition with the Commission on 1 September
1976. The Commission declared the application admissible on 9 May 1978. In
its report of 1 March 1979 it concluded, unanimously, that there had been a
breach of Article 8, and, by seven votes to three, of Article 12. The Commission
and the Belgian Government referred the case to the Court. By judgment of 4
October 1980, the Court rejected the application. In its view, held by thirteen
votes to four, the applicant had 'failed to exhaust national remedies'.[9]

The apparently technical requirement of having to 'exhaust national remedies'
lends itself to use as a policy instrument, enabling the gates of 'admissibility' to be
opened or closed. Whether or not the Court did this intentionally, the decision
in *Van Oosterwijck* enabled it to avoid having to consider the merits of an

undoubtedly difficult and sensitive issue. The respite, however, did not last long. Other transsexual applicants soon came knocking at the Strasbourg doors.

Rees v. *UK* (1985): The Court's reasoning in transsexual cases

Another female-to-male transsexual applicant, Mr Rees, brought the next case to be reviewed here. A British citizen, Mr Rees had undertaken hormonal and surgical treatment in the 1970s after learning that transsexualism was a recognised medical condition, treatable under the National Health Service. (He was then approaching thirty.) More or less contemporaneously he changed his first names and applied for a new passport. The passport arrived in his new name but without the prefix 'Mr'. Subsequently, Mr Rees sought, unsuccessfully, to have his birth certificate altered to show his sex as male. He applied to the Commission in 1979. By the time his case came before the Strasbourg Court, all his official documents contained his new name *and* the prefix 'Mr', including a passport made in 1984, with the exception of his birth certificate (*Rees*, paragraphs 11 to 17).

According to the law applicable in England and Wales:

> [T]he birth certificate constitutes a document revealing not current identity, but historical facts. The system is intended to provide accurate and authenticated evidence of the events themselves and also to enable the establishment of the connections of families for purposes related to succession, legitimate descent and distribution of property. The registration records also form the basis for a comprehensive range of vital statistics and constitute an integral and essential part of the statistical study of population and its growth, medical and fertility research and the like … Only in cases of a clerical error, or where the apparent and genital sex of the child was wrongly identified or in case of biological intersex, i.e. cases in which the biological criteria are not congruent, will a change of the initial entry be contemplated …'. (paragraphs 21 and 23)

Mr Rees submitted that issuing a birth certificate on which his sex continued to be recorded as 'female' entailed a violation both of Article 8 and of Article 12. He explained that the birth certificate, which revealed the discrepancy between his apparent and his legal sex, caused him embarrassment and humiliation whenever social practices required its production (paragraph 34). He persuaded the Commission, but not the Court.

The Court's reasoning on Article 8 was as follows (in a paraphrase of paragraphs 35 and 36):

1. Article 8 not only protects the individual against interference by the state, but also entails positive obligations inherent in an effective respect for private life. In this case, the refusal by the authorities to *alter* the register of births is not an interference: the applicant wishes them to do – rather than refrain from doing – something.

2. The notion of 'respect' found in Article 8 is not clear-cut, especially as far as positive obligations are concerned.

3. Having regard to the diversity of practices followed and the situations obtaining in the Contracting States – with some giving transsexuals the option of changing their personal status and others not – the 'respect' due to transsexuals under Article 8 is bound to vary *considerably* from case to case (my emphasis rather than that of the Court). This is an area where the Contracting Parties enjoy a wide margin of appreciation.

4. In determining whether or not a positive obligation exists, regard must be had to the fair balance that has to be struck between the general interest of the community and the interests of the individual.

The Court proceeded to apply this reasoning to the facts of the case:

The alleged lack of respect … seems to come down to a refusal to establish a type of documentation showing, and constituting proof of, *current* civil status [my emphasis]. The introduction of such a system has not hitherto been considered necessary in the United Kingdom. … The governing authorities in the United Kingdom are fully entitled, in the exercise of their margin of appreciation, to take account of the requirements of the situation pertaining there in determining what measures to adopt. While the requirement of striking a fair balance … may possibly … call for incidental adjustments to the existing system, it cannot give rise to any direct obligation on the United Kingdom to alter the very basis thereof (paragraph 42).

As this paragraph shows, the Court was not ready to impose precise obligations on member states as to how national authorities were supposed to run their country, especially in regard to the legal effects of transsexualism – a controversial issue which did not yield European-wide, let alone universal, consensus. By twelve votes to three, the Court found that there had been no violation of Article 8. It went on to dismiss, unanimously, the claim that Article 12 had been violated.

Uncharacteristically, the Court added a paragraph to the effect that:

[T]he Court is conscious of the seriousness of the problems affecting [transsexuals] and the distress they suffer. The Convention [must] be interpreted and applied in the light of current circumstances … The need for appropriate legal measures should therefore be kept under review having regard particularly to scientific and societal developments (paragraph 47).

This suggested that the Court might restrict the degree of freedom enjoyed by the participating states in this area in the future. However, as we shall see, it took seventeen years for the Court to define more closely the boundaries[10] within which states party to the Convention can treat transsexuals.

Cossey v. *UK* (1990): Judge Martens' critique of the 'Biological-Sex-is-Decisive' Idea

The next case to come before the Court was *Cossey*. The applicant, born male in 1954, had had gender reassignment surgery in 1974, paid for by the United Kingdom's National Health Service. In 1983, she met a man who had wished to marry her, but the Registrar General informed the couple that their marriage would be void, as it would be between persons legally of the same sex. In 1989, Ms Cossey married a (different) man at a London synagogue. The relationship broke down five weeks later; the High Court decreed this marriage to have been void. Ms Cossey complained before the Strasbourg institutions that she could not claim full recognition of her changed status and that she was unable to enter a valid marriage with a man (*Cossey*, paragraphs 9–14 and 27).

The Court decided that the case was not distinguishable from *Rees* – the issue was exactly the same even though the applicant was a male-to-female transsexual who had actually wanted to marry (paragraphs 32 to 34). The question was: should the Court depart from its judgment in *Rees*? The Court answered negatively, on the grounds that there had been no significant scientific or legal development in the interval (paragraph 40). In its opinion, there remained 'little common ground between the Contracting States', which thus continued to enjoy a wide margin of appreciation in respect to transsexualism (ibid.). It reiterated that the issue was to be kept under review (paragraph 42).

The Court ruled that Article 8 had not been violated – but only by ten votes to eight. A ruling that Article 12 was not violated was adopted, not by unanimity, but by fourteen votes to four. Among the dissenting opinions attached to the judgment, Judge Martens' is particularly interesting (and unusually long). I shall review it in some detail.

Martens started by identifying the legal identity of a transsexual as truly a 'human rights' issue (paragraph 2). He talked of the 'rebirth' which the transsexual seeks to achieve with the assistance of medical science, but which can be successfully completed only through the legal recognition of his [sic] new sexual identity (paragraphs 2.2 and 2.4). He wrote:

> This urge for full legal recognition is part of the transsexual's plight. That explains why so many transsexuals, after having suffered the medical ordeals they have to endure, still muster the courage to start and keep up the often long and humiliating fight for a new legal identity (paragraph 2.4).

Later, Martens referred to 'tragic' human beings (paragraph 2.6.1). He stressed respect for human dignity and human freedom as the principle underlying human rights, including the rights provided in the Convention. He argued that the transsexual only 'demands to be treated by the law as a member of the sex he has won' through 'long, dangerous and painful medical treatment' (paragraph

2.7). For him, refusal to do so is not brought about by compelling reasons; it is 'cruel' (ibid.; see also Karsten 1999: 207).

Martens proceeded with a critique of the Court's reasoning in *Rees* (paragraph 3). He scolded the Court for having treated the issues as if they were technical, by insisting on distinguishing negative and positive obligations flowing from Article 8, and by saying that the refusal to alter the register of births was a '"mere" (!) refusal' (paragraph 3.2, his exclamation mark). For Martens, what was at stake for Mr Rees was the fact that the legal system in force in the United Kingdom relied on the 'BSD idea' that 'Biological Sex is Decisive' (paragraph 3.4). With socio-logical insight, he saw that sexual identity, through the ubiquity of the sexual dichotomy, is an important social fact. Mr Rees was condemned to live in oppo-sition to his country's legal system – he was 'outlawed', a situation which must have caused permanent and acute distress (ibid.). Martens suggested that the Court should have accepted that the 'BSD system' constituted a continuous inter-ference with the right of post-operative transsexuals[11] to respect for their private life, which should have logically led to a stricter examination of the conditions in Article 8 (2), and thus a finding of violation (paragraph 3.5).

Even if the alteration to the birth certificate is considered a positive obligation, Martens continued, the Court was still erring in its reasoning (paragraph 3.6.1). For Martens, it does not follow from the 'little common ground' that exists between the Contracting States that states should enjoy a wide margin of appre-ciation in this area. He recalled that the preamble to the Convention invites the Court to develop common standards: the Court should only practice self-restraint when it feels that the *specific* features of the case, or the situation obtaining in the defendant state, mean that the Court feels unable fully to exercise its power of control (paragraph 3.6.3). Nothing suggested that the culture of the United King-dom differed essentially from that of other member states as to the role of the sexes. In the *Rees* case, the Court was wrong to have granted the United Kingdom such latitude regarding the legal recognition of the identity of post-operative transsexuals (paragraph 3.6.4). The BSD system should not have been found compatible with Article 8 (paragraph 3.6.5).

If it is accepted that the new identity of the transsexual warrants full respect of law in all respects, Martens argued, violation of Article 12 must also be found (paragraph 4). Of course, Article 12 speaks of 'men and women', indicating that marriage is the union of two persons of opposite sex. But, he asked, what does 'sex' mean in this context? Why should the chromosomal factor be decisive (para-graph 4.5.1)? The question is all the more pertinent since 'marriage is far more than a sexual union'. It is a societal bond, 'a species of togetherness in which intel-lectual, spiritual and emotional bonds are at least as essential as the physical one' (paragraph 4.5.2).

Martens then argued that social and legal developments within the Council of Europe should anyway have led the Court to overrule its *Rees* ruling in *Cossey* (paragraph 5). He cited 'the ever-growing awareness of the essential importance of everyone's identity', 'a growing tolerance for, and even comprehension of, modes of human existence which differ from what is considered "normal"', 'a markedly increased recognition of the importance of privacy' (paragraph 5.5). While at the time of the *Rees* judgment only five member states to the Council of Europe permitted, one way or another, the legal recognition of the new identity of post-operative transsexuals, at the time of the *Cossey* judgment this number had increased to fourteen (ibid.).[12] Martens regretted the cautiousness of the Court whose policy 'seems to be to adapt its interpretation to the relevant societal change only if almost all member States have adopted the new ideas' (paragraph 5.6.3). In an echo of the 'universalism versus cultural relativism' debate which has long raged in anthropology (Cowan et al. 2001), he concluded that 'the Court should take great care not to yield too readily to arguments based on a country's cultural and historical particularities' (paragraph 5.6.3).

The dissenting opinion of Judge Martens, however intellectually and morally convincing, did not find favour with the Court, as the review of the subsequent case law demonstrates.

B v. *France* (1992): A false positive

The applicant in this case was born in Algeria in 1935 as a male, but had always been considered a girl by her four siblings. She had suffered from the segregated Algerian school system and, as a man, had adopted noticeably homosexual behaviour, including during military service in Algeria. She left for France in 1963, and started to dress as a woman and to have hormone therapy. Surgical operations followed in Morocco in 1972. In 1978, wishing to marry a man she had met shortly before her operation (and with whom she was still living at the time of the Strasbourg proceedings), she asked the French tribunal to hold that she was in reality of feminine constitution. This was dismissed on the ground that 'the change of sex was intentionally brought about by artificial processes'. Her appeal failed (*B. v. France*, paragraphs 9–17). She petitioned the Commission in 1987. Her claim that Article 12 had been violated was declared inadmissible for 'failure to exhaust national remedies'. Her claim related to Article 8 was declared admissible. She argued that the failure by the French authorities to correct her sex in the civil status register, and on her official identity documents, compelled her to disclose intimate personal information to third parties. Her professional life suffered as a result of her transsexualism (paragraph 43).

The Court repeated that the notion of 'respect' enshrined in Article 8 was not clear-cut, especially in regard to positive obligations, and that its requirements would vary considerably from case to case, although there must be a 'fair balance' between the general interest and the interest of the individuals (paragraph 44). The Court did not find scientific, legal and social developments between the member states sufficient, in 1992, to enable it to overrule its *Rees* and *Cossey* judgments (paragraph 48).

Nevertheless, the Court found a violation of Article 8, because the applicant's submissions showed that the position of transsexuals was much harder in France than in the United Kingdom (paragraph 49). French law made it barely possible to change forenames: the applicant's identity documents (identity card, passport, voting card, etc.), her cheque books and her official correspondence (telephone accounts, tax demands, etc.) described her by the male forename of Norbert (paragraph 56). As so many official documents (extracts of birth certificates, computerised identity cards, European Communities passports, etc.) indicated sex, the applicant could not cross a frontier, undergo an identity check, or carry out the many transactions of daily life requiring proof of identity without disclosing the discrepancy between her legal and her apparent sexes (paragraph 59). The Court accepted that, 'even having regard to the State's margin of appreciation, the fair balance between the general interest and the interests of the individual [had] not been attained' in France (paragraph 63).

The Court ruled by fifteen votes to six that Article 8 had been violated. Dissenting opinions concentrated on the fact that France should have enjoyed a wide margin of appreciation in this area, considering the absence of a common denominator in the legislation of the member states. They also expressed fears before the unknown. Two judges expressed the view that the Court might have opened 'the way to serious and as yet unforeseeable consequences'. Exclaiming, 'one cannot accept dubious hermaphrodites and ambiguous situations', they aired the risk of seeing 'half-feminised men claiming the right to marry normally constituted men, and then where would the line have to be drawn?'[13]

I shall return in the conclusion to the problem of wishing to rule out ambiguity. I note here that *B. v. France* is a false positive in the case law of the Court. Although the Court found a violation of Article 8 in this case, that finding was strictly confined to a national situation which made the *daily* life of the post-operative transsexual potentially distressing. *B. v. France* was a far cry from a resounding victory for transsexuals. Indeed, at the first opportunity, as it were, the Court returned to deliver a verdict of non-violation.

X, Y and Z v. *United Kingdom* (1997): The denial of legal fatherhood

Up to the early 1990s the Court had not been forced, directly, to consider the implications of the transsexual status of one individual on other persons.[14] The *X, Y and Z* case changed this. It was brought by a female-to-male transsexual, his female partner and 'their' child. Mr X, born as a female in 1955, had undertaken gender reassignment surgery in 1979, when he was already living with Ms Y. In 1990, X and Y applied for fertility treatment in the form of artificial insemination by donor ('AID'). This was initially refused but, after a successful appeal, Y was impregnated with sperm from an anonymous donor in January 1992. After Z's birth, X was not permitted to be registered as the child's father, being legally of female sex, even though he had been asked to acknowledge himself as the father of the child by the relevant hospital ethics committee, as a condition of AID treatment. Z bore X's name, and she, as well as a second child (born through the same method after the application was lodged at Strasbourg) and the wider family considered X as the father of the children. To all appearances, the applicants lived as a traditional family. They argued that they were denied respect for their family and private life as a result of the lack of legal recognition of X's role as father[15] (*X, Y and Z*, paragraphs 12–18, 29 and 33).

The Court was not persuaded by their argument (even though the Commission had been). Issues concerning filiation following medically assisted procreation were intensely debated. Since there was little common ground among the member states in this area, the respondent state was to be offered a wide margin of appreciation (paragraph 44). As for the balance to be struck between the general interest and the interest of the individuals concerned with respect to the law (paragraph 47), it had not been established that the child Z or the parents suffered undue hardship (paragraphs 48–9). The uncertainty with regard to how to protect the interest of children in the situation of Z meant that the Court could not impose any single viewpoint (paragraph 51).

By fourteen votes to six, the Court ruled that there had been no violation of Article 8. Referring to the dissenting opinion of Judge Martens in *Cossey*, three judges made theirs the qualification that the refusal to give legal effect to the new identity of the transsexual was 'cruel'.[16] Another relied on lofty language to mark his disapproval of the Court's decision: 'It is part of our common European heritage that governments are under a duty to take special care of individuals who are disadvantaged in any way'.[17] Differences of opinion exist within the Court. In the next judgment, dissent will come even more forcefully as to the ruling of non-violation regarding Article 8 – but, significantly, still not regarding Article 12.

Sheffield and Horsham v. *the United Kingdom* (1998): A tightening majority on the non-violation of Article 8.

Ms Sheffield and Ms Horsham are two unrelated applicants whose cases were joined before the Court because they raised a similar issue. Both happened to have been born in the UK in 1946, as male. Ms Sheffield had sex reassignment surgery some time around 1986, at which point contact with her daughter ceased.[18] She brought before the Court the issue that her birth certificate and social security and police records mentioned her former sex. This had led her to be dissuaded to act as a witness in court and to have to disclose her situation in certain contexts (such as entering an insurance contract in respect of her car). She also alleged discrimination in relation to work and employment. Ms Horsham had undertaken surgery in 1992, in the Netherlands rather than the United Kingdom – which she had left in 1971 to lead her life abroad as a female. She had a male partner in the Netherlands whom she was planning to marry; they wanted to lead married life in the United Kingdom, but this was impossible as a matter of English law, as Ms Horsham was legally male. Both applicants alleged that Articles 8 and 12 of the Convention were violated (*Sheffield and Horsham*, paragraphs 12–25, 36 and 37).

The Commission considered that 'the applicants, even if they [did] not suffer daily humiliation and embarrassment, [were] nevertheless subject to a real and continuous risk of intrusive and distressing enquiries and to an obligation to make embarrassing disclosures' (paragraph 49). It found a violation of Article 8, by fifteen votes to one. But, contrary to the expectations of some commentators (Wijte 1998), the Court kept to the line it had adopted in *Rees* and *Cossey* and found no breach of Article 8 (paragraphs 53–9). It reiterated the need to keep this area under review. This time, however, it observed with irritation: 'it would appear that the respondent State has not taken any steps to do so' (paragraph 60).

This remark suggested that if the United Kingdom persisted in not reviewing its domestic provisions, it could well be found in violation of Article 8 next time it appeared before the Court. Furthermore, the ruling on Article 8 in *Sheffield and Horsham* was adopted by the narrowest of majority: eleven votes against nine.[19] The dissenting judges, relying on information submitted by Liberty, remarked that only four countries (Albania, Andorra, Ireland and the United Kingdom) out of the thirty-seven member states surveyed at the time of the *Sheffield and Horsham* proceedings expressly prohibited any change in birth-certificate entries following gender reassignment surgery.

The Commission concluded that it was unnecessary to rule on the alleged violation of Article 12, as no separate issue arose once a violation of Article 8 had been found. Not surprisingly, the Court dismissed the claim about Article 12, on the basis that 'Article 12 refers to the traditional marriage between persons of opposite biological sex' (paragraph 66). Only two judges dissented with this ruling. Judge Van Dijk remarked that the violation of Article 8 he had found logically encompassed a violation of Article 12. In his opinion, shared by Judge Wildhaber, applicants had to be considered as persons of the new sex for legal purposes, including for the application of Article 12. This solution was not especially problematic as the concept of 'sex' found in Article 12 did not need to be based on biological criteria. Indeed, this solution was the more warranted since the option for the transsexual to marry a person of her newly acquired sex was no longer acceptable[20] (paragraph 8 of Van Dijk's dissenting opinion).

Goodwin v. *the United Kingdom* (2002): Victory at last

The male-to-female applicant in this case[21] brought a complaint similar to that of *Rees*, *Cossey* and *Sheffield and Horsham*. She argued that she had suffered sexual harassment at work. She also complained that her request for a new National Insurance number was refused and her file was marked 'sensitive' instead, with the result that only an employee of a particular grade had access to it, obliging her to make special appointments with the Department of Social Security for even the most trivial matters. She stated that she had refrained from a number of actions (such as opting for a remortgage and reporting a theft to the police) to avoid having to produce her birth certificate. As a man, she was prevented from retiring at sixty and had to wait until sixty five for a free London bus pass.

The Court, after going through the motions of its reasoning in the transsexual cases, now concluded that:

> The stress and alienation arising from a discordance between the position in society assumed by a post-operative transsexual and the status imposed by law which refuses to recognise the change of gender cannot, in the Court's view, be regarded as a minor inconvenience arising from a formality. A conflict between social reality and law arises which places the transsexual in an anomalous position, in which he or she may experience feelings of vulnerability, humiliation and anxiety (*Goodwin*, paragraph 77).

> In the twenty first century the right of transsexuals to personal development cannot be regarded as a matter of controversy requiring the lapse of time to cast clearer light on the issues involved. In short, the unsatisfactory situation in which post-operative transsexuals live in an intermediate zone as not quite one gender or the other is no longer sustainable (paragraph 90).

> [T]he Court has since 1986 emphasised the importance of keeping the need for appropriate legal measures under review ... [T]he fair balance that is inherent in the Convention now tilts decisively in favour of the applicant (paragraph 93).

In this case, the Court unanimously found a violation of both Article 8 *and* Article 12 of the Convention. This was undoubtedly a landmark victory for campaigners for transsexual rights, with the decision forcing the Government to reconsider its position and amend the legislation.

The new position of the Court was to be anticipated. Interestingly, even before it was publicly announced through the delivery of the *Goodwin* judgment on 11 July 2002, the flavour of the case law involving transsexuals had arguably started to change. Come 2003, in which *Van Kück* is our next case, what was at stake was no more an issue at the very heart of a principle but one tangential to it.

Van Kück v. *Germany* (2003): The 'normalisation' of transsexual human rights issues

The case of Ms Van Kück, a post-operative transsexual, was directed against Germany, a country which makes it possible for the entry regarding sex to be changed on birth certificates and other official documentation after gender reassignment surgery. Not surprisingly, therefore, *Van Kück* concerns neither Article 8 (at least not in the sense encountered above) nor Article 12. The main complaint raised by the applicant related to Article 6 of the Convention (hereafter 'Article 6).

Ms Van Kück's health insurance company had refused to reimburse her for the hormonal and surgical treatment she undertook to treat her transsexual condition. She lost her dispute in the national courts: the German courts considered her treatment unnecessary. Ms Van Kück alleged before the Court that the rules governing the decision on her case were incompatible with Article 6, which guarantees individuals a fair trial by a tribunal in the determination of their civil rights and obligations. Moreover, she argued that the interpretation of 'necessary medical treatment' adopted by the German courts was arbitrary, and that they had failed to respect her sexual identity (thus also leading to a violation of Article 8). She won on both counts on a very tight majority (four votes against three).

Article 6 is the most debated provision before the European Court of Human Rights. It has always accounted for about half of the whole of the Strasbourg case law. To this extent, *Van Kück* can be said to signal a normalisation of the Strasbourg transsexual case law. It seems to deal, not with an issue central to the being of the individual, but with more materialistic considerations (Dembour 2003).

Conclusion

Transsexualism has been recognised as a medical condition, which is medically treatable, since the second half of the twentieth century.[22] Social recognition of the plight of transsexuals followed the medical trend, and is more developed in some societies than in others. Significantly, an appreciable number of countries belonging to the Council of Europe, which extends from 'Westport to Wladiwoskok' (Bruisma and de Blois 1997), have adapted their legislation in recent years to accommodate the plight of transsexuals. In contrast to these national developments, the European Court of Human Rights has proved 'retrograde': for twenty years the Court has insisted in staying fixed in a direction different from the one that was emerging from medical, social and national legislative moves. The denomination of the Court as a court of *human rights* could have raised expectations that it would see its role as defending superior, fundamental, radical, or minority values. However, the fact that the Court *is* a supreme judicial institution has led it – one could almost say inevitably – to be one step behind the social developments that were taking place at national level.

Many had approved the longstanding 'cautiousness' of the Court (e.g. Elósegui 1998). For Michel Levinet (1999: 672), commenting on the case law up to *Sheffield and Horsham*, the attribution of 'male' or 'female' at birth had a mythical and metaphysical dimension beyond the medical and legal aspects with which the Court had to deal. Levinet thought the Court was right not to redraw the universe. He associated transsexualism with postmodernism, extreme individualism and selfishness ('*absolutisation du moi*'), and with demands for any attitude and possibly every form of family to be legitimated (ibid.). After the *Goodwin* victory, two doctors at the Portman Clinic argued that a 'sex change' operation tends to leave patients with a mutilated body and no psychological resolution (*Guardian,*

16 July 2002). They argued that transsexuals attempt to live as a member of the opposite sex so as 'to avoid internal conflict which may otherwise prove to be too distressing'. Recently an academic commentary has suggested, with repeated references to Pierre Legendre, that the Court followed the applicant in *Goodwin* in 'his' madness and delusion (Wachsmann and Marienburg-Wachsmann 2003). For the authors, the judicial decision constituted a serious breach in the symbolic order, for apparently compassionate reasons but with dramatic consequences in terms of the abdication by the state, law and authority to keep the order – not least the genealogical order – and the historical truth.

By contrast other scholars relentlessly urged the Court to recognise and do something about the plight of the transsexual well before *Goodwin*. The Belgian legal theorist François Rigaux (1998) was of the view that the Court's case law consisted of a series of missed opportunities. He sought to dispel four common errors: the transsexual is not pursuing a whimsical fancy; she does not seek to change sex but to unify diverging criteria; she is not a 'perverse' homosexual; concepts in this area, including those of sex and gender are approximations (Rigaux 1998: 139). Rigaux rightly identified the central 'problem' as having to do with binary oppositions which, as anthropologists know, are central to the human organisation of the world but less clear-cut than their conceptualisations imply. For Rigaux, the pretence that the male/female distinction is more determinate than the opposition between day and night (where does one end and the other begin?) had lasted for as long as one sex has dominated the other (1998: 144). The transsexual condition showed the limit of the distinction, which is either more blurred or more encompassing than an either/or formulation implies.

Levinet assumed that the transsexual is necessarily an ultra-conformist individual who wants to live according to the traditional criteria of the other sex (1999: 662, citing Pousson-Petit). Some transsexuals do, but others do not.[23] Significantly, Stephen Whittle (2002: 2) says that what he refuses is to be regarded as a woman for, having lived as a man since the age of nineteen, he has never been one; he is happy to be regarded as a trans-man, whose experience is different from other men. Wachsmann and Marienburg-Wachsmann (2003) castigated doctors (and the Court) for participating in the phantasm of an all-powerful medical science and deceiving their patients as to the possibility of making them totally part of the other sex, as if all their problems would suddenly disappear. However, I do not see any such delusion in the accounts Whittle (2002: 271–7) gives of the stories of people he has come across as the coordinator of the Female to Male Transsexual Network in the United Kingdom. In line with Wachsmann and Marienburg-Wachsmann (2003), Levinet argued that the applicants were seeking not a status specific to the transsexual but the status of the sex to which they felt they belonged (1999: 662–3, citing Evain). Again, this is not necessarily true. Whittle (2002: 17), for example, notes that 'X was not asking to be a man in law, but rather to be afforded the title "father" as a transsexual man'.

Levinet regarded transsexualism as a 'bulimic' claim, where one claim would lead to another. There he was right. The issues before the Court have moved from the issue of the birth certificate to parental rights to the reimbursement of medical expenses, and they will move again. Even though I have talked of *Van Kück* as signalling the normalisation of the transsexual case law, *Goodwin* will not mark the final position of the Court on transsexualism. One can expect issues of discrimination at work, sex classification in sport competition, detention in the prison of the wrong sex to be raised before the Court. Moreover transsexual applicants who have appeared before the Court have so far been 'post-operative'. The questions of when a transsexual has 'transited' and how to treat an individual in 'transition' are bound to come up and to prove problematic. This is the more so since law likes to deal with clear-cut categories and 'transition' is not a straightforward process,[24] cannot happen overnight and is never fully realised.

Rigaux (1998: 133) criticised the Court for seeing in the transsexual an ambiguous being who, in terms of marriage, was neither man nor woman and thus could not marry. I sympathise with Rigaux's position. At the same time the aim should not be to work towards removing ambiguity, but to seek better ways of accommodating the 'misfits' that our reliance on categories produce. However, none of us, not even the transsexuals, manage to escape the male v. female distinction – we live by it. Given this, despite admittedly not being an expert on the issue, I cannot help thinking that a move towards recognising what transsexuals feel is their real sex or gender is intellectually more sophisticated and ethically more compassionate than the position which insists they are deluded.

Notes

Acknowledgements: I wish to thank the editors for encouraging me to delve into a case law I had never read closely and for providing comments on the text. My thanks also go to Bob Morton, Craig Lind and especially Amanda Collins.

1. Following Rigaux, Van Drooghenbroeck (2001: 568–9) has noted that the supposedly great victories achieved at Strasbourg commonly *follow* the near accomplishment of legislative reform at home.
2. Except, for instance, if the applicant and the defendant state had reached a 'friendly settlement', as happened in X v. *Federal Republic of Germany*, Report of 11 October 1979 (see van Dijk and van Hoof 1998: 186–7).
3. When Protocol 11 was first discussed, the fall of the Berlin Wall and the accession of Eastern and Central European countries to the Council of Europe had not been anticipated. The current institutional arrangements have failed to keep up with the resulting caseload and a new, controversial (Dembour 2002), Protocol 14 was signed in May 2004.
4. The Court was noted for being generally more conservative than the Commission (Tomkins 1997: 23).
5. Transsexual applicants have also alleged the violation of Articles 3 (inhuman and degrading treatment), 13 (national remedy) and 14 (discrimination) of the Convention, but unsuccessfully and without attracting detailed responses from either the Commission or the Court.
6. My presentation of the cases discussed in this article, including their facts, the arguments of the parties and the decisions adopted by either the national or the Strasbourg institutions, is based exclusively on the text of the judgments of the European Court of Human Rights.

7. In 1979 Mr Van Oosterwijck obtained a law degree from the University of Brussels, arguably easing his access to judicial redress including at Strasbourg.

8. The name of the case is the applicant's name italicised. Judgments of the Court and decisions on admissibility are available at: http://cmiskp.echr.coe.int/tkp197/search.asp? skin=hvdoc-en. Lawyers refer to paragraphs (if available), rather than pages, when citing or quoting a judgment or a legal opinion.

9. He had not specifically relied on the Convention in first instance and in appeal and he had not brought the case before the Court of Cassation.

10. It would be wrong to expect the Court to impose a precise line of conduct on state governments. Such a direct imposition would go against the subsidiary character of the European Convention system of human rights protection and would contravene the principle of national sovereignty. For example, in *Rees*, had the Court found a violation of Article 8, it would have made clear that the way the national authorities organised the issue of birth certificates was unacceptable, but it would nonetheless have refrained from indicating exactly how this defect was to be corrected.

11. Martens refers to *post-operative* transsexuals throughout his dissenting opinion, presumably accepting that the case of non-operated transsexuals is different. A few years later, the Commission declared inadmissible the petition of a male-to-female transsexual applicant who complained that she had been refused the rectification of her birth certificate – she had not had surgery, and could still father a child: *Roetzheim* v. *Germany*, decision of 23 October 1997.

12. These included Denmark, Finland, Germany, Italy, Luxemburg, the Netherlands, Spain, Sweden and Turkey (through appropriate legislation) and Belgium, France and Portugal (through case law). Elósegui (1998: 101) disputes this claim in regard to Spain. The case of *B.* v. *France* indicates that the situation was not completely resolved in France either.

13. Judge Valticos, joined by judge Loizou. Another judge criticised the imposition on the French State of the consequences of a surgical operation 'performed in another State, voluntarily and intentionally and without prior checks' (Pinheiro Farinha, paragraph 6). He feared 'the trivialisation of irreversible surgical operations' (paragraph 2). Yet another judge (Pettitti) warned that '[t]he whole of civil law and inheritance law could be thrown into confusion'.

14. Ms Cossey's partner might have argued that his right to marry was violated, but he did not. A few months after the Court gave its decision in *X, Y and Z*, the Commission declared inadmissible the petition by a male-to-female transsexual whose access to her child following divorce was suspended after she failed to comply with the judicially imposed condition of wearing male clothes in the presence of the child to whom she was legally the father: *L.F.* v. *Ireland*, application no. 28154/95, decision of 2 July 1997, discussed in Levinet (1999: 671, note 57). In the *Sheffield and Horsham* case, reviewed below, the first applicant was a male-to-female transsexual who had a daughter from a marriage which was dissolved just before she undertook sex reassignment surgery. On divorce contact with her daughter was terminated. Ms Sheffield would have wished to complain at Strasbourg about the by-then twelve-year-long lack of contact, but her claim on this ground was declared inadmissible for being out of time.

15. They also claimed they were discriminated against in contravention of Article 14. Mr X felt unable to accept a job offer outside the United Kingdom, as Z and Y would not have legally qualified as his dependants (paragraph 19).

16. Partly dissenting opinion of Judge Casadevall, joined by Judges Russo and Makarczyk.

17. Dissenting opinion of Judge Foighel, paragraphs 6 and 7. See also the dissenting opinion of Judge Gotchev, who insists that the welfare of the child – understood as integration into the family whenever possible – should be the prevailing consideration in striking this balance.

18. See note 14 above.

19. Moreover, Judge Sir John Freeland concurred 'after much hesitation and even with some reluctance'.

20. On 9 November 1989, the Commission had declared inadmissible the application by a male-to-female transsexual and her female partner, regarding the impossibility of legal marriage (*Eriksson and Goldschmidt* v. *Sweden*).

21. As well as in a second case decided on the same day: *I.* v. *United Kingdom.*

22. Although the first case of surgical intervention certainly dates back to at least 1931 (Whittle 2002: 20) and probably before (Wachsmann and Marienburg-Wachsmann, 2003: 1168).

23. See, for example, *Eriksson and Goldschmidt* v. *Switzerland,* which concerned a lesbian couple, one of whom was a male-to-female transsexual.

24. For example, what is required? Whittle persuasively argues against vaginectomy for female-to-male transsexuals (2002, Chapter 14).

References

British Medical Association. 1995. *Complete Family Health Encyclopedia.* London: Dorling Kindersley.

Bruisma, F. and M. de Blois. 1997. 'Rules of Law from Westport to Wladiwostok. Separate Opinions in the European Court of Human Rights'. *Netherlands Quarterly of Human Rights*, 15, 175–86.

Cowan, J.K., M.-B. Dembour and R.A. Wilson. 2001. *Culture and Rights: Anthropological Perspectives.* Cambridge: Cambridge University Press.

Dembour, M.-B. 2002. '"Finishing Off" Cases: The Radical Solution to the Problem of the Expanding ECHR Caseload'. *European Review of Human Rights Law*, 5, 604–23.

―――― 2003. *Losing its Core? Human Rights as a Drifting Concept.* Paper presented at the Conference on 'The "Legalisation" of Human Rights' held at University College London in April 2003, ms.

Elósegui, M. 1998. 'Transsexualité, droit à la vie privée et droit au mariage. Examen du cas espagnol à la lumière de la jurisprudence de la Cour européenne des Droits de l'Homme'. *Revue interdisciplinaire d'études juridiques*, 41, 89–126.

Karsten, I. 1999. 'Atypical Families and the Human Rights Act: The Rights of Unmarried Fathers, Same Sex Couples and Transsexuals'. *European Human Rights Law Review*, 4, 195–205.

Leach, P.H. 2001. *Taking a Case to the European Court of Human Rights.* London: Blackstone.

Levinet, M. 1999. 'La revendication transsexuelle et la Convention européenne des droits de l'homme'. *Revue trimestrielle des droits de l'homme*, 39, 646–72.

Niveau, G., M. Ummel and T. Harding. 1999. 'Human Rights Aspects of Transsexualism', *Health and Human Rights*, 4,1, 35–64.

Reid, R. 1995. 'Psychiatric and Psychological Aspects of Transsexualism', in *Transsexualism, Medicine and Law*, Proceedings of the XXIIIrd Colloquy on European Law. Strasbourg: Council of Europe, 25–50.

Rigaux, F. 1998. 'Les transsexuels devant la Cour européenne des droits de l'homme: une suite d'occasions manquées'. *Revue trimestrielle des droits de l'homme*, 34, 130–44.

Tomkins, A. 1997. 'Civil Liberties in the Council of Europe: A Critical Survey'. In *European Civil Liberties and the European Convention on Human Rights*, Gearty, C.A. (ed.). The Hague: Nijhoff, 1–52.

Van Dijk, P. and G.J.H. van Hoof. 1998. *Theory and Practice of the European Convention on Human Rights*. The Hague: Kluwer.

Van Drooghenbroeck, S. 2001. *La proportionnalité dans le droit de la Convention européenne des droits de l'homme: Prendre l'idée simple au sérieux*. Bruxelles: Bruylant.

Wachsmann, P. and Marienburg-Wachsmann, A. 2003. 'La folie dans la loi: Considérations critiques sur la nouvelle jurisprudence de la Cour européenne des droits de l'homme en matière de transsexualisme'. *Revue trimestrielle des droits de l'homme*, 1157–83.

Whittle, S. 2002. *Respect and Equality: Transsexual and Transgender Rights*. London: Cavendish.

Wijte, S. 1998. 'Post-Operative Transsexuals and the European Court of Human Rights', *SIM Special. To Baehr in our minds. Essays on human rights from the heart of the Netherlands*, 21, 501–20.

4

TWO VIEWS ON THE GENDER IDENTITY OF BYZANTINE EUNUCHS

Shaun Tougher

Introduction

The gender identity I shall consider here is that of the eunuch; the specific context is the Byzantine Empire, the name given to the continuation of the Roman Empire in the east. The Byzantine Empire was centred on the ancient Greek city of Byzantium (modern day Istanbul), which was renamed Constantinople by the Emperor Constantine the Great (306–37). Its existence can be dated from 330 (the year of the official dedication of the city) until 1453 (the year of the fall of the city to the Ottoman Turks). Its language was predominantly Greek, its religion Christianity. Whilst I will make some general remarks about Byzantine views on the gender identity of eunuchs, I want to highlight in particular two texts that are notable in the history of literature for taking the eunuch as their specific subject. They are Claudian's *In Eutropium* (AD 399) and Theophylact of Ochrid's *In Defence of Eunuchs* (probably early twelfth century). The pair provide interesting comparison. They are divergent in many ways, but most notably one is a deliberate attack on a specific eunuch, the other a deliberate defence of eunuchs in general. I will explore how each presents the gender identity of eunuchs, then compare the texts with each other, and finally attempt to reach some general conclusions about the gender identity of eunuchs in Byzantium.

Eunuchs

First, we can define and characterise the eunuch; we can record where and when eunuchs are found; and we can list the roles that eunuchs tended to play. The eunuch could be defined as 'a castrated man', but this is rather simplistic. For instance, it can be argued that the true eunuch is the male who has been castrated before puberty, for only castration before puberty produces the classic physical indicators of eunuchness, as a result of the lack of androgen hormone stimulation at puberty (Rouselle 1988: 124). These include the high-pitched, child-like voice, due to the lack of the development of the vocal chords; the lack of facial hair (the absence of a beard is often noted), and body hair in general; more developed fat deposits on hips, buttocks and breasts; and extended arm and leg length (see Peschel and Peschel 1987). Castration could occur after puberty, but would not be as physically apparent. It should also be noted that the method and extent of 'castration' could vary. The testes could be excised, or simply crushed.[1] The scrotum could be completely severed, and the penis could also be cut off.[2] Further, some eunuchs reputedly owed their condition to accident; famous examples are the Attalid dynast Philetairos (Guyot 1980: 219–20), and many of the castrati (Peschel and Peschel 1987: 24). However, we also need to remember that there are individuals who could be categorised as eunuchs by birth, such as the second-century AD sophist Favorinus.[3] This is acknowledged in the words of Jesus Christ, who identified three types of eunuchs: those who made themselves eunuchs for the kingdom of heaven, those who were made eunuchs by others, and those that were born eunuchs (Matthew 19.12). This quotation provides a further category, that of the metaphorical eunuch. There were those who imposed chastity upon themselves. This chapter will however be concerned with those who had been deliberately castrated prior to puberty.

Turning to the issue of the historical distribution of eunuchs we can note that they are found throughout the span of history, from ancient to modern times, and in a diversity of cultures. For example, in addition to Byzantium, we meet them in China, Assyria, Persia, Italy, Russia, India, the Hellenistic Kingdoms and the Roman and Islamic Empires.[4] Finally, we can record the diverse roles that eunuchs played within these countries and powers. Eunuchs could be luxury slaves, status symbols denoting the wealth of their owners; they could be employed specifically at royal or imperial courts, becoming powerful chamberlains or officials; they could have a role in religion, whether pagan (e.g. the *galli*), Christian (e.g. the Skoptzy) or Hindu (e.g. the *hijras*); and they could have a role in music (e.g. the famous castrati, such as Farinelli).[5]

Eunuchs in Byzantium

Eunuchs were a fact of life in Byzantium (Guilland 1943, Ringrose 1994, 1996, Tougher 1997). They were most notable for their roles at the imperial court, where they were employed as servants of the imperial family, from ordinary chamberlain to the heady heights of *praepositus sacri cubiculi* ('grand chamberlain') or *parakoimomenos* (Dunlap 1924, Schlinkert 1994, Scholten 1995). In the middle Byzantine period other specialised palace posts were reserved for eunuchs.[6] They could also be employed in the imperial administration generally – for instance, as treasurers (*sakellarioi*), such as Leo the *patrikios* the patron of the famous Leo Bible, or even generals (*strategoi*), such as Narses. The place of eunuchs within imperial service was inherited by Byzantium from the Roman Empire (it seems that eunuchs were a staple feature of the late Roman court from the end of the third century);[7] they survived into the Palaiologan period (thirteenth-fifteenth centuries AD), if in an apparently subdued fashion (Gaul 2002). However, eunuchs in Byzantium were not just secular attendants or administrators; spiritual roles were also open to them (Guilland 1943: 202–205; Ringrose 1999), as clergy, bishops and monks. They could be recognised for their holiness, and some even became saints. Some also found roles as singers (Moran 2002, Witt 2002).

In many societies that employed court eunuchs, they tended to be imported foreigners (Tougher 2002b). A good example is the Ottoman Empire, famous for its use of black eunuchs imported from Africa, though it also used foreign white eunuchs (Toledano 1984). The later Roman/early Byzantine Empire tends to match this pattern. It seems that most eunuchs in imperial service in this period were imported as slaves, mainly from Armenia. In the middle Byzantine Empire we still find such examples, but there also seems to be a significant internal production of native eunuchs, in particular from Paphlagonia (Magdalino 1998; Tougher 2002b). Such internal production can be found in other cultures too, such as China. Thus in Byzantium we find that parents may castrate their own sons for the sake of court careers.

However, there were also other reasons for castration in Byzantium. In particular it could be used as a form of punishment. It is found as a penalty for sex crimes, such as rape or homosexuality.[8] It could also be used in the political arena, either to block the accession of rivals to imperial power or to overthrow and debar current emperors: eunuchs could not become emperors in Byzantium. In the ninth century, when Leo V (813–20) came to power, he ousted Michael I and castrated his sons so that they could not reclaim the throne; when Leo V himself was overthrown, his own sons were castrated by Michael II (820–9) (Treadgold 1988: 188–9, 224). In the tenth century, Alexander (912–13) is said to have contemplated castrating his nephew, the Emperor Constantine VII (Toynbee 1973: 8). Another reason for castration in Byzantium was health, as Leo VI acknowledges in one of his new laws.[9] Byzantium also knew examples of those who were accidental eunuchs, such as the sixth-century general Solomon (Dewing 1916: 102–103).

The Image of eunuchs

Despite the common presence of eunuchs in Byzantine society, views of eunuchs inherited from Classical Greek and Roman thought tend to be negative and hostile. The literature of the late Roman/early Byzantine period is notorious for its hostility towards eunuchs, as highlighted by Hopkins (1963, 1978). A famous example cited by Hopkins (1978: 195) is the letter of the Cappadocian Father Basil of Caesarea to Simplicia (Deferrari 1928: 228–32). The bishop characterises eunuchs as woman-mad, envious, corrupt, quick-tempered, money-mad, cruel, slaves of the belly, lamenting the loss of a dinner, fickle, niggardly, all-receiving, insatiable, mad and jealous. The history of Ammianus Marcellinus and the compilation of the *Historia Augusta* are also noted for their hatred of eunuchs. Ammianus targets his anger mainly at the court of Constantius II (337–61) and the grand chamberlain Eusebius (Tougher 1999a, Sidéris 2000), whilst the *Historia Augusta* renounces the influence of eunuchs at court generally (Cameron 1965). Such hostile views did persist into the middle and late Byzantine periods (Tougher 1999b, Gaul 2002). In the ninth century Photios assailed the eunuch John Angourios in a letter, and declared that 'John has made his race even more "hated and notorious for wickedness" than before' (Vinson 1998: 488–9). The chronicle of Kedrenos (eleventh-twelfth centuries) records the saying 'If you have a eunuch kill him; if you haven't, buy one and kill him' (Ringrose 1996: 80). The twelfth-century Byzantine romance *Aristandros and Kallithea*, written by Constantine Manasses, relates that although a viper had bitten a eunuch it was the snake that died, since the eunuch's blood was more poisonous (Gaul 2002: 206).

Hostility to eunuchs could also be expressed in gender terms (Ringrose 1994). In his letter cited above Basil of Caesarea also describes eunuchs as unwomanly (*athely*), unmanly (*anandron*) and effeminate (*thelydriodes*). Further, they could be portrayed as an aberration, a third sex. In a speech praising the Emperor Julian (361–63) Claudius Mamertinus describes eunuchs as 'exiles from the society of the human race, belonging neither to one sex nor the other' (*Latin Panegyric* 3.19.4 cited in Lieu 1989: 29). This is akin to what the Emperor Severus Alexander is made to say of eunuchs in the *Historia Augusta*; he asserts that they are 'a third sex of the human race' (Magie 1924: 220–221). In the tenth century the diplomat Leo Choirosphaktes suggests a similar categorisation by reflecting on the condition of a eunuch that it was as if he had been born of two women (Tougher 1999b: 92).

However, it is important to recognise that positive images of eunuchs can also be found. In classical Greek texts eunuchs can be praised for their loyalty and devotion,[10] and indeed Ammianus himself does allude to one such example, though he stresses its rarity (Rolfe 1950: 226–33). In particular, though, it is the context of the Christianisation of the late Roman/early Byzantine Empire that accounts for an alternative positive view of eunuchs. This has been emphasised by Boulhol and Cochelin (1992) for the early Byzantine period, and others have followed their lead for the subsequent period (Ringrose 1996, Sidéris 2002). Essentially, eunuchs could be deemed to be chaste and pure. This stance was signalled by the Bible itself, given the apparent shift in attitude to eunuchs found in Isaiah, and also reflected by the statement, cited above, of Jesus himself (Matthew 19.12).

But what ramifications does this positive view of eunuchs have for their gender identity? At one level, it asserts their normalcy as men (Boulhol and Cochelin 1992: 66). However, at another it serves to create an alternative gender status; the eunuch can be assimilated with the angelic other (Sidéris 2002: 166–8). Thus, we can see that in Byzantium there existed a range of gender identities for eunuchs: they could be masculine, feminine and other.

The texts: Claudian and Theophylact

It is of course risky, not to say unsatisfying, to generalise too much. Thus I feel it would be useful to explore some specific texts in more depth. Two authors virtually nominate themselves for such an exploration, since they take a eunuch or eunuchs as their especial subject. They are Claudian and Theophylact, and their respective texts are *In Eutropium* and *In Defence of Eunuchs*. I will establish the context of these texts, the arguments that the writers are making, and then explore the issue of the gender identity of eunuchs in each case. I will also compare both texts, and reflect in particular on the argument that by the twelfth century a shift in the gender identity of Byzantine eunuchs had occurred.

The negative view: Claudian's *In Eutropium* (I and II)

In AD 395 the Emperor Theodosius I died, bequeathing the empire to his two young sons Arcadius and Honorius. Arcadius was to rule the East, Honorius the West. Given the youth of the emperors, however, the exercise of power lay more with their right-hand men. In the West this was the half-Vandal General Stilicho. It seems that Stilicho had ambitions to exercise power in the East as well, and the period was marked by competition between the courts. A crucial mouthpiece during this competition was the poet Claudian (Cameron 1970). Claudian was originally from Alexandria, but had acquired the role of 'court poet' of the western court, producing in Latin verse works of praise and blame. Part of his output was two attacks on a eunuch named Eutropius. Eutropius had risen to become Arcadius' Grand Chamberlain and right-hand man. It was in particular the appointment of Eutropius as Consul in AD 399 that inspired Claudian's works on the eunuch. *In Eutropium I* was written when Eutropius was still Consul, whilst *In Eutropium II* dates to his fall from grace and exile in Cyprus.[11] The poems are fascinating as examples of the hostile treatment of eunuchs, and do dwell on the issue of their gender identity.[12] I will discuss the poems generally before examining this aspect of them.

Claudian begins *In Eutropium I* with the outrage of the fact that a eunuch has become Consul, then traces Eutropius' career and deeds, and ends with an address by Roma to the Emperor Honorius, in which Stilicho is called upon to deal with the eunuch. The poet also acknowledges in *In Eutropium II* that Eutropius has fallen from power, but argues that the effeminate East still needs salvation. The disasters (especially military) that affected the East under the eunuch consul are recalled, and Aurora calls upon Stilicho in Italy to save the Eastern Empire. The attacks dwell especially on Eutropius' slave origin, his physical condition, his ambiguous gender identity, his bad character, and his bad government. However, as Long says, 'For Claudian, the central fact of Eutropius's person was that he was a eunuch' (Long 1996: 107, echoed by Kuefler 2001: 65–6). All these negative aspects are intertwined and bound up with his eunuch-hood.

Considering Claudian's presentation of Eutropius' gender identity in particular, it can be seen that the poet categorises the Grand Chamberlain in several different ways. The eunuch can be man, woman and also something other entirely.

The image of Eutropius as a woman appears right at the start of *In Eutropium I*. Claudian wails 'O shame to heaven and earth! Our cities behold an old woman decked in a consul's robe who gives a woman's name to the year' (*In Eutropium I* 9–10), and demands 'at least give us a man' (*In Eutropium I* 29). When Eutropius is cast off by his lover Ptolemy,[13] Claudian has the eunuch wonder 'Leav'st thou Eutropius a widow?' (*In Eutropium I* 69–70). Eutropius goes on to become 'a lady's maid' (*In Eutropium I* 104–105). When he became Grand Chamberlain, Eutropius' acquisition of a military role provides Claudian with much mileage for his attack. He declares 'Mars blushed, Bellona scoffed and turned her from the disgrace of the East whene'er with arrows strung and flashing quiver the aged Amazon practises battle or hurries back as arbiter of peace and war to hold parley with the Getae. Our enemies rejoiced at the sight and felt that at last we were lacking in *men*' (*In Eutropium I* 238–43). Eutropius should have left the male arena of warfare well alone, and devoted himself to the female craft of spinning: 'The distaff, not the dart should be thine' (*In Eutropium I* 274). Claudian also has Roma observe that, unlike the West, the East is accustomed to women as rulers, and demands, 'Drive this foreign pollution from out the boundaries of manly Latium' (*In Eutropium I* 431–2). A scene from *In Eutropium II*, when the eunuch is urging his leading officials to war, likens Eutropius to a forewoman haranguing her working-girls (*In Eutropium II* 365–75).

Claudian is also happy to employ the categorisation of Eutropius as effeminate, a half-man (e.g. *In Eutropium I* 171; *In Eutropium II* 21). Addressing the castration of Eutropius as a boy, Claudian comments 'Up hastens the Armenian, skilled by operating with unerring knife, to make males womanish' (*In Eutropium I* 47–8). Roma asserts 'The majesty of Rome cannot devolve upon an effeminate' (*In Eutropium I* 423–4). Mars describes Eutropius as the 'unmanned master' of the army (*In Eutropium II* 157). Claudian also relates the theory that it was the Assyrian Queen Semiramis who first created eunuchs in order to disguise her own sex by surrounding herself with womanly men (*In Eutropium I* 339–42).

Claudian also depicts eunuchs, represented by Eutropius, as men, active in the arena of male activity, although he is of course unhappy with this. As we have seen, Eutropius did indeed take on a military role, leading a campaign against the Huns.[14] Claudian is keen to brand his ventures in the military a failure, though he has Eutropius declare himself a success (*In Eutropium I* 252–4). Eutropius' acquisition of the consulship and his role in legal proceedings also mark his transgression into the male arena, as far as Claudian is concerned. Roma observes that eunuchs 'now despise the fan and aspire to the consul's cloak. No longer do they carry the maidenly parasol for they have dared to wield the axes of Latium' (*In Eutropium I* 463–5); and 'If eunuchs shall give judgement and determine laws, then let men card wool and live like the Amazons, confusion and license dispossessing the order of nature' (*In Eutropium I* 497–9). Claudian also refers to

Eutropius' sister, who is likened to a wife.[15] Thus, Eutropius is even transgressing into the male arena of husbandhood and marriage, though Claudian again undercuts this by stressing the excessive influence of the sister/wife. Claudian also likens Eutropius to the father of the Emperor Arcadius, since he held the rank of patrician (*In Eutropium II* 50).

Finally, Claudian also envisages eunuchs as neither man nor woman, as a different, third entity. Eunuchs can never have children, they can never be a mother or a father (*In Eutropium I* 224). Even women are known to exercise political power, but 'We know of no people who endure a eunuch's rule' (*In Eutropium I* 323–4). Bellona, disguised as the wife of the Gruthungian Tarbigilus, tells her husband 'It is another sex that is in arms against thee; the world has entrusted itself to the protection of eunuchs' (*In Eutropium II* 223–5). Most striking of all is the description of eunuchs as the 'unhappy band' 'whom the male sex has discarded and the female will not adopt' (*In Eutropium I* 466–7). Thus, Claudian has recourse to a range of interpretations of eunuch gender identity, and the very diversity only serves to underscore the ambiguity that the eunuch presented.

The positive answer: Theophylact's *In Defence of Eunuchs*

The other text I wish to highlight forms a very strong contrast with the work of Claudian; its purpose was to defend eunuchs. It was written about eight hundred years later (probably in the early twelfth century) by Theophylact, the Byzantine archbishop of Ochrid in Bulgaria.[16] The reason for the production of the text is provided by Theophylact; he wrote it to comfort his brother (who was a eunuch) since he was fed up with the insults that eunuchs had to endure. The text also has a very distinctive character and structure. Theophylact purports that it is the record of a conversation between a monk and a eunuch that he had overheard whilst he was in the city of Thessalonike during a visit of the Emperor, the catalyst for the exchange being the fact that the eunuch had castrated his own nephew. The dialogue is sandwiched between Theophylact's introduction and conclusion. The speech of the non-eunuch sets out reasons why the eunuch should not have castrated his nephew, and the speech of the eunuch responds to each of these criticisms in detail.

The monk's criticisms are as follows. He asserts that castration is against the will of the Creator. It is also illegal in the eyes of many authorities: Moses, the Apostles, the Fathers and the Roman Emperors, especially Justinian. He argues that the character of the child who is castrated will be corrupted since he will be prey to many passions. He states that those eunuchs who work in the palace will be more susceptible to passions than others (and those who work in the women's quarters will become feminised), whilst those who work in the theatre are debauched,[17] and have introduced licentious songs into the church. He also declares that eunuchs are ill-omened. The eunuch, rejecting self-castration after puberty but accepting pre-pubertal castration (on this distinction see Ringrose

1999: 131), counters each of these charges. He asserts that castration can in fact be used to thwart the passions (Gautier 1980: 297.9–12, and also 303.22–6); eunuchs can be pure and continent (Gautier 1980: 329.9–21). Also particularly striking in his argument's armoury are the examples of the specific context of previous anti-eunuch statements, the emphasis on how times have changed, and the assertions that eunuchs must be assessed as individuals and that non-eunuchs can be equally bad in character if not worse. Notably, the speech of the eunuch is about nine times longer than that of the monk.[18] In the end the monk is so won over by the eunuch that he begs him to stop before he persuades him to become a eunuch himself.[19]

In Mullett's recent (2002) analysis of the text she remarks how little the exchange actually concerns issues of gender, and this seems broadly true, as the above summary indicates. The monk certainly gives the impression that defects of character (e.g. greed, ambition, jealousy, quarrelsomeness, wiliness, maliciousness) are simply innate in eunuchs, rather than through any feminisation. When the monk does raise the possibility of the existence of effeminate eunuchs, this is due to the fact that some eunuchs are separated from men and spend too much time with women rather than the fact that they are inherently effeminate (Gautier 1980: 293.15–295.6, and also 295.19–20). The terminology used for eunuch and non-eunuch also avoids any easy division into 'real men' and 'other', there are simply two types of men: those without testicles (eunouchoi) and those who have them (enorchai) (e.g. Gautier, 1980: 291.5 and 317.10–11). Theophylact also describes his brother as the father of the text (Gautier 1980: 291.29). As Ringrose has noted, it seems that for Theophylact 'eunuchs are neither a third sex nor a third gender; they are simply men' (Ringrose 1994: 108).

A comparison

We can make many contrasts between Claudian's *In Eutropium* and Theophylact's *In Defence of Eunuchs*. There is a wide chronological gap between them, about eight centuries. The former is poetry, and written in Latin, the latter mainly prose (the first preface is in verse), and in Greek. The social roles of the writers also diverge: Claudian is a court poet, Theophylact a Christian bishop. The most obvious contrast is their different purposes. Claudian is producing deliberate attacks for the Western court on a specific eunuch in a specific political context, whilst Theophylact is writing a deliberate defence of eunuchs in order to please his eunuch brother. As such Theophylact is producing the more original document as he has to make a more unusual case whilst Claudian, it seems, simply taps into a tradition of hostility towards eunuchs. Claudian can visualise a large receptive audience, whilst Theophylact produces a personal document intended for an individual, though it is worth stressing that he imagines the possibility that others will read it and profit it from it too.[20] In terms of the gender identity of eunuchs, as we have seen, Claudian plays with a range of possibilities, whilst Theophylact seeks to categorise eunuchs as men.

The question arises, what do these differences tell us? One view is that attitudes towards eunuchs have changed. Ringrose has argued that 'The ecclesiastical community, at least as reflected in Theophylaktos, is defining manliness in a new way – in terms of spiritual perfection rather than physical or reproductive ability' (Ringrose 1994: 108, 1999: 132). Her assertion that eunuchs are simply men follows from this. There are, however, problems with such an interpretation. As Mullett (2002) has stressed, Theophylact's document is personal and for an individual, and as such his views do not necessarily reflect a general ecclesiastical view of eunuchs. One can point to other factors which undermine the view. For instance the origin of the document is the eunuch brother's unhappiness with continued hostility towards eunuchs. Further, the proponent of the anti-eunuch stance (the fictional monk) is himself a religious, not a secular individual. It can also be pointed out that other writings of Theophylact can resort to hostile stereotypes of eunuchs; in one of his poems Theophylact reflects the popular opinion that eunuchs were 'monsters' known for corruption and sexual depravity (Tougher 1997: 174–5, Mullett 2002: 182). Here, the eunuch is described as a libertine, friend of prostitutes, corrupter of virgins, more lustful than a billygoat, and is compared to Priapus and Pan. Theophylact does, however, acknowledge that this is the *exception* to the rule, and states that *in fact* purity was the natural privilege of the eunuch. Such a view was not new however, as we saw above. Thus, Theophylact's text hardly suggests that a radical shift in social attitudes has occurred. Also, it should not be forgotten that Theophylact is producing a deliberate defence. As Mullett (2002: 181) has noted, the fictional monk did not get the chance to say everything he might have about eunuchs; the eunuch and Theophylact prevent him.

There are other qualifications we should make about Theophylact's text, I would suggest. It seems to me that some of his comments do have more in common with Claudian's than might appear. As noted, Ringrose (1994) has argued that Theophylact depicts eunuchs as men; however, the speech of the fictional eunuch himself ironically confuses the issue. Addressing the topic of the bad character of eunuchs he asserts that the monk argued that they were prey to passions since they were reduced to the state of women. This is in fact more radical than what the monk actually said; it indicates a view that all eunuchs are feminised and owe their particular passions to this reason, but the monk had said that, while the eunuch character was inherent, only eunuchs who spent time with women were feminised. Theophylact's eunuch seems to acknowledge a different, gendered view of eunuchs, a view reflected in Claudian. Theophylact's eunuch also reinforces an orientalist vision of eunuchs. He objects to the monk's criticism of eunuchs partly on the grounds that the monk is applying to Byzantine eunuchs the characteristics of eunuchs found elsewhere – such as amongst the Persians or the Arabs (Gautier 1980: 297.1–4). Claudian had applied orientalist stereotypes to the Eastern Roman Empire, whilst Theophylact rejects these for Byzantium but is quite happy to apply them to foreign powers. Thus, similarities between Claudian and Theophylact do surface.

What does emerge from the comparison, I would argue, is not so much a different image of eunuchs but an insight into the *societal transformations* that have occurred within the empire. For Claudian, eunuchs were foreign slaves who could end up working at the imperial court; for Theophylact, a eunuch could be your own relative, castrated for worthy Christian sentiments. Whilst castration for Christian purposes and the existence of native eunuchs were not unknown in the later Roman/early Byzantine Empire, it is fair to say that both *religious eunuchs* (Guilland 1943: 202–5) and *native eunuchs* (Tougher 2002b) were far more prevalent in the middle Byzantine Empire. Theophylact's mention of his eunuch brother, the fact that the fictional eunuch of the dialogue had castrated his nephew, and a string of contemporary religious eunuchs, is positively casual. His acceptance of the use of free native eunuchs at the imperial court would, I think, have shocked Claudian and his age (Gautier 1980: 313.5–22). Society had changed, rather than its perceptions of eunuchs.

Conclusion

This chapter has sought to consider the gender identity of the eunuch in the specific context of the Byzantine Empire. It has drawn on a range of sources, but also focused on two authors in particular in order to give the analysis more depth. The *In Eutropium* of Claudian and the *In Defence of Eunuchs* of Theophylact certainly deserve their status as texts significant for the history of eunuchs. What has emerged is the fact that the figure of the eunuch provides great scope for a variety of gendering. Eunuchs can be men, women and other, according to the wishes of the writer. As such it is clear that in the case of eunuchs gender identity is as much imposed as it is inherent.

Notes

1. As indicated, for instance, by the seventh-century doctor Paul of Aegina; see Tougher 1997: 175.
2. It seems for instance that Chinese eunuchs and the black eunuchs of the Ottoman Empire were penisless.
3. See, for instance, Gleason 1995, Stevenson 1995.
4. See for instance Browe 1936, Grayson 1995, Scholz 2001, Tougher 2002a.
5. For further discussion of these roles see for instance Guyot 1980, Scholz 2001, Tougher 2002a.
6. See for instance the evidence of the Kletorologion of Philotheos: Oikonomidès 1972: 65–235.
7. On the phenomenon of the court eunuch of the later Roman Empire see the classic work of Hopkins 1963; 1978: 172–96.

8. See, for example, Malalas Chronicle 18.18 and 18.150, translated by Jeffreys et al. 1986: 253 and 305.

9. This new law was Novel 60: Noailles and Dain 1944: 225.29–227.2. Theophylact indicates that health could simply be used as an excuse for castration: Gautier 1980: 311.22–313.3.

10. For example, Xenophon on the eunuchs of Panthea and on Cyrus' motivations for employing eunuchs, see Gera 1993: 203–204, 287–8. An etymology of the word eunuch known to the Byzantines was 'having good will towards', referring to the dedication of eunuchs to their masters, see Gautier 1980: 309.14–15.

11. On the texts see Long 1996, and now Kuefler 2001: 65–9, 96–100. For the political context see also Liebeschuetz 1991: 93–108.

12. For a text and translation see Platnauer 1976: 138–229. The quotations in this chapter are taken from Platnauer's translation.

13. Claudian does dwell on Eutropius' sexual role and his agency in sexual relationships. Eutropius served Ptolemy's lusts, and then was handed on to Arinthaeus: *In Eutropium I* 61–3. As a household eunuch Eutropius was meant to ensure chastity, but actually fulfilled the role of a pander (*In Eutropium I* 98–100). Innuendo of Julian Clary proportions drips from a report of how the amenable Eutropius won the consulship (*In Eutropium I* 358–70).

14. In *In Eutropium II* Eutropius does not campaign in person, but Claudian finds the quality of the eastern army wanting anyway; it is effeminate.

15. In *Eutropium II* 88–90. On this passage see the comments of Long 1996: 133–4. The sister also appears in *In Eutropium I* 263. I hope to explore the question of Eutropius' sister elsewhere. Here I simply raise the suggestion that the 'sister' may be another eunuch and Claudian is playing with gender identity again; eunuchs form a sisterhood rather than a brotherhood.

16. For the most recent consideration of the text see Mullett 2002. See also Ringrose 1994: esp. 102–107, 1999: esp. 130–2; and Simon 1994. For a text and French translation see Gautier 1980: 288–331. For Theophylact in general see Mullett 1997.

17. The monk's speech forms two pages of Gautier's (1980) edition (pp. 290–5), whilst the eunuch's speech occupies eighteen pages (pp. 297–331).

18. Theophylact lists their appetite for food and drink, their unseemly and disorderly manner and their unbridled foul language. He also refers to their licentious behaviour. Gautier (1980: 294) interprets this as homosexuality, but others are less certain. Ringrose (1994: 103) understands Theophylact to mean that eunuchs 'pretend to be men and attempt to achieve sexual pleasure', and Mullett (2002: 180) reads it as meaning that eunuchs 'play the man' in licentiousness.

19. A joke, suggests Mullett (2002: 180).

20. Gautier 1980: 291.17–18 and 30–5. Mullett (2002) rather underplays this I feel. It is perhaps also notable that although Theophylact writes the text for his brother and does address him in places, he also refers to him in the third person.

References

Boulhol, P. and I. Cochelin. 1992. 'La rehabilitation de l'eunuque dans l'hagiographie antique (IVe–VIe siècles)'. *Studi di Antichita Christiana*, 48, 49–76.

Browe, P. 1936. *Zur Geschichte der Entmannung: Eine religions- und rechtsgeschichtliche Studie*. Breslau: Müller and Seiffert.

Cameron, A. 1965. 'Eunuchs in the "Historia Augusta"'. *Latomus,* 24, 155–8.

———— 1970. *Claudian: Poetry and Propaganda at the Court of Honorius.* Oxford: Oxford University Press.

Deferrari, R.J. 1928. *Saint Basil. The Letters, Volume 2.* London and New York: William Heinemann and G.P. Putnam's Sons.

Dewing, H.B. 1916. *Procopius. History of the Wars, Volume 2.* London: William Heinemann.

Dunlap, J.E. 1924. 'The Office of the Grand Chamberlain in the Later Roman and Byzantine Empires'. In *Two Studies in Later Roman and Byzantine Administration.* New York and London: The Macmillan Company, 161–234.

Gaul, N. 2002. 'Eunuchs in the Late Byzantine Empire, c. 1250–1400'. In *Eunuchs in Antiquity and Beyond.* Tougher, S. (ed.). London: The Classical Press of Wales and Duckworth, 199–219.

Gautier, P. 1980. *Théophylacte d'Achrida: Discours, Traités, Poésies. Introduction, Texte, Traduction et Notes.* Thessalonike: Association de Recherches Byzantines.

Gera, D.L. 1993. *Xenophon's Cyropaedia. Style, Genre and Literary Technique.* Oxford: Oxford University Press.

Gleason, M. 1995. *Making Men: Sophists and Self-Presentation in Ancient Rome.* Princeton: Princeton University Press.

Grayson, A.K. 1995. 'Eunuchs in Power. Their Role in the Assyrian Bureaucracy'. In *Vom Alten Orient zum Alten Testament. Festschrift für Wolfram Freiherrn von Soden (Alter Orient und Altes Testament 240),* Dietrich, M. and O. Loretz (eds). Neukirchen: Verlag Butzon & Bercker Kevelaer, 85–98.

Guilland, R. 1943. 'Les Eunuques dans l'empire Byzantin', *Revue des Etudes Byzantines,* 1, 197–238.

Guyot, P. 1980. *Eunuchen als Sklaven und Freigelassene in der griechisch-römischen Antike.* Stuttgart: Klett-Cotta.

Hopkins, K. 1963. 'Eunuchs in Politics in the Later Roman Empire'. *Proceedings of the Cambridge Philological Society,* 189: 62–80.

———— 1978. *Conquerors and Slaves.* Cambridge: Cambridge University Press.

Jeffreys, E., M. Jeffreys and R. Scott. 1986. *The Chronicle of John Malalas: A Translation.* Melbourne: Australian Association for Byzantine Studies.

Kuefler, M. 2001. *The Manly Eunuch: Masculinity, Gender Ambiguity, and Christian Ideology in Late Antiquity.* Chicago and London: The University of Chicago Press.

Liebeschuetz, J.H.W.G. 1991. *Barbarians and Bishops: Army, Church, and State in the Age of Arcadius and Chrysostom.* Oxford: Oxford University Press.

Lieu, S.N.C. (ed.) 1989. *The Emperor Julian: Panegyric and Polemic.* 2nd edition. Liverpool: Liverpool University Press.

Long, J. 1996. *Claudian's In Eutropium. Or, How, When, and Why to Slander a Eunuch.* Chapel Hill and London: The University of North Carolina Press.

Magdalino, P. 1998. 'Paphlagonians in Byzantine High Society'. In *Byzantine Asia Minor (6th – 12th Centuries).* Athens: Institute for Byzantine Research, 141–50.

Magie, D. 1924. *The Scriptores Historiae Augustae, Volume 2.* London and New York: William Heinemann and G.P. Putnam's Sons.

Moran, N. 2002. 'Byzantine Castrati'. *Plainsong and Medieval Music,* 11, 99–112.

Mullett, M. 1997. *Theophylact of Ochrid. Reading the Letters of a Byzantine Archbishop.* Aldershot: Ashgate.

———— 2002. 'Theophylact of Ochrid's In Defence of Eunuchs'. In *Eunuchs in Antiquity and Beyond,* Tougher, S. (ed.). London: The Classical Press of Wales and Duckworth, 177–98.

Noailles, P. and A. Dain. 1944. *Les Novelles de Léon VI le Sage.* Paris: Les Belles Lettres.

Oikonomidès, N. 1972. *Les Listes de Préséance Byzantines des IXe et Xe Siècles. Introduction, Texte, Traduction et Commentaire.* Paris: CNRS.

Peschel, E.R. and R.E. Peschel 1987. 'Medicine and Music: The Castrati in Opera'. *Opera Quarterly*, 4, 21–38.

Platnauer, M. 1976. *Claudian, vol. 1.* Cambridge, MA and London: Harvard University Press and William Heinemannn Ltd.

Ringrose, K.M. 1994. 'Living in the Shadows: Eunuchs and Gender in Byzantium'. In *Third Sex, Third Gender: Beyond Sexual Dimorphism in Culture and History*, Herdt, G. (ed.). New York: Zone Books, 85–109.

———— 1996. 'Eunuchs as Cultural Mediators'. *Byzantinische Forschungen*, 23, 75–93.

———— 1999, 'Passing the Test of Sanctity: Denial of Sexuality and Involuntary Castration'. In *Desire and Denial in Byzantium*, James, L. (ed.). Aldershot and Brookfield Vermont: Variorum, 123–37.

Rolfe, J.C. 1982. *Ammianus Marcellinus, Volume 1.* London and Cambridge, Massachusetts: William Heinemann and Harvard University Press.

Rousselle, A. 1988. *Porneia: On Desire and the Body in Antiquity.* Translated by F. Pheasant. Oxford and New York: Basil Blackwell.

Schlinkert, D. 1994. 'Der Hofeunuch in der Spätantike: Ein Gefährlicher Außenseiter?' *Hermes*, 122, 342–59.

Scholten, H. 1995. *Der Eunuch in Kaisernähe. Zur politischen und sozialen Bedeutung des praepositus sacri cubiculi im 4. und 5. Jahrhundert n. Chr.* Frankfurt am Main and New York: Peter Lang.

Scholz, P.O. 2001. *Eunuchs and Castrati: A Cultural History.* Translated by J.A. Broadwin and S.L. Frisch. Princeton: Markus Weiner Publishers.

Sidéris, G. 2000. 'La Comédie des Castrats. Ammien Marcellin et les Eunuques, Entre Eunocophobie et Admiration'. *Revue Belge de Philologie et d'Histoire*, 78, 681–717.

———— 2002. '"Eunuchs of Light". Power, Imperial Ceremonial and Positive Representations of Eunuchs in Byzantium (4th-12th Centuries AD)'. In *Eunuchs in Antiquity and Beyond*, Tougher, S. (ed.). London: The Classical Press of Wales and Duckworth, 161–75.

Simon, D. 1994. 'Lobpreis des Eunuchen'. *Schriften des Historischen Kollegs, Vorträge*, 24, 5–27.

Stevenson, W. 1995. 'The Rise of Eunuchs in Greco-Roman Antiquity'. *Journal of the History of Sexuality*, 5, 495–511.

Toledano, E.R. 1984. 'The Imperial Eunuchs of Istanbul: From Africa to the Heart of Islam'. *Middle Eastern Studies*, 20, 379–90.

Tougher, S. 1997. 'Byzantine Eunuchs: An Overview with Special Reference to their Creation and Origin'. In *Women, Men and Eunuchs: Gender in Byzantium*, James, L. (ed.). London and New York: Routledge, 168–84.

———— 1999a. 'Ammianus and the Eunuchs'. In *The Late Roman World and its Historian: Interpreting Ammianus Marcellinus*, Drijvers, J.W. and D. Hunt (eds). London and New York: Routledge, 63–73.

———— 1999b. 'Images of Effeminate Men: The Case of Byzantine Eunuchs'. In *Masculinity in Medieval Europe*, Hadley, D.M. (ed.). London and New York: Longman, 89–100.

———— (ed.). 2002a. *Eunuchs in Antiquity and Beyond*, London: The Classical Press of Wales and Duckworth.

———— 2002b. 'In or Out? Origins of Court Eunuchs'. In *Eunuchs in Antiquity and Beyond*, Tougher, S. (ed.). London: The Classical Press of Wales and Duckworth, 143–59.

Toynbee, A. 1973. *Constantine Porphyrogenitus and his World.* London/New York/Toronto: Oxford University Press.

Treadgold, W.T. 1988. *The Byzantine Revival, 780–842.* Stanford: Stanford University Press.

Vinson, M.P. 1998. 'Gender and Politics in the Post-Iconoclastic Period: The Lives of Antony the Younger, the Empress Theodora, and the Patriarch Ignatios'. *Byzantion,* 68, 469–515.

Witt, R. 2002. 'The Other Castrati'. In *Eunuchs in Antiquity and Beyond,* Tougher, S. (ed.). London: The Classical Press of Wales and Duckworth, 235–60.

5

THE THIRD SEX IN ALBANIA: AN ETHNOGRAPHIC NOTE

Roland Littlewood and Antonia Young

Introduction

The institution of a third gender (or third sex[1]) is not uncommon in non-indus-trialised societies (Whitehead 1981, Roscoe 1994), be they those with a distinctive male/female difference, or, less commonly, those where the difference between the sexes is not conspicuously heightened. The instance we wish to consider here is a phenomenon observed in the mountain villages of Northern Albania, and to a lesser extent Kosova, Serbia and Montenegro, where one finds something like a third sex recognised. This is a society where male/female differences are certainly heightened, at least in European terms.

'Sworn virgins' have been reported in the Western Balkans (Albania, Kosova, Bosnia, Montenegro and Macedonia) since the early 1800s. In the Serbian language they are known as *muskobanja* or 'man-like woman'. Grémaux (1994) claimed to know of one hundred and twenty instances in the previous one hundred and fifty years, pointing out that they are particularly found among those of peasant origin. In mountainous northern Albania particularly, traditional values of patrilineal descent and inheritance, exogamy and virilocality still persist (the south is more influenced by Greek culture, and is also more cosmopolitan). Men and women are quite different in terms of morphology, lineage, power, social roles, emotion and agency. In 1928, Mary Edith Durham (1928:194) reported that 'if a betrothed girl went off with another man, willingly or unwillingly, a blood-feud always started. She was the property of the family that had bought her and had no rights over her person'. Today, female virginity before marriage (or engagement) is still prized, and in consequence the possibility of premarital sexual relations is met with stern disapproval and drastic retribution. For example, there was a case reported in April 2002 where a Kosovar, without even questioning the situation, killed his sister (who had been returned to her natal home) on her new bridegroom's claim that she was not a virgin at marriage.

The historical setting

Albanian speakers have been settled in what are now Albania, Kosova, Western Macedonia and Southern Montenegro since at least the early medieval period (Vickers 1999). Albanians were, in the late nineteenth century, among the last to seek a national identity separate from Ottoman Turkey. Albania finally achieved independence from Turkey in 1912; shortly after, the Albanian-speaking area east of the Accursed Mountains, Kosova, was granted to Serbia by the Great Powers (Austro-Hungary, France, Germany, Great Britain, Italy and Russia) in 1913, and remained almost continuously part of Serbia and thence Yugoslavia. Resistance grew to the Belgrade administration from the 1960s. Kosova was granted autonomy in 1974, but this was rescinded in 1989, and intense repression by the Belgrade administration gave rise to non-violent resistance during the 1990s, which only turned to violence in 1998. In 1999, the attempt at reconciliation at Rambouillet failed and was followed by intense war: NATO forces expelled the Serb military and paramilitary and installed an interim administration, the United Nations Mission in Kosovo (UNMIK), with the aim of returning the government to the inhabitants of Kosova – this is the current situation.

Meanwhile, Albania itself, on the Adriatic coast, remained independent, first as a republic proclaimed in 1912, but not actually realised until 1920. The self-declared monarch King Zog reigned from 1928–39 when Albania was occupied first by the Italians and then by the Germans during the Second World War. This was followed by a forty five-year period of extreme isolation under the communist Enver Hoxha (died 1985) and his successor, Ramiz Alia, which ended with elections in 1991. Few lives were lost in the change to a nominal parliamentary system, which looked promising under the leadership of Democratic Party President Sali Berisha from 1992. However, during a state of widespread civil disturbance approaching civil war in 1997, the Organisation for Security and Cooperation in Europe monitored elections, under the protection of a heavy Italian military presence, and restored a tentative order which has remained since, but with a vacuum of power at the political centre and resulting corruption, crime and a heightened level of violence.

'A woman is a sack made to endure': gender and the customary law

During the twentieth century, Kosova and Albania have remained the poorest parts of Europe, isolated from the rest of the continent by geography and politics. Despite attempts at centralisation from Belgrade or Tirana, rural life was dominated by a network of exogamous patrilineal clans or tribes (*fis*, or at the local regional level *bajraks* or Banners) especially among the Ghegs of northern Albania and Kosova (Doja 1999, Saltmarshe 2001). Without a nationally enforced system of justice, customary law prevailed among the transhumant peasants living in wooded, multi-generational, family settlements (*shtëpia* or *zadrugas*), which rear small livestock, particularly sheep and goats. Men are generally responsible for ploughing and irrigation, and feuding. Women take care of hoeing, sowing, harvesting, fetching water for the household, cooking, childrearing and look after the house. Whilst generally fairly secular in everyday life, the majority of Albanians are nominally Muslim, with a substantial Catholic minority in the north and an Orthodox minority in the south. In spite of the Hoxha regime's opposition to the rural social order and to religion (Albania was the world's first 'atheist state', which lasted twenty-three years), notions of the customary law remain to adjust personal relations in what is, once again, a clan-based society with limited central authority. Indeed, Albanians can be described as 'traditional' in adhering to the public norms of early modern European peasant communities.

The most influential of the codifications of the customary law is the medieval *Kanun* (Canon) of Lekë Dukagjini, which was collected together, with twentieth century revisions, by a Kosovar priest in the 1920s (Gjeçov 1989), presumably in an attempt to standardise and attenuate more inchoate forms of immediate revenge (Black-Michaud 1975). 'The importance of the Kanun to the ordinary life of the Albanians of Kosova and the Malësi [mountainous northern Albania] can hardly be exaggerated' says the Balkanist historian Noel Malcolm (1999: 17). 'It still influences life in the entire area...' (Senechal 1997: 5), and traditionally took precedence over state or church law (Gjeçov 1989).

Much of the *Kanun* is taken up with issues of gender and marriage, hospitality and the resolution of rights in livestock and property. However, the *Kanun* is most well-known in Western Europe for its regulation of homicide and for a male blood feud (*gjakmarrje*) of the type associated with other Mediterranean societies such as Sicily or Corsica (Peristiany 1965). This has been particularly true since the translation of the Albanian novelist Ismail Kadare's famous *Broken April* (1991). One of the most striking aspects of this ethnographic novel, and the *Kanun* which it illustrates, is the location of experience and revenge within the standardised setting of the *Kanun* itself – as if individual perception and experience are of no real significance in the working-out of the process of the local moral economy. Whatever was its original focus (quarrels over boundaries or grazing rights, insults to guests or women), the continuation of the *Kanun* has an almost inexorable public form. One of the aspects noted by commentators on the blood feud (Durham 1909, Hasluck 1954, Kadare 1991, Senechal 1997) is how little individual motivation to continue a feud is actually determined by feelings of loss or personal revenge: they all note that the motive is *the expected public response* to an insult to the 'law of blood' (Durham 1909, Hasluck 1954): 'Till you had taken blood everyone would talk about you. You could not live like that' (Durham 1909: 112); 'strangely impersonal, abstract ... the blood feud is a collective concept involving the whole community' (Senechal 1997: 29, 30). A man engages in return assassination because he must, being himself a part of the accepted order. He goes into ambush, shoots a male member of the opposing family (women are exempt), carefully turns him on his back and places his gun by his head – as the *Kanun* specifies (Gjeçov 1989). He then goes back to his own family stronghold (*kulla*) and sends a neutral messenger to the opposing family (or tribe in the case of an inter-tribal feud) stating what he has done and claiming a period of *besa* or pledged truce. During this he attends the funeral and wake of his victim in the latter's house, pays a monetary compensation to the ritual authorities and then, on completion of the truce, awaits his own death (or that of another male family member).

The display of expected and permitted grief after a death is clearly specified by the *Kanun*: 'The men bewail the dead, scratch their faces and beat their clothes; the women lament, but do not scratch their faces; men do not lament over women, except in the case of a son over his mother or a brother over a sister' (Gjeçov 1989: 218). Women had little voice in the *Kanun*: they could not be the target of a blood feud, could neither inherit nor refuse their arranged marriage, were assumed to be virgins at their engagement, and had to 'submit to the husband's domination' (Gjeçov 1989: 222). In the words of the *Kanun*: 'A woman is a sack made to endure' (Gjeçov 1989: 238). In other words, a woman had to perform an essentially child-bearing role as the property of her husband (Whitaker 1981). Formerly, at her marriage a wife's parents gave their son-in-law a cartridge to kill their daughter should she be adulterous or 'betray hospitality' (Hasluck 1954). The association of men with the blood feud is exemplified by tracing agnatic relationships (descent through men) 'by blood', whereas relationships through women (uterine relationships, barely proper descent) are traced 'by milk'. Durham described how everyday interest and occupation are monopolised by the 'law of blood', and how sardonically, but light-heartedly, men pursue its course.

It might be expected that the *Kanun* refers to a now disappeared past, yet, since the early 1990s (with the decline in central authority and the lack of impartial and effective law enforcement), blood feuds and their associated gender relations in Albania and Kosova have proliferated. Arguments over the privatisation of communal land (Malcolm 1998, Schwandner-Sievers 1999, Young 2000) increased 'at a remarkable rate' (King 2000: 27), shading into new urban and rural criminality, and are now 'without order' (Krasztev 2000). Schwandner-Sievers (1999) discusses the resurgence of various *Kanuns* after communism; their modifications and exploitation, particularly by Sali Berisha (President 1992–1997); and newer 'national' attempts at offering processes for reconciliation (see also Miller 1999). A recent study found that over a hundred young boys in northern Albania were in protected hiding, fearing to go out of their *kullas* because of an ongoing feud (King 2000). Perhaps a hundred families in Shkodër, a northern town of some 80,000, are 'in blood' at the moment (Krasztev 2000: 8), with over two thousand families in the whole of Albania (Economist Intelligence Unit 2001). A recent case involved two members of the national parliament. The annual homicide rate in Shkodër in the late 1990s was one per thousand of the population, and 73 percent of violent deaths in Albania are attributed to feud killings (Saltmarshe 2001).

The traditional gender bipolarity was to an extent mitigated under Hoxha, at least in the public sphere, with his Communist attempts to produce 'the new Soviet man'. To an extent, distinctions based on gender have returned in rural areas with the resurgence of church marriages (but no longer, as formerly, involving bride price) and private household economies. One very conservative old lady who served Littlewood coffee in the old manner confided that she had once been the leader of the local Communist village council. Islam in Albania is not especially severe, but few outside the capital have much knowledge of the small Albanian Women's Movement (for a brief history of the Albanian Women's Movement, see Young 2000: 147–51).

Sworn virgins

It is against this background of re-traditionalisation that, with the frequency of male deaths, women can still elect to become honorary males and, declining marriage altogether, inherit and act as heads of households – as 'sworn virgins' (*vajzë e betuar* or *virgjinesha*: Durham 1909, Grémaux 1994). They can, indeed, even take part in blood feuds (Young 2000). As Alexander Lopäić (2001) explains, there are other more specific terms for such women used in Montenegro. *Ostajnica* (woman who remains) and *cura* (girl) are used among the Kuci tribe in Montenegro, while *tombelija* specifies girls who abandon their usual female role, either of their own will or under pressure of their parents.

'Sworn virgins' generally attain their status in one of three circumstances. The only way an adolescent girl can avoid her arranged marriage is by swearing perpetual virginity (formerly before a group of twelve elders in the church or mosque). A father without a son to whom to leave his property (who in turn would become the *zoti i shtëpies*: 'master of the house' or household head) may proclaim a daughter to be a man. Thirdly, if a family loses one or more of its young male members, a girl may be selected to take his place. 'Virgins' now dress as men, with short hair, trousers, wristwatch and gun. They work as men, publicly drink *raki* and smoke, and generally socialise as men. They assume male gestures and body language. They may become a *zoti i shtëpies*, and they often take traditionally male labouring or mechanical jobs. Sometimes they take a masculine form of their given name, and sometimes (although not always) they are referred to by the masculine pronoun. They have no distinctive religious role, nor do they form any kind of corporate group (unlike the *berdache* of North America).

With rapid social changes taking place in Albania throughout the last decade of the twentieth century and into the twenty-first, there appear to be new circumstances validating women taking the role and costume of men (though they might not accept the term 'sworn virgin'). In rural areas there is a new fear for the fate of young women: the growing trade in trafficking women into prostitution abroad (Young 2003). In a recent film a young woman explains in an interview that this is her reason for choosing to act and dress as a man (Michalski 2003). In the urban setting, women have become 'sworn virgins' simply to enable them to live alone (which would be impossible for them as women).

We interviewed three sworn virgins, Xhema, Lule and Paske in 2001[2]; we present these as case studies:

Xhema, although of rural background, lived in Shkodër in the apartment block where Roland Littlewood was staying in 2001 with a family of the Dibra *fis*. She was aged sixty nine at the time, and lived together with her younger sister, an ex-schoolteacher who adopted the female role – quieter, calmer, almost subservient, serving coffee to their guests. Xhema, by contrast, was a forceful, almost outrageous, woman who dressed in trousers and a man's short-sleeved shirt. Her hair was cut short. She had had six sisters and one younger brother. Xhema described how when she was a small girl, the neighbours called her a boy because of her behaviour, and at the age of ten or twelve she started wearing trousers (*panthallona*) and went to the village hairdresser saying 'cut it short like a boy' (another version of her story says she became a man only at sixteen when her father died, and she then had to hide her new haircut from her angry brother). She worked as a mechanic after leaving her home at sixteen. Her sister, with whom she was living (and lived until her death), never married but felt no obligation or inclination to become a sworn virgin. Xhema vigorously acted as a man in her household, taking economic decisions, and in the local bar drinking *raki* and officiously lighting cigarettes for others, coughing vigorously over her own. Four of her six sisters married (all now widowed) and she acted as the 'uncle' to her brother's two daughters living nearby: he died some years ago.

Lule works in a lowland village near the River Burrë, close to the Adriatic, with her older brother Pjetar, his wife and their five children. She appeared to be the *zoti i shtëpies* (household head), generally ignoring her brother when entertaining and publicly sitting with and toasting guests, whilst served by his wife. (Women serve men food and then retire to eat with the children or by themselves.) Pjetar moves around the house unobtrusively, self-deprecating and almost apologetic. The family (his wife included) say he was spoilt as the only boy among eleven children, and has not been able to become a strong household head, only just managing to keep the family livestock (cows and sheep) together. Pjetar's and Lule's parents died while Lule was in her teens, after which she became a public man. She wears a black leather jacket and dungarees, and previously (in the Communist period) worked as a tractor driver and mechanic; currently she is looking after a machine in a nearby quarry. She is now in her late forties and comes across as friendly but fairly forceful.

Pashke is in her early sixties and lives in Theth (some four hours truck ride north of Shkodër). As a child, the orphaned Pashke was brought up by her grandmother and an uncle. Sometime after the death of her grandmother, her uncle became severely ill and was taken to hospital in Shkodër. Every two weeks Pashke walked over to the town (thirty-five miles away) to visit him. This was only possible for

5.1 Pashke (left) with an uncle, on a bus. (Photographer: Bevis Fusha.)

her to do as a man, thus she dressed as a man for security. Having made this change, even when the uncle returned to the village, Pashke felt honour bound to continue to live as a man, later inheriting the small house and homestead on his death. Wearing her hair cropped short, she dresses in a dark shirt and trousers, or in a smart Italian-style man's suit for special occasions. She has lived alone in the mountains since the death of her uncle. Offering us *raki* and coffee, she joined in to drink herself; normally a woman leaves whilst the men drink.

Three into two

To what extent, then, are sworn virgins seen as a separate category? And to what extent are they subsumed under the overarching categories of male or female? They share the label of 'virgin' with unmarried girls – who are certainly regarded as female (cf. Hastrup 1978). When Xhema became ill, as a sworn virgin she was offered the choice of the men's or the women's wards in the hospital. She chose the women's ward. (All three said they were female anatomically and physiologically, though Pashke said she feels like a man 'both inside and outside'.) Even though the virgins take part in the blood feud, Grémaux (1994) says there is debate as to whether it is proper to kill them: whilst all maintained that they would play a full man's part, we found no-one with recollections of such an event and none of the three cases given here had been involved in a feud themselves. Although sworn virgins are buried as men in men's clothing and, unlike other women, they sit in on the elders' discussions, they cannot vote on decisions in these assemblies (Gjeçov 1989: 108). In the most fundamental articulation of gender – sexual rela-

5.2 Pashke (centre) with an uncle and two guests. (Photographer: Antonia Young.)

tions – what is the situation of the virgins? Reportedly, sworn virgins who had sex were once burned alive and, generally, virgins now do not have sexual relations. The three quoted here denied any history or desire for sex, but Grémaux (1994) records some in Serbia as having had sexual relations with women. The sworn virgin has life-long use of land and property inherited from parents, but both pass through her, agnatically, to her nephews, on her death. There is no mechanism whereby a sworn virgin might marry in order to become the *pater* (legal father) of direct heirs, regardless of whom their genitor might be, as sometimes occurs elsewhere, as 'ghost marriage' (the marriage of a woman to a dead man to produce legal posthumous children) for instance, in parts of Africa.

Thus, there seems some local uncertainty as to how far sworn virgins are to be regarded as fully male. Although they may be annoyed, personally, by being reminded of their female origin, there is no bar to a villager describing them publicly as 'really female'. Virgins claim no solidarity or identity either with reported lesbians in the West or with its Women's Movement, and are as socially conservative as men. In these respects they support the patriarchal system. Although Northern Albania was generally opposed to the Hoxha regime, and virgins now too decry it along with others, it seems that in the Communist period they found it relatively easier to obtain men's work and perhaps thus to be social men. Albanian communist ideology presented a more equal status for women (Saltmarshe 2001) – at least in theory. A popular saying recounts that in the Zog period, a woman walked ten paces behind a man, under Hoxha this became three paces. The end of Communism and the collapse of state-owned enterprises resulted in more women than men losing paid employment outside the household (Saltmarshe 2001).

Whether we take the emergence of phenomena like a 'third sex' as more or less likely with traditional binary gender classification, it nevertheless appears that they have less classificatory autonomy than lesbians in more pluralistic societies, constantly tending to be represented as 'women who have become men' rather than some more independent third category.[3] Nor do they appear to dilute the dichotomy. Indeed, they seem to support and enhance a rigorous binarism: male and female still appear as powerfully contrasted and determining categories in Northern Albania. This is what we would expect if 'sworn virgins' are 'women who become men' rather than some quite separate third sex. *Virgjinesha* are always described in terms of male or female attributes: never in terms of anything altogether 'other' (as with multiple genders).

How much does the move to become a sworn virgin depend on local structural dynamics, how much on individual personality? All three of the virgins described here exhibited Albanian male body language and a self-confident, almost arrogant, style. Xhema's choice seems the most personal, although we know little about her younger brother's capacity, but in the cases of Lule and Pashke, the decision lies partly in external circumstances (a weak brother, an old ill uncle with no children). None of the three expressed or demonstrated publicly any of the sexual behaviour associated with lesbian interests.

5.3 Pashke attending a wedding (1993). (Photographer: Antonia Young.)

We have considered the question in fairly abstract terms without considering the extent to which women may resent ritualised female deference and a sub-dominant position (Denich 1974). This would include marrying into a male-controlled household, often being known only by the husband's first name, childbirth and child rearing, carrying out heavy domestic and agricultural duties, washing the feet of male guests, always deferring to their husband in public, and so on. 'A man has blood [kin] … and a woman is anybody's daughter' (Hasluck 1954: 33). The extent to which this is currently perceived and resented by women depends perhaps on their knowledge of contemporary Western European and American society (television, with its extensive diet of Italian films, is now commonly available in towns and even in the poorer countryside). None of our informants expressed such resentment but our relations with them were quite public and formal. All three of the sworn virgins discussed here certainly did express a satisfaction with their having greater autonomy and public responsibility than other women. But there is little indication that the *virgjenesha* serve to mitigate a superordinate sexual binarism.

Notes

1. Herdt (1994) argues that 'sex' and 'gender' have recently become elided categories, just as 'disease' and 'illness' have under the influence of new biomedical technologies.
2. Roland Littlewood is indebted to Antonia Young for her introduction to the subject of the sworn virgins. He also thanks the women he interviewed in 2001 with Antonia Young, and with Elena Von Lukovitz, who made a short film about them with us. Sadly, Xhema died some months later.
3. '[T]he sociological situation between the superordinate and the subordinate is completely changed as soon as a third element is added' (Simmel 1951: 141).

References

Black-Michaud, J. 1975. *Cohesive Feud: Feud in the Mediterranean and the Middle East.* Oxford: Blackwell.

Denich, B.S. 1974. 'Sex and Power in the Balkans'. In *Women, Culture and Society*, Rosaldo, M.Z. and L. Lamphere (eds.). Stanford, California: Stanford University Press, 243–62.

Doja, A. 1999. 'Morphologie Traditionelle de la Société Albanaise'. *Social Anthropology*, 7, 37–55.

Durham, M. E. 1909/1985. *High Albania.* London: Virago.

————— 1928. *Some Tribal Origins, Laws and Customs of the Balkans.* London: Allen and Unwin.

Economist Intelligence Unit. 1999. *Albania Country Profile 1998–9.* London: Economist Intelligence Unit.

Gjeçov, S. 1989. *Kanuni I Lekë Dukagjinit. (The Code of Lekë Dukagjini).* Originally collected 1933. Translated by L. Fox. New York: Gjonlekaj.

Grémaux, P. 1994. 'Woman becomes Man in the Balkans'. In *Third Sex, Third Gender: Beyond Sexual Dimorphism in Culture and Society*, Herdt, G. (ed.). New York: Zone Books, 241–81.

Hasluck, M. 1954. *The Unwritten Law in Albania.* Cambridge: Cambridge University Press.

Hastrup, K. 1978. 'The Semantics of Biology: Virginity'. In *Defining Females*, Ardener, S. (ed.). London: Croom Helm, 49–65.

Herdt, G. 1994. 'Introduction: Third Sexes and Third Genders'. In *Third Sex, Third Gender: Beyond Sexual Dimorphism in Culture and Society*, Herdt, G. (ed.). New York: Zone Books, 21–81.

Kadare, I. 1991. *Broken April*. London: Harper Collins.

King, C. 2000. 'Singular oaths'. *Times Literary Supplement*, 7 July, 27.

Krasztev, P. 2000. 'Back to the Torn-out Roots: Reflections on Vendetta in Contemporary Albania'. Conference on *Intersecting Times: The Work of Memory in South East Europe*. Swansea University.

Lopăić, A. 2001. Review of A. Young, *Women Who Become Men: Albanian Sworn Virgins*, Oxford: Berg, 2000. In *South Slav Journal*, Autumn-Winter, 22, 123.

Malcolm, N. 1998. *Kosovo: A Short History*. Second edition. London: Macmillan.

Michalski, K. 2003. *Pashke and Sofia, Women Make Movies*.

Miller, M. 1999. 'Family Feuds are no Game in Albania'. *Los Angeles Times*, 12 July.

Peristiany, J.G. (ed.) 1965. *Honour and Shame*. London: Weidenfeld and Nicolson.

Roscoe, W. 1994. 'How to Become a Berdache: Toward a Unified Analysis of Gender Diversity'. In *Third Sex, Third Gender: Beyond Sexual Dimorphism in Culture and Society*, Herdt, G. (ed.). New York: Zone Books, 329–72.

Saltmarshe, D. 2001. *Identity in a Post-Communist Balkan State: An Albanian Village Study*. Aldershot: Ashgate.

Schwandner-Sievers, S. 1999. 'Humiliation and Reconciliation in Northern Albania: the Logics of Feuding in Symbolic and Diachronic Perspective'. In *Dynamics of Violence: Processes of Escalation and De-Escalation in Violent Group Conflicts*, Elwert, G., S. Feuchtwang and D. Neubert (eds). Berlin: Duncker and Humblot, 133–52.

Senechal, M. 1997. *Long Life to Your Children: A Portrait of High Albania*. Amherst: University of Massachusetts Press.

Simmel, G. 1951. *The Sociology of Georg Simmel*. Glencoe, Illinois: Free Press.

Vickers, M. 1999. *The Albanians: A Modern History*. Revised edition. London: Tauris.

Whitaker, I. 1981. 'A Sack for Carrying Things: the Traditional Role of Women in Northern Albanian Society'. *Anthropological Quarterly*, 54, 146–56.

Whitehead, H. 1981. 'The Bow and the Burden Strap: A New Look at Institutionalised Homosexuality in Native North America'. In *Sexual Meanings: The Cultural Construction of Gender and Sexuality*, Ortner, S.B. and H. Whitehead (eds). Cambridge: Cambridge University Press, 80–115.

Young, A. 2000. *Women Who Become Men: Albanian Sworn Virgins*. Oxford: Berg.

———— 2003. 'Albania' and 'Kosovo'. In *The Greenwood Encyclopedia of Women's Issues Worldwide: Europe*, Walter, L. (ed.). Greenwood Press, Connecticut, 3: 17–31, 573–86.

6

LIVING LIKE MEN, LOVING LIKE WOMEN: *TOMBOI* IN THE SOUTHERN PHILIPPINES

Mark Johnson

Introduction

This chapter provides an ethnographic account of individuals in the Southern Philippines who are identified, by themselves and others, as *tomboi* or *t*-birds,[1] that is, as female-bodied individuals who identify with and choose to live 'like men'. *Tomboi* masculine identifications are registered among other things in dress and bodily comportment, in occupational and leisure pursuits, and in their desire for, and sexual relationships with, feminine-identified female-bodied individuals – that is, women. However, while *tomboi* see themselves as being 'like men', they do not talk about themselves exclusively in terms of masculine identifications. Specifically, they distinguish themselves from other masculine-identified male-bodied individuals in loving women 'like women' do. *Tomboi*, in other words, actively identify themselves in different degrees and in different ways with both men and masculinity and with women and femininity.

The first part of this chapter describes *tomboi* identifications in terms of dress, bodily comportment and work. *Tomboi* wish to be identified less by the *kind* of work they do, but more, 'like men', in terms of their pursuit of occupations, rather than, 'like women', for their reproductive and domestic labour. The second part of the chapter explores aspects of *tomboi* sexuality and, in particular, how *tomboi* representations of their sexuality both reproduce and challenge normative conventions of heterogendered sexuality. In particular, while their sexual comportment is gendered masculine, *tomboi* emphasise their shared acts of emotional and bodily identification with their female lovers. In the final section of the chapter, I explore the construction of *tomboi* sexuality as deviant in the dominant discourse. What is at stake, I suggest, is not simply that *tomboi* are seen to engage in unreproductive sexuality, but that they are seen (by men in particular) as inappropriately occupying and positioning themselves as men in relation to women.

The locality

The chapter is based on ethnographic research conducted over an eighteen month period during the early 1990s in Zamboanga City, in Southern Mindanao and in the small town of Jolo, Sulu. Jolo, where most of the research was completed, had a population of just over sixty thousand at the time of research. Jolo inhabitants distinguish *daira* (town) and *gimba* (rural hinterlands) which, from the vantage-point of Jolo town, refers to anything lying beyond its limits. Jolo had doubled in population from 1980 to 1990 as more people moved in from the surrounding areas, and most people I spoke to (including *tomboi* themselves) reckoned that there were few, if any, *tomboi*, in the *gimba*. The *gimba* is associated with a kind of rural backwardness and tradition, while the town is seen as being more modern and providing better educational and occupational life chances and opportunities. The story is, of course, much more complex than that, and many individuals living in the town maintain kinship as well as economic ties with the *gimba*.

Economically, the town is the major provincial market and trading centre and politically, the seat of municipal and provincial government. It is also an important educational centre with a number of high schools and college campuses. However, there is little in the way of locally available professional employment other than teaching and the civil service, and there is little or no industry to speak of, apart from construction. Most work is concentrated in a few service sectors, in various forms of petty market trading and in small-scale agriculture and fisheries.

Almost ninety percent of the population of Jolo is ethnically identified as Muslim Tausug, with a small minority identified either as Bisaya (a generic term used by Muslims to refer to Christian Filipinos, regardless of their ethnic affiliation) or Lannang (Chinese or *mestizo* Chinese). Since the late 1960s, Jolo has been a centre of Muslim ethnic nationalism and the site of state and separatist conflict. It is impossible here to provide even a brief overview of the local forms of Islamic practice and belief, or of Muslim ethnic nationalism. However, while Islam is a dominant idiom of symbolic life and ethnic identification, it is understood and inflected in a variety of often contested ways, and is very far removed from Western stereotypes about Islam, including typecast images of oppressed women. Islam is not insignificant either for *tomboi* self-identifications or in the way in which *tomboi* are identified by others, but we cannot assume that because the majority of the population is Muslim, *tomboi* will *necessarily* face religious oppression and persecution for their alternative gender and sexualities. Most of the *tomboi* I knew were self-identified Muslims, though a number were also identified as *Bisaya*. Among the Muslim *tomboi* I knew, some regarded themselves as devout adherents of Islam and some did not. Moreover, while some people (particularly men) described the *tomboi* as violating Islamic belief and Quranic teachings, others (both women and men) would suggest that being a *tomboi* was 'God's will'. As I shall demonstrate below, although *tomboi* are in important respects denied legitimacy and constructed as deviant, this has as much, if not more to do with gender ideology as with religious belief.

Jolo town has symbolic and material connections with a variety of different worlds and ideas. To the south is Sabah, Malaysia, an important source of consumer goods in Sulu's 'barter trading' network, an important destination for illegal immigrant workers (*tago-nang-tago or TNT*) who are unable to go 'abroad' (that is to the Middle East or elsewhere) as contract workers, and part of the greater Malay-Muslim region with which local people sometimes associate. To the north is Zamboanga which has a sizeable Muslim population and is also the gateway to the rest of the Philippines, which is primarily conceptualised along ethnic-religious lines as 'the world of Christian Filipinos'. Beyond these two boundaries with Malaysia and the Christian Philippines lies the rest of the outside world, the world *abroad*, which people mention frequently in terms of migrant labour, and in connection with everything from religion to style. In particular, people most actively engage with two primary significant 'others': the world of Islam and the Arabs to the west, and the world of the *Milikan* (the local transliteration of American, a word also often used to refer to any white foreigner) which conceptually lies to the east.

The appropriation of the English term 'tomboy' suggests translocal connections with respect to gender and sexuality, but in local usage the term *tomboi* refers to a much broader and culturally more particular range of meanings related to gender and sexuality than it denotes in Anglo-American discourse, even though there are some overlaps in meaning. The word 'tomboy' is used in similar ways throughout many parts of South East Asia to refer to masculine-identified women, and indicates regionally specific configurations of gender and sexuality as much as it illustrates the influence and hegemony of Western categories of gender and sexuality (Blackwood 1995, 1999). Furthermore, while the term *tomboi* refers to both masculine-identified women and forms of female same-sex sexuality, it is *not* primarily about sexual orientation, *nor* is it a sexual identity category in the same way that the term 'lesbian' is. *Tomboi* cannot simply be equated with lesbian, and the concept of 'lesbian' is not, at least in this particular locale, part of *tomboi* identifications, although it is becoming more important in other more metropolitan areas of the Philippines.

The rest of the chapter considers *tomboi* self-identifications and how they are constructed by others in this particular locality. I attempt to indicate the important elements of the translocal social geography and the diverse symbolic reference points that inform *tomboi* lives and experiences.

Ethnographic encounters with *tomboi* in the Southern Philippines

My interest in the *tomboi* originally arose in the context of doing research among males who were identified as 'gay' or *bantut* (see Johnson 1997a, 1998). However, while I initially assumed that *tomboi* was simply the female equivalent of 'gay', I later realised that it was not. I have until now chosen not to write about *tomboi* because

I do not wish them to be seen as a mirror image of 'gay' identified individuals. To be sure, some useful comparisons and contrasts can be drawn between *tomboi* and gays, but I argue that each is better understood in their own terms rather than simply as transformations of some underlying logic which links them together.

One important difference was in terms of the research process itself. Whereas it was very easy to meet and interview 'gays', I found it difficult to meet individuals who identified themselves as *tomboi*. This was partly because individuals who identified as *tomboi* were, for reasons discussed in more detail below, much less publicly visible and accessible than individuals identified as 'gay', and partly due to my position as a man and as a one of a few white foreigners living locally. These two points are related, for while, as I describe below, *tomboi* are in important respects simply attempting to and succeeding to 'live like' an average Filipino man, in the dominant or everyday discourse, *tomboi* are also sometimes viewed as 'women who do bad things'. Moreover, *tomboi* sometimes express very real concerns about male sexual violence. Thus, while *tomboi* are certainly not closeted, they also tend to be circumspect and cautious about the people around them.

As a foreign man, I was unknown and potentially threatening, and also a potential liability for, as a white foreign man, my presence was always publicly visible. Not surprisingly, therefore, many *tomboi* were at first very reluctant to meet and talk with me. I came to understand more fully the reasons for this reluctance later, but I was sensitive enough always to approach *tomboi* discreetly through an intermediary, and not to pursue meeting them if they refused my initial request. I was able to meet and interview more than a handful of self-identified *tomboi* only fairly late into my research, and this was largely through the influence of a young *tomboi* of eighteen whom I shall call Maj. I first met Maj through a mutual male acquaintance who was going out with Maj's sister. Over several months (during which time Maj's sister's boyfriend and I frequently visited in their home) Maj befriended me and gradually took me into her confidence. As she did so, she started introducing me to other *tomboi*, many of whom were college-age students like Maj, though others were older and either working or unemployed.

Our meetings were always arranged at times and in locations that were least likely to draw attention. Sometimes Maj stayed with me while I interviewed other *tomboi*, and other times she simply introduced us and left it for us to arrange a separate occasion without her. Although I did not have the same kind of long-term sustained relationship with other *tomboi* that I had with Maj, for the most part I found that the *tomboi* who did agree to meet and talk to me were forthcoming about themselves and their lives and experiences. Moreover, although the fact I was a foreign man was potentially hazardous because I might have brought unwelcome attention to *tomboi*, the fact that I was a white foreigner from the United States also had the advantage that I was assumed to be more open-minded and 'modern' in my approach.

In the end, largely through Maj's interventions, I personally came to know of about thirty self-identified *tomboi* in Jolo. The data presented here are derived both from general observations and informal conversations with *tomboi* and other 'normatively' gendered individuals in the course of everyday participant observation and, more directly, from a series of semi-structured life-history interviews with nineteen *tomboi* ranging in age from fifteen to forty-five, most of whom were under thirty.

Living 'like men': masculine identifications and masculine subject positions in *tomboi* narratives of self

In general, the term '*tomboi*' is understood to mean women (individuals with female bodies) who behave or think of themselves as being like men. I say 'like men' purposively, because this is the way the *tomboi*, when asked about how they thought and felt about themselves, would reply, saying, '*biya' da usug aku*' or '*biya' da usug*' ('it's like I'm a man' or 'like a man'), which is not exactly the same thing as saying 'I am a man'. *Tomboi* are 'like men' in a variety of possible ways.

The *tomboi* were seen, and saw themselves to be 'like men' in terms of dress and bodily and social comportment. Some *tomboi* articulated their self-identifications specifically in terms of adopting the style of men (*istyle sin usug*). In terms of dress and appearance, *tomboi* frequently had short-cropped hair, wore T-shirts and jeans or, on occasion, basketball sport shorts, and carried and smoked cigarettes. Although blue jeans and a T-shirt is a fairly generic 'unisex' attire, especially for the young, in the Southern Philippines, short-cropped hair, wearing sport shorts (especially outside of the house) and smoking are all stereotypically male. Women's clothing encompasses a range of dress styles, including jeans and T-shirts, skirt and blouse, and both casual and formal dresses. The key thing, however, is that it is immodest for women to wear clothing that reveals their upper legs and thighs, which is why sport shorts are inappropriate.

In terms of bodily and social comportment, women and men are seen, and are largely expected, to carry themselves in different ways. Men learn to walk and talk in a more aggressive, confident and forthright manner than women, who are expected to appear more demure and modest (although neither men nor women equate a modest demeanour with passivity or docility). Both young men and younger *tomboi*, in particular, expressed this male demeanour in a characteristic style of strut and saunter, and in assertive, boisterous forms of social interaction, full of play and banter.

An important aspiration of some, particularly younger, *tomboi* was also to be able to hang out (*nagistanbai*) with 'the lads', at the beauty parlours (a common haunt or *istandbai* venue in Jolo in particular), drink beer together at friends' houses, or simply walk around town in the company of other men. I say aspiration, however, because while some *tomboi* did associate with male *barkada* (an informal group of usually same-gendered friends and acquaintances) this was usually done in a circumspect manner.

Most *tomboi* do not express any sense of being a man 'trapped in the wrong body'. Nevertheless, *tomboi* speak not just of acting like men, but also of feeling like or having a 'heart' like a man. Moreover, in narrating their life stories, *tomboi* often cited examples from their early childhood that suggested to them as well as to others that they had always shared a greater affinity with men than with women. A young *tomboi* in her late teens recounted how she asked her mum why she was a *tomboi*. Her mum replied saying that, 'it is what had been handed to you by God. It was your fate'. Her mother then recounted how, since childhood, this daughter had always expressed an interest in and preference for boys' clothing, games and toys rather than for girls' pursuits and clothing.

For her, as for other *tomboi* from whom I heard similar accounts, such stories are an important means of creating and conveying to themselves and others a certain authenticity to their claims to a different gendered status. It is in fact quite common for young girls who display some or all of the above characteristics, whether or not they refer to themselves as *tomboi*, to be identified by others as *tomboi*, or more often, diminutively, as 'acting like a *tomboi* (*nagtomboi-tomboi*)', much in the same way that young girls in Britain and North America have been labelled as 'tomboys'. Hence, while stories about their early childhood identification with 'boys' is one means by which *tomboi* authenticate their status as *tomboi*, the diminutive use of *tomboi-tomboi* is also, in certain contexts, a means of questioning the authenticity of *tomboi* subjectivities and subject positions.

Work and employment, however, is at least as important as style and comportment for tomboi *self*-definitions. I emphasise *tomboi* self-identification because, while *tomboi* are variously identified by others on the basis of dress, style, and bodily and social comportment as well as sexuality (see below), they are rarely, if ever, identified by others in terms of work or occupation. *Tomboi* do not identify themselves with or perform paid work that is regarded as exclusively 'male' or 'female', despite the fact that there are gendered divisions of labour both within and outside the domestic sphere in the Southern Philippines. Certain occupations tend to be defined as male and female, especially the police and military service, both official and 'unofficial' (as a member of a private army). Because of their association with violent conflict, these occupations are categorically defined as singularly appropriate for men. Moreover, de facto gendered divisions of labour occur in particular forms of low-waged 'unskilled' labour where, for example, dock workers, pedicab drivers and unskilled construction workers are almost all men, while women tend to predominate (though not to the extent that men outnumber women in low-waged manual labour) as waitresses in the numerous coffee shops in Jolo.

Tomboi occupations, and educational and occupational aspirations, were not, however, categorically or practically the exclusive, or even the predominate, preserve of either gender. Of the thirty or so self-identified *tomboi* I knew of in Jolo, only two had occupations in what would have been viewed as male preserves: one was in the police force, the other was a pedicab driver. Among the rest, there was a variety of occupations, including teachers, an administrative officer in the Mayor's office, a market trader, someone involved in informal credit, and a number of high school and college students, and some *tomboi* (for a variety of reasons) were unemployed or not seeking work.

When speaking of work and employment, *tomboi* do not express any inclination towards particularly 'male' occupations, but 'like men', they see their work, and wish their work to be seen by others, as a primary focus and defining feature of their lives. One of the first life-history interviews I conducted (and one of the few I carried out before meeting Maj) was with a *tomboi* in her mid-forties who, when asked about what being a *tomboi* meant, said it was simply about work, about 'earning a living'. She spent most of the interview telling me about her work in informal credit relations. Both her answer, and her definition and description of a *tomboi*'s life surprised me, because I had thought, on the basis of what others had, up to that point, told me, that being a *tomboi* was primarily about sartorial style and intimate relationships with women. As I met, spent more time with, and interviewed more *tomboi*, I began to realise that many *tomboi* define themselves similarly in relation to work, whether articulating this simply as 'earning a living', or as having or aspiring to have a 'professional' career.

In particular, *tomboi* often talked about how, like men, they were single-minded in pursuing a career and making a living. *Tomboi* suggested that, in contrast, women were often (though not always of their own choice) distracted by the demands of having or obtaining a husband, bearing and raising children, looking after their parents and elders, managing a household, and the like. One of the first things Maj told me was that, for her, being a *tomboi* was about concentrating on her college studies and preparing for a good career. Similarly, many younger *tomboi* (those in their late teens and early twenties who were attending college) suggested that their masculine identifications were, in part, a means of deflecting or at least deferring the hassle of dealing with men *and* their parents' intentions to marry them off to start a family, so that they could instead concentrate on their studies and career. In self-identifying as *tomboi* and in defining themselves in terms of earning a living and/or having a career, *tomboi* not only identified themselves as being 'like men'; rather, they were also articulating their difference from women, or at least from women's reproductive roles as defined in the prevailing everyday discourse.

Contrary to dominant Western stereotypes of Islam, Southern Philippine women are encouraged to pursue education, engage in paid employment or other money-making enterprises and pursue 'professional' careers. Women out-perform men in educational attainment, and out-number men in work and employment abroad, as temporary migrant workers. Nevertheless, a woman's first duty and obligation is *still* seen to be towards her husband, children and parents or, in the case of young unmarried women, to get married, raise children and, generally, to look after one's parents and elder siblings. In this respect *tomboi* discourse both reproduces and challenges dominant images and ideas of femininity in which women are primarily (though not exclusively) defined in terms of being or becoming wives and mothers.

Marriage and fatherhood are also important and significant for men and for definitions of masculinity, but there is a difference in degree and emphasis. For men, having a wife and fathering children is a way of demonstrating one's masculinity, and in particular one's male sexual capacity. Beyond that, there are normative ideas about what being a good husband and father entails, but men and masculinity are *primarily* defined in terms of being the family's 'protectors' and financial providers. Women, on the other hand, are *primarily* defined in terms of their domestic and reproductive labour; whatever their actual contribution to the household economy might be, it is usually considered secondary to that of men. In other words, the key gendered difference here, as in many other parts of the world, is that while both men and women may aspire to both work and raise a family, for women, work outside the home is always seen as of secondary importance to their domestic and reproductive labour.

In summary, *tomboi* identify themselves as being 'like men' because in certain respects they identify with and wish to be treated 'like men' and, just as importantly, because they neither feel themselves to be nor wish to be categorised as, and treated, 'like women', at least in certain aspects of the normatively ascribed definitions and expectations of women. However, *tomboi* masculine identifications are not simply a form of female resistance to ascribed gender roles, nor do *tomboi* otherwise resist, challenge and reformulate the normative category 'woman' (see Johnson 1997b). Rather, the category *tomboi* itself is a normative gender category that in many respects confirms even as it challenges women's ascribed gender roles: *tomboi* define themselves as being 'like men' in opposition to women. Moreover, to take *tomboi* narratives of self and their subjective experiences of being a *tomboi* seriously requires us to understand and appreciate that identifying as a *tomboi* is, for some, simply a modest desire to live like, and be treated with the respect accorded to an average man. To a certain extent, *tomboi* do live and are treated 'like men'. Nevertheless, as I suggest below, living 'like men' is neither completely unambiguous nor untroubled; *tomboi* do not feel like, or identify themselves completely with, men.

Loving 'like women': *Tomboi* discourses of sexuality

Dress and work has precedence over sexuality in terms of *tomboi masculine* identifications. In narrating their life-histories, *tomboi* did not see sexual desire for other women as fundamental to their sense of being different from other women, or as propelling them to identify with men. Sexuality is no more or less important for them as it is for anyone else, either in *tomboi* subjectivities or in the way in which *tomboi* are defined by others. Rather, *tomboi* sexuality informs and is informed by their masculine identifications, but in a manner *opposite* to the assumptions of the normative discourse and is, and is seen by the *tomboi*, as a basis for creating shared identifications with women.

Self-identified *tomboi* see themselves (and are defined by others) as being 'like men' in desiring women. *Tomboi* do not see other *tomboi* as being appropriate lovers, viewing this as akin to incest, or having sex with your 'own kind'. *Tomboi* representations of courtship also frequently reproduced normative discourses about men's and women's relationships. In conventional protocols of courtship and marriage, men (whatever the actual situation) are supposed to be the providers or those who pay. In discussing situations where *tomboi* and women established homes together, *tomboi* often represented the relationship as being like that of husband and wife (*maglaki-bini*). Similarly, when talking of their relationships with women, *tomboi* would emphasise the gifts they gave to would-be lovers. They would also recount with great bravado, similar to that of other young men, stories of jealous lovers who would get angry with them if they so much as looked at another woman.

On one occasion I was sitting in a small coffee shop/bar with a group of three young *tomboi* who were, in turn, narrating their life histories. One of the three began telling me about a previous love affair turned sour. She described how the relationship had been going well, when her lover accused her of pursuing another woman. When she protested her innocence, her lover tore up the clothes she had given her in a fit of passionate rage and left them in shreds in her bedroom.

Tomboi sexual practice is also gendered in that both *tomboi* and others follow normative conventions of masculinity and femininity when describing who does what to whom and how. *Tomboi* identified themselves as the masculine-identified penetrator in sexual acts, described as 'fingering' their female lover. This gendering of erotic acts does not *necessarily* translate into the simple binary of 'active' versus 'passive'. What one does in bed, may, at least in terms of conventional protocols, be gendered in specific ways, but both women and men are seen as equally 'active' in their sexual pursuits and demands and in their erotic practice. Although *tomboi* make a point of saying they would never let their female lovers 'finger' them, they would often describe their female lovers as being very aggressive and voracious lovers.

Tomboi sexual desire and practices are entirely conventional in following local heterogendered protocols of sexuality, for the only culturally recognised and acknowledged sexuality is that which occurs between individuals who are (independently of their genitalia) *differently* gendered. In the Southern Philippines there are four different gender categories: men (masculine-identified male-bodied individuals), women (feminine-identified female-bodied individuals), *tomboi* (masculine identified female-bodied individuals) and the *bantut* (feminine-identified male-bodied individuals). Table 6.1 below describes the range of culturally acknowledged sexual partners for each category:

	Women (feminine-identified female – body)	Men (masculine-identified male-body)	*tomboi* (masculine-identified female-body)	Gay/*bantut* (feminine-identified male – body)
Women (feminine-identified female – body)		Culturally Recognised Sexual Partners	Culturally Recognised Sexual Partners	
Men (masculine-identified male-body)	Culturally Recognised Sexual Partners			Culturally Recognised Sexual Partners
tomboi (masculine-identified female-body)	Culturally Recognised Sexual Partners			Culturally Recognised but Improbable Sexual Partners
Gay/*bantut* (feminine-identified male – body)		Culturally Recognised Sexual Partners	Culturally Recognised but Improbable Sexual Partners	

Table 6.1 Gender categories and culturally acknowledged sexual partnerships

I use the expression 'heterogendered sexuality' because, as is apparent from the above table, there is generally no cultural recognition of, or space for, homo-gendered sexuality. In particular, because *tomboi* are 'like men', their culturally recognised sexual partners are those who belong to a different gender category – that is, women. Nor is it appropriate to speak of 'homosexual' or 'same sex' sexualities, since individuals are primarily classified in terms of their identification with and attributions of masculinity and femininity rather than in terms of their sex or genitalia per se (see below). The linguistic categories heterosexual and homosexual are, as yet, neither meaningful nor significant in the situation I am describing in the Southern Philippines. *Tomboi*, I have suggested, is a gender category rather than one based around either sexual preference or sexual identity, and *tomboi* do not regard sexuality as being the origin of or basis for their masculine identifications.

Moreover, although *tomboi* representations of their erotic desires and sexual practices conform to the norms of heterogendered sexuality, tomboi sexual subjectivities are not *only* defined in terms of masculine identifications. Individual *tomboi* often referred to the superior ability of *tomboi* to communicate and love women by virtue of their shared female experience. *Tomboi* frequently said, for instance, that while men are mainly concerned with fulfilling their own needs and pleasure, *tomboi* are much better lovers because, being also, 'like women', they know what their female lovers need and require.

Their capacity to love women 'like women' is, at one level, based on an acknowledgment of a shared bodily gender. *Tomboi* would describe their love-making with other women in terms of 'two women, the same' (*babai sibu-sibu*). I use the term 'bodily gender' rather than 'sex' for two reasons. The first is because, as Butler (1990) suggests, the term 'sex' suggests a kind of natural given on to which cultural ideas of gender are variously inscribed, rather than seeing 'sex' as one of the primary means through which gender discourses are naturalised. The second reason I use the term 'bodily gender', however, is that it better captures the sense of how *tomboi* and other individuals in the Southern Philippines understand the relationship between bodies and gender identifications.

In local cultural understandings, as much emphasis is placed on what bodies *do and become* in practice, as on what bodies are seen to *signify* in and of their genital selves. Just as individuals with putatively 'male' bodies may embody femininity and be 'like women', so too individuals with 'female' bodies may embody masculinity and be 'like men'. In other words, bodies can be either masculine or feminine independent of their genitals. This is not to say that bodily gender is seen as being completely fluid, or that the body is not seen, in important respects, to circumscribe the kind of woman or man that one might be. *Tomboi* are seen, in particular, to be like other women in having female reproductive organs and sexual substance, and to be unlike other men in lacking male organs and male sexual substance, i.e. semen. In this respect *tomboi* might be said to share the same 'sex' as other female-bodied individuals.

However, I would argue that while acknowledging that they possess similar kinds of bodies and reproductive capacities, *tomboi*'s affinity for and identification with women is not based simply on shared female reproductive organs or sexual substance. As described above, one of the central ways in which *tomboi* distinguish themselves from other women is in terms of their choice *not* to be defined in terms of either domestic or reproductive labour, including maternity. In other words, *tomboi* do not appeal to bodily gender as an essentialised substratum of female sexual identity. Indeed, *tomboi* are not, on the whole, preoccupied with their bodies. As previously suggested, *tomboi* neither see themselves as being 'stuck' with nor 'trapped' in 'the wrong body', nor do they see their female bodies as containing the ultimate or essential truths about themselves. Rather, their bodily gender is seen as limiting, though not exhausting, their various masculine identifications, *and* as providing a basis for, though not determining, their identification with other women.

For *tomboi*, to love 'like a woman' is, in other words, about *acts* of bodily and emotional identification with other women, rather than simply shared biology. *Tomboi* frequently talked about their relationships with women as friendships. Talking about lovers as friends was necessary in part because *tomboi* found it difficult to speak directly of romantic attachments and sexual liaisons, not simply because I was a foreigner and a man, but also because of the way *tomboi* sexuality is constructed in dominant (popular) discourse in terms of 'doing bad things'.

The accounts *tomboi* gave me of their relationship with women often progressed through three stages during the course of an extended informal interview, as well as in conversations that extended over time, as was the case with Maj and one or two others. At first, *tomboi* would describe their relationship with women as they speak of them in public, as simply friendship (*bagay*) or as friendly acquaintances (*bagay-bagay*). Later, they would to talk about a romantic interest in a particular woman, usually beginning by describing flirtatious relationships and infatuations, and concluding with accounts of women with whom they had sexual affairs. When discussing their romantic interests, *tomboi* would often use the normative conventions of *tomboi* masculine identifications in describing their sexual comportment, but as the conversation progressed *tomboi* would often begin to speak of the emotional and physical bonds that developed between themselves and their lovers, partly to distinguish themselves as better lovers than men, and partly to reiterate the importance of sharing and friendship.

The idiom of friendship is therefore not simply an acceptable cover for other-wise forbidden erotic desire and sexual practices, but is foundational to the way in which *tomboi* think of their relationships with women. *Tomboi* repeatedly told me that their relationships with women involved the mutual reciprocation of a partnership, and a shared relationship of caring and giving. As one *tomboi* described her relationship, 'Our love is beautiful. We share things together as if we were one. When I have money, I share with her. If she has money, she shares with me'. She recounted that they had previously shared a house in another town on an island further south, and had shared their income and, just as significantly, all the domestic labour. As noted above, in defining themselves as 'like men', *tomboi* deliberately seek to distance themselves from being primarily identified in terms of domestic labour.

Other *tomboi* recounted stories of their relationships that similarly emphasised shared material and emotional concerns. As another *tomboi* put it, 'We often spend a lot of time just talking to each other. When she tells me things, I can understand her because I too know what it feels like to be a woman'. *Tomboi* link this sharing of material possessions and emotional experience to their physical relationship. Indeed, they talk about 'just being women together', of holding, kissing, embracing and caressing each other 'as women' as much as, if not more than, they talk about specific acts of penetrative sexuality (i.e. of *tomboi* fingering their lovers, of placing themselves in the position of men in relation to their lovers). *Tomboi* would also talk about the general care and attention they give to each others' bodies, and of the importance of being able to understand their lovers because they were also 'women, just the same' (*babai sibu-sibu*).

The importance of this is that, firstly, it is one of the key differences between 'gay' and *tomboi* self-definitions. For the feminine-identified 'gays', sexual rela-tions with masculine-identified men were a key site for, and ultimate expression and affirmation of, their transgendered identifications; of feeling 'like a woman'. For the *tomboi*, however, their love of and desire for feminine-identified women was one of the ways in which they were 'like men', but it was seen neither as the underlying basis for, nor as the ultimate expression of, their masculine identifica-tions. Rather, sexuality was articulated in precisely the opposite manner: as much in terms of *shared* acts of feminine identification and solidarity as in terms of mas-culinity. Secondly, the emphasis on affective ties based on 'sharing' emotional, material and physical experience was seen, in particular, by *tomboi* as distin-guishing *tomboi* relationships from men's relationships with both 'gays' and women. Men's relationship with 'gays' was commonly characterised as one in which men obtained sexual favours and material goods from 'gays' without giving anything in return; both *tomboi* and 'gays' themselves frequently lamented this fact. While *tomboi* acknowledged that men's relationships with women might include shared love and affection, this was seen by *tomboi* as being constrained by men's inability to identify with and love women 'like women' in the way that *tomboi* were able.

I would not wish to over-romanticise *tomboi* representations of their relationships with women. *Tomboi* subject positions and masculine identifications also inform the structure of *tomboi* sexual subjectivities and relationships with women. When *tomboi* describe how their relationships with women are superior to those of men because of their shared identification as women, they are often describing situations in which there remains a one-way relationship; *tomboi* share with women in aspects of being women, while women are effectively excluded from sharing in aspects of *tomboi* masculine identifications and subject positions. Nevertheless, *tomboi* representations are important in specifically articulating a form of relationship that is qualitatively *different* from the conventional representations of their own and other relationships in terms of normative heterogendered sexuality.

'Women who do bad things': hegemonic masculinity and compulsory heterogender/sexuality

To appreciate more fully *tomboi* representations of their sexual selves and their relationships with women, it is also important to understand how the mainstream dominant discourse constructs *tomboi* sexuality as deviant. In terms of the normative categories of heterogendered sexuality, *tomboi* are seen to be 'like men' both in their desire for, and in the position(s) they are assumed to take in, sexual relations with women. The dominant discourse refuses to acknowledge that *tomboi* might love women 'like women'; it also describes *tomboi*, and their sexual practices, as 'women who do bad things' (*babai maghinang mangi*).

The discourse of 'doing bad things' was so widely an accepted and normalised way of describing *tomboi* sexual practice that it was commonly used not only by women and men in the course of conversations about *tomboi*, but also sometimes by *tomboi* themselves. When I challenged women and men about why they said *tomboi* did 'bad things', they responded in a number of ways. Some said that what *tomboi* did was bad particularly because *tomboi* were said to place their fingers in a woman's vagina. Women would often leave it at that, and would sometimes talk more generally and gently about the way in which *tomboi* might also cuddle, kiss and hold their lovers. Men, however, would often elaborate, repeating often-rehearsed sentiments about the sanctity of a woman's vagina, which is sometimes likened to the *ka'aba* (the black stone in Mecca) and described as a sacred passageway through which all individuals are seen to pass from one world into the other. In men's discourse, *tomboi* were seen as doing bad things to women's bod-

ies *and* as corrupting them by enticing them away from normal reproductive sexuality with 'real' men. Indeed, the dominant discourse, as most clearly and forcefully articulated by men, suggests that *tomboi* do bad things to other women and
violate the norms of reproductive sexuality and, more fundamentally, do bad
things in attempting to place themselves 'as men' in relation to women.

The wider effect of referring to *tomboi* as *women* who do bad things is that,
apart from rendering *tomboi* sexual subjectivities and relationships deviant and
largely unintelligible in terms of heterogendered sexuality, it essentialises their
bodily gender and reinforces their normatively ascribed position as women in
terms of reproductive sexuality and labour. It also de-legitimises their more general claims to occupy a subject position that is 'like men'.

Tomboi subject positions are denied and de-legitimated in a variety of ways.
Everyday discourse denies the authenticity of their subject positions through the
use of the diminutive term *nagtomboi-tomboi*, which suggests the individual is
simply play-acting or pretending to be a *tomboi*. Since the term *tomboi* means
being 'like' a man its diminutive, *nagtomboi-tomboi*, is a kind of double diminutive of the category 'man'. In fact, in referring to self-identified *tomboi* or those
seen to display *tomboi*-like characteristics, some individuals would describe
tomboi using the diminutive linguistic form for men, *usug-usug* or *magusug-usug*,
that is, 'little men' or 'pretend men'.

These terms were sometimes used in an ostensibly good-natured and affec-
tionate way, particularly of the boisterous behaviour of pre-pubescent girls. However, they were also used more systematically to denigrate and infantilise *tomboi*
actions and feelings and, by extension, the authenticity of their claims to a status
like that of men. The diminutive linguistic form for men or *tomboi* was used especially in describing young self-identified *tomboi*, who would otherwise be classified as *budjang*, young women of marriageable age. Thus, for example, those
younger *tomboi* who suggested that their *tomboi* identity was a means of deflecting parental nagging about marriage and family also said that their parents,
fathers in particular, would often say something to the effect of, 'When are you
going to stop acting like a *tomboi* (*nagtomboi-tomboi*), settle down and get married?' In other words, 'When are you going to grow up and stop play-acting?'

In so far as it is seen as play-acting, *tomboi* masculine identifications in terms
of dress, style and social comportment are 'tolerated' as long as they avoid, publicly at least, any hint of romantic or sexual relationships with women. In fact, in
tomboi representations, a clear distinction emerged between how *tomboi* were
treated by their mothers, and how they were treated by fathers and brothers.
Whereas fathers were more often than not reported to discourage *tomboi* adoption of masculine style and comportment as *tomboi* became older, mothers were
reportedly slightly more tolerant at least of masculine identifications. As I noted
earlier, *tomboi* often recounted their mothers' stories about their daughters' childhood identifications with boys, which explained their mothers' statements that
being a *tomboi* was 'Gods plan' for them. *Tomboi* also reported that their moth-

ers would often say to them, 'It is OK if you want to play at being a man, just don't do any bad things' (or, 'just don't shame us').

Yet I have also heard young self-identified *tomboi* referred to by both women and men as *maarte*, which might roughly be translated in this context as 'show-offs' who (as girls) inappropriately call attention to themselves by acting in male ways. Some young *tomboi* also said that they had to moderate their 'style' around family, in particular in front of fathers and brothers. One *tomboi* told me that she could not smoke near her brother, and when she went with her parents into the rural hinterlands she had to dress like a girl because of the reaction of relatives there. Nevertheless, usually the younger self-identified *tomboi* are the most bois-terous and apparently least concerned about their public visibility. This may partly reflect their age, for younger *tomboi* are perceived as 'play-acting' and are still, also, viewed as potential candidates for marriage. Moreover, some of the younger *tomboi* who talked about being a *tomboi* as a stratagem to avoid or at least postpone the hassles of men and family life also suggested that they might 'begin again' (*magbagu*) as women. One *tomboi*, referring to a *tomboi* who had, accord-ing to local gossip, begun again as a woman (*nagbagu babai*), said 'We don't know what is in their heart'.

The fact that someone might 'pretend' to be a *tomboi* suggests there is a 'real' *tomboy*, even though *tomboi* identifications are complex, and not usually described as 'real' versus 'pretend'. The dominant discourse distinguishes 'real' *tomboi* from those who are seen to be acting 'like' *tomboi*. The distinction between 'real' and 'pretend' focuses on the linked issues of age, potential marriageability, reproduction and sexuality. Self-identified *tomboi* whose style and comportment are 'like men's' and who are by common consent, viewed as either past marriage-able age or as showing no sign of getting married, are more likely to be viewed as 'real' *tomboi* (*tomboi tu'ud*). Yet the more they are identified as 'real' *tomboi*, the more they are also likely to be talked about as 'women who do bad things' because of their 'inappropriate' self-positioning 'as men' in relation to women.

We see here that both in the case of younger and older *tomboi*, and of 'pretend' and 'real' *tomboi*, a system of hegemonic masculinity and compulsory heterogen-der/sexuality simultaneously creates the framework within which *tomboi* are ren-dered culturally intelligible, and which denies the legitimacy of *tomboi* claims to be and to occupy a position 'like men'. Moreover, while older *tomboi* are less vis-ible and more discreet than younger *tomboi* – since to call attention to oneself as a *tomboi* is potentially to invite not just social opprobrium but verbal abuse – this does not mean that younger *tomboi*, comparatively more visible than older *tomboi*, are any less subject to the punitive effects of the dominant discourse.

Some, particularly younger, *tomboi* aspire to hang-out and be treated as 'one of the lads', as noted earlier, but were in practice often very circumspect and cautious about the contexts in which they did this. *Tomboi* do not wish to draw undue attention to themselves, not only for the reasons outlined above but also because they feared sexual harassment and potential sexual violence from men. From the *tomboi* perspective at least, by forcibly placing *tomboi* in a subordinate feminised relationship to themselves, young men perceive *tomboi* as a principle target for asserting their own and denying *tomboi* masculinity. This fear is not unfounded. One *tomboi* I knew had been raped by a young man who was part of the group of young men she had regularly associated and gone drinking with and whom she had, until then, considered a friend. The young man had reportedly told her that he was determined to turn her into a 'real' woman.

Living like men, loving like women: the question of *tomboi* likeness and being

In this chapter, I have explored aspects of *tomboi* gender identifications and sexual subjectivities, and highlighted key differences between *tomboi* self-identifications and descriptions and the way in which they are described and identified by others. *Tomboi* identify themselves and are identified by others as being 'like men', but *tomboi* see themselves as being similar to but also significantly different from *both* men and women in important respects. The crucial difference between *tomboi* self-representations and the way *tomboi* are represented by others centres around the question of the ways in which *tomboi* are and are not seen to be 'like men', and the quality and extent of that likeness.

On the one hand, the mainstream discourse, which enforces and reproduces hegemonic masculinity and heterogendered sexuality, accepts that certain female-bodied individuals (i.e. those identified as *tomboi*) may display a preference for, act like and adopt the style of 'men', and even acquire certain masculine qualities and characteristics. To this extent, it is recognised that masculinity and femininity may be achieved and are not necessarily tied to genitalia. Nevertheless, the closer a *tomboi* seems to embodying masculinity, the less acceptable she becomes, and the more she is reduced to a female gender that is essentialised in terms of reproductive sexuality. In fact, the dominant discourse works in a number of ways to de-legitimise *tomboi* claims to occupy a subject position that is 'like men'. They may be diminutively defined as *tomboi-tomboi* and treated as if they are simply 'playing' at being *tomboi*, thus disqualifying their claim to be really 'like men'. Alternatively, they may be defined as 'real' *tomboi*, i.e. masculine-identified female-bodied individuals who have sexual relationships with women, but in this case they are 'women who do bad things': that is, female-bodied individuals who inappropriately place themselves as men in relationship to other women.

Yet while *tomboi* were seeking to live and be treated 'like men', be this in terms of dress, social comportment, work and occupation, or their desires for and intimate relationships with women, they did not aspire to 'full' membership of the men's 'club', as it were, because they did not completely identify with men or masculinity. Certainly, *tomboi* sometimes spoke of 'having a heart like a man', and in narrating their life stories *tomboi* suggested that they had, since childhood, expressed a greater affinity for things defined as male rather than things defined as female. In each of these respects *tomboi* saw themselves as being and thinking of themselves as more like men than like women. Nevertheless, *tomboi* saw themselves as being 'like men', rather than as categorically being men, while *also* seeing themselves as being in certain respects 'like women'. Moreover, they considered their likeness to women as not simply a consequence of sharing the same genital body, but, more importantly, as based on acts of identification – of loving 'like women'.

In summary, the dominant gender ideology renders the gender identifications and sexual subjectivities of *tomboi* – 'real' *tomboi* in particular- meaningful and intelligible only in terms of what is presumed to be their masculine identities. This discourse acknowledges that *tomboi* may act like and embody certain masculine qualities and characteristics, but ultimately refuses to acknowledge subject positions that would enable them effectively to live 'like men', because they have female bodies. In *tomboi* self-representations, by contrast, an important distinction emerges between the way *tomboi* choose and aspire to live and *tomboi* gender identifications. *Tomboi* desire to *live* like men, that is to occupy subject positions which are gendered masculine and which are, to a large extent within the existing gender system, open only to masculine male-bodied individuals. *Tomboi* gender identifications and sexual subjectivities, however, are not exclusively defined in terms of either masculinity or femininity. Instead, *tomboi* identify themselves in different ways and in different contexts in terms of both masculinity and femininity.

Finally, although *tomboi* draw on and identify with both men and masculinity and women and femininity, I am not suggesting that they represent some kind of 'third gender' category. This concept neither makes theoretical sense nor reflects *tomboi* self-representations or the mainstream discourse in this particular locality. Rather, I suggest that *tomboi* might be best thought of as individuals who are, more modestly, seeking to live and love in ways that are otherwise forbidden or foreclosed by the dominant sex/gender system. In this way, *tomboi* challenge even as they reproduce and work within the existing framework of heterogender/sexuality. Firstly, *tomboi* show that masculinity and femininity are characteristics that may be acquired equally by both male- or female-bodied individuals, by challenging a system that ultimately only authorises male bodies as appropriately occupying the gender status of men. Secondly, however, while variously defining themselves in terms of masculinity and femininity, they defer the question of who and what they are, speaking instead of the way they wish to live and love. In this respect, they challenge the assumption that they *must* have an identity and likeness as one thing and not another.

Notes

1. The proper orthography for written Tausug (*Bahasa Sinug*), the majority language spoken in Jolo, Sulu, would be *tumbuy* (pronounced like 'tomb' and 'buoy' together). In other parts of the Philippines, tomboy is simply written as it is in English. I have chosen to use the Indonesian way of writing *tomboi* since it is near enough to the English word tomboy to be verbally recognisable yet also sufficiently different to remind the reader of the par-

ticular meanings attached to the word in this locale. Moreover, given that Tausug, like Indonesian, is part of the Austronesian family of languages, this choice of orthography is not completely indefensible in linguistic terms.

References

Blackwood, E. 1995. 'Falling in Love with An-Other Lesbian: Reflections on Identity in Fieldwork'. In *Taboo: Sex, Identity and Erotic Subjectivity in Anthropological Fieldwork*, Kulick, D. and M. Wilson (eds). London: Routledge, 51–5.

_____ 1999. 'Tombois in West Sumatra: Constructing Masculinity and Erotic Desire'. In *Female Desires: Same-Sex Relations and transgender Practices Across Cultures*. Blackwood, E. and S. Wieringa (eds). New York: Colombia University Press, 181–206.

Butler, J. 1990. *Gender Trouble: Feminism and the Subversion of Identity*. London: Routledge.

Johnson, M. 1997a. *Beauty and Power: Transgender and Cultural Transformation in the Southern Philippines*. Oxford: Berg.

_____ 1997b. 'At Home and Abroad: Inalienable Wealth, Personal Consumption and Formulations of Femininity in the Southern Philippines'. In *Material Cultures: Why Some Things Matter*, Miller, D. (ed.). Chicago: University of Chicago Press, 215–238.

_____ 1998. 'Global Desirings and Translocal Loves: Transgendering and Same-Sex Sexualities in the Southern Philippines'. *American Ethnologist*, 25, 4, 695–711.

7

ONE OF THE GALS WHO'S ONE OF THE GUYS: MEN, MASCULINITY AND DRAG PERFORMANCE IN NORTH AMERICA

Fiona Moore

Introduction: drag as an expression of masculinity

Over the years, numerous studies have been done of 'drag performance', a comedy performance by cross-dressed men in North America and Europe. These focus on drag as a form of gender crossing, a part of sexual politics, or an act of misogyny. Few, however, investigate the relation of drag to the expression of masculinity. On the basis of fieldwork in and around the Sunday-night drag show at a Canadian bar, I would argue that drag is used by straight and gay men to symbolise their respective conceptions of, and positions on, masculinity and the tensions relating to it.

Drag, for those not familiar with it, refers in its simplest form to men dressing in female clothing for the purposes of performance. More specifically, this performance was generally an exaggerated burlesque – many interviewees compared drag to leather-fetishist gear or the outrageous costumes worn by larger-than-life female performers such as the American comedienne Bette Midler. All interviewees stressed, however, that it should not be confused with transvestitism, which was seen as trying to 'look real' (cf. Woodhouse 1989: 18). There was some debate as to whether or not women could 'do drag', of which more later. Most of the performers I spoke with preferred the term 'drag queen' or, in a few and rather pretentious cases, 'drag performer'. I will refer to performers by feminine pronouns, as this was the form of address which they preferred. For the present, then, drag will be defined as *exaggerated cross-dressed performance by men*.

Most researchers who have investigated drag have seen it as either an act of misogyny or of heroic gender-bending. In the 1970s and 1980s, most commentators agreed with Ackroyd's assertion that drag was a form of acting out hatred of women (1979); Lurie calls it 'a caricature … of female ugliness' (1983: 260). More recently, with the spate of postmodernist interest in drag, it has been seen

7.1 A drag queen dressed as Marilyn Monroe taking part in Toronto's Lesbian, Bisexual and Gay Pride Parade. (Photographer: Pete Bevin, 1999.)

variously as 'blurring the visual lines between the sexes' (Foote 1989: 144), or 'a symbolic incursion into the territory that crosses gender boundaries' (Bullough and Bullough 1993: iii). Marjorie Garber, in *Vested Interests* (1993: 139), calls it a challenge to 'the notion of... manliness as a cultural norm'. Most writers, then, consider drag as either a symbolic attack on women or a questioning of gender stereotypes; few consider how it is actually interpreted by performers and audience members as it relates to their own lifestyles and genders.

In this chapter, I propose to look at how different sections of the audience and participants of a drag show use its imagery and performance attributes to define and consider masculinity and gender relations. I shall not actually attempt a hard-and-fast definition of masculinity in Canada; rather, my aim is to explore how masculinity was constructed with regard to a particular performance genre by its participants. An examination of drag as it is experienced might put a different complexion on the performance as a genre of male-only performing art in a North American context.

Dragged up on deck: the setting

The fieldwork on which this chapter is based was conducted at a bar, here called the 'Fifty-Four', in the 'Gay Village' of Toronto, Ontario, Canada (also called 'The Gay Ghetto', or 'Churwell').[1] This is an area of about half a square mile cen-

tring on the intersection of Church and Wellesley Streets in which a large per-
centage of the residents and business owners are gay or lesbian. I attended several
performances of the Fifty-Four's Sunday night drag show; for comparative purposes I attended other drag events at the Fifty-Four, including a benefit performance and a bingo game, and two shows at other bars, one a regular weekly show,
the other a special event on a Bette Midler theme. I also spent a certain amount
of time hanging about the Village and the Fifty-Four, talking informally with people. Most of my interviews were conducted in the bar itself or nearby venues.
More recently, I have also attended drag shows at Gay Pride festivals and so forth,
and have made a couple of return visits to the bar over the past few years. I have
thus been able to obtain some perspective on drag as a consumer and participant
(as an audience member) in a number of performances centred on the same bar.

The people who were interviewed in connection with this chapter were all
approached at the Sunday night show; most were audience members, but I also
conducted extensive interviews with several performers and members of the bar
staff (one of whom was a semi-retired performer himself). All were in employment or full-time education; all but two of my interviewees were Caucasian. All
the performers identified themselves as gay; the audience members included a mix
of sexual orientations and genders. I was also assisted by some performers who
were not directly associated with the Fifty-Four.[2]

7.2 A Toronto Lesbian, Bisexual and Gay Pride Parade float advertising a local gay bar, featuring a drag performer. (Photographer: Pete Bevin, 1999.)

The Fifty-Four was close to the hub of the Gay Village and had been in the same form for about five years at the time of the study. A recent revisit has revealed that it is still there and still running Sunday night drag shows, with many of the same performers. In 1996/1997 it had (and still has), a reputation as a relaxed, 'neighbourhood' bar, casual and with a heavily mixed clientele: regular customers likened it to 'Cheers', the pub in the American sitcom of the same name. The clientele were in fact about 90 percent male and 95 percent Caucasian; however, the presence of women and non-Caucasians, however small in number, made it quite mixed in comparison to other bars in the neighbourhood. It was, furthermore, very mixed in terms of the types of people who went there: other Gay Village bars tended to cater exclusively to one or the other of the Village's many cliques. It was often pointed out by staff and performers, with a certain amount of pride, that there was even a small group of 'leathermen' (gay leather-fetishists), who were regulars; normally, leathermen are said to avoid drag shows. The apparent age of the clientele for both sexes ranged from the late teens to the late sixties; the dress was generally casual, and the music tended to be popular songs from the 1970s and 1980s. The Fifty-Four, although its clientele was fairly restricted, was thus considered one of the more socially accommodating bars in the Village.

Physically, the bar was also rather relaxed. Its decor was sparse and modern: purples and dark blues, with industrial carpet, track lighting and aluminium and plastic bar and chairs. The walls were graced with exposed wires and posters advertising upcoming events; there was a stand with the local gay, lesbian and bisexual free newspaper. There were rotating shows of paintings by local artists. In the back of the bar were TVs, pool tables and pinball. The performance stage was simply a wooden platform about one and a half feet off the ground, large enough for two or three dragged-up individuals with microphones; it was painted black but chipped and scarred. It fronted onto a series of huge windows, which were something of the bar's trademark; in the summer these were opened and the drag shows would spill out onto the street, and even on to the occasional tour bus.

The Sunday night drag show was not the formal, elaborate drag cabaret of the sort seen in such films as *La Cage aux Folles* or *The Adventures of Priscilla, Queen of the Desert* (Molinaro 1978, Elliott 1994). Instead, in keeping with the relaxed tone of the bar, it was an 'open mike', in which any person wanting to perform was welcome to do so. While two of the drag queens whom I interviewed at the bar were full-time performers and two others were former full-time performers, most of the people – including the Master of Ceremonies (MC) – who participated in the Sunday night show 'did drag' either as a hobby or a part-time job. Neither was the structure very formal: there were two MCs, and a few weekly 'regular performers', but most of the people in a given show simply turned up and had a word with the MC beforehand. Sunday night shows were considered a good way for performers wanting to break into the profession – or just seeing if they enjoyed the genre – to get their start, and also for more established performers to promote their current and upcoming shows. In addition, the bar ran a bingo game with a dragged-up caller every Saturday afternoon and, occasionally, ran more formal shows.

The venue studied is thus a casual, predominantly but not exclusively gay, bar with a long-established, informal weekly drag cabaret. As such, it provides a fertile site to investigate the question of how drag performers and audiences use the art form to express and assert masculinity.

More man than you'll ever be: drag as gay male art form

Drag is, in the first instance, most associated with masculinity through its symbolic and social links to gay culture. I made the decision to look at drag in a gay bar mainly because the drag scene in Canadian cities has become increasingly focused on the gay community over the past ten years. Older performers recalled that twenty or thirty years before, at the time when the classic ethnography of drag shows, *Mother Camp* by Esther Newton (1979) was written, there had been a lot of drag cabarets which had catered to straight audiences more or less exclusively; Newton's informants regarded such cabarets as the ideal, and gay bars as second-rate venues. However, 'straight shows' had declined in number and prestige at the time of my fieldwork; the two performers with whom I spoke who specialised in straight audiences relied on bookings at banquets, casinos, weddings and so forth. One informant attributed this decline to a growing willingness among straight people to visit gay bars. Drag is a staple feature of any gay celebration, especially Pride Day. Drag is thus increasingly symbolic of homosexuality in North American culture.

However, it is significant that drag is more associated with gay male culture than with gay culture in general (Goodwin 1989). One drag fan with whom I spoke, a gay man, was astounded to learn that the well-known drag performer Barry Humphries ('Dame Edna Everedge') is straight. Many performers at the time regularly did benefits for causes predominantly of interest to gay men (such as AIDS research), rather than ones of more general interest to the gay community (such as anti-violence initiatives or youth centres). One of the more prominent organisations in the Toronto gay community is TICOT, the Trillium Imperial Court of Toronto, a charitable organisation whose members took the titles of royalty and about three-quarters of whom were drag performers. The membership is mainly, if not exclusively, gay men; friends of mine referred to them as the Gay Freemasons. All the male and mixed bars in the Village have a drag show, if only occasionally, and a drag queen 'mascot' chosen in an annual 'beauty pageant' competition; the two women's bars did not, at the time, have competitions of this sort. Most of the performances consisted of miming to songs which were popular dance tunes in the men's bars; more sophisticated ones involved celebrity impersonation, but, again, always those popular with gay men, such as Bette Midler and Cher. Drag is thus part of the gay community, but its activities have a male focus.

7.3 Patrons of a Toronto gay bar, occupying a performance space normally used for drag shows. (Photographer: Pete Bevin, 1999.)

The association of drag with gay men, however, was the source of some discomfort for them. What Garber (1993: 137) calls 'the transvestophobia within gay culture' was very much present under the surface in many of my interviews with gay men; performers were spoken of almost as a separate group. While most performers said that relations between drag queens and the rest of the gay community 'have improved', one retired performer had dated several men 'who don't like people to know they're dating a drag queen'. A gay male bar steward said that in the 1980s drag 'was not the impression that we [gay men] want[ed] to give the public'. There is thus also ambivalence about drag in the Gay Village.

This ambivalence seems to be at least partly linked to drag's supposedly feminine qualities. One gay man, a drag fan who was also vaguely associated with the leatherman community, said:

> I thought [performers] were *not men*, effeminate guys… but I didn't know any… now I enjoy it. I thought the only people who watched drag shows were effeminate men and drag queens, but here they are very normal.

These feminine qualities of drag are spoken of as frightening or threatening (Showalter 1990: 7); one gay man attributed his ex-boyfriend's dislike of drag to insecurity with his own sexuality, and it seems likely that discomfort with drag may be a reaction to the stereotype of the gay man as effeminate. It is also worth noting that the gay man quoted above implies in his last line that at other bars, perhaps, the audience is more effeminate and less 'normal'. Drag thus, for gay men, is seen as defining a gay man as someone who 'wants to be a woman'; the feminine qualities of drag are thus rejected by them, and are the source of some discomfort even among serious fans of the genre.

Some performers spoke of drag as a way in which they could express a sexual attraction to men more openly than gay men are normally allowed to in Canadian culture. However, this fact also causes them to describe gay sexuality in almost homophobic terms. One performer, who used the stage name Bunny LeBlanc, said:

> Bunny is a different persona; it's a kind of role-playing. Bunny is more brazen than I am. I can poke a guy in the crotch and he'll laugh, 'cause I'm a clown in makeup, where if I was [dressed as] a guy, I'd get decked.

One retired performer expressed similar sentiments in stronger words:

> I could almost call myself clinically bipolar. I can't control it, I become another person. If I see an attractive man and I'm in drag, I'll go over to him and start fondling him; if I was [dressed as] a boy, I would just look away.

In both cases, 'fondling a man' is an activity in which only someone who 'looks female' can indulge; the self-loathing expressed by the second performer also reinforces this. The actions in drag shows thus define masculinity in terms of sexuality; only someone who 'looks female' is allowed to perform sexual acts with 'men'.

This is also achieved through the structure of the show. The interaction between the performer and the audience is an exaggerated imitation of male-oriented heterosexual performance, with the drag queens flirting with and kissing male audience members as female nightclub artists do, and the audience stuffing tips down the performers' garter belts or bras, like the audience at a strip show. Drag performance thus defines sexual activity as being only appropriate between a 'man' and a 'woman'. Hence, the gay men's ambivalence to it; on the one hand, it involves sexual activity between two men, but on the other hand, it also seems to suggest that to engage in sexual activity with a man is not to be masculine.

Interestingly, however, drag queens were given an almost macho spin when gay men spoke about their positive role in the community. All the performers and gay male fans with whom I talked told me about the part that the drag queens had played in the Stonewall Riots, a 1969 protest which in North America is seen as the beginning of the Gay Rights movement. One or two gay men who were in their fifties or sixties spoke of how, in the days when homosexuality was criminalised and gay bars regularly raided, the drag queens would fight back against the police even when leathermen, who make a literal fetish of machismo, would go quietly. Today, one young gay man said, 'Gay men walk down the street, we'd maybe be called faggot, but if two drag queens walk down the street, they're taking their lives in their hands'. Drag queens are thus, in gay mythology, given a macho interior.

This form of masculinity, machismo hidden under effeminacy, seems to be one which gay men associate with themselves. The title of Goodwin's 1989 book on gay male humour, *More Man than You'll Ever Be*, is drawn from a quip made by a drag queen in the 1977 film *Car Wash*: 'I'm more man than you'll ever *be*, and more woman than you'll ever *get*.' (Russo 1987: 228). Many gay men spoke of drag as having been a positive influence on their coming-out process. Drag thus comes across as a macho interior disguised in a feminine exterior, and thus defines gay masculinity as tough machismo hidden by effeminacy.

One might also argue that this is reflected in the gender-crossing aspects of drag performance. At one TICOT event I saw a person who was in perfect, elegant, female drag, but sporting a luxuriant handlebar moustache. I also once saw a performer do what was unmistakably a drag act while out of makeup, wearing jeans and T-shirt and sporting a full beard. Most of the performances included a deliberate breaking of the 'fourth wall'; performers would archly adjust their wigs or breasts during performances, or joke about the falsity of each other's attributes. Many performers used gender-ambiguous stage names such as Chris Edwards, Terry Stevens or Rusty Ryan. One or two performers will even use their own, male names, particularly if they do other sorts of performance, as does the well-known comedian Barry Humphries. In all of these cases, the illusion of femininity is broken by periodic intrusions of an, often exaggeratedly, macho attribute.

While many researchers (e.g. Showalter 1990, Garber 1993) assert that the gender-crossing aspects of drag are a way of challenging gender roles or celebrating the transgressive, I would argue that these are in fact a way of reassuring the – predominantly gay male – audience by introducing 'safe' elements into the performance. By demonstrating visibly that they are in fact male, and 'macho', under their clothing, the performers are seen as reasserting that to be gay is still, in the final analysis, to be masculine. Furthermore, there was the case of one regular performer at the bar who began to undergo a sex change during my fieldwork. As her transition became apparent, one female fan who had been quite keen on this performer ceased to mention her, and the MCs of the show became more and more polite when introducing her. I was informed by a retired performer that this was a sign of dislike or anger. Significantly, this performer refused my request for an interview, although a mutual acquaintance had named her as someone generally willing to talk to reporters and researchers. Most of the gay male fans were very quick to assert that the equation of drag with physical transgendering, as in the film *Paris is Burning* (see Livingston 1990, Docter 1988: 36) was 'not true here, but it is in the USA', thereby invoking the familiar Canadian anti-American discourse and relegating any suggestion that drag might involve *genuine* femininity as belonging to a classic negative other. Another performer, who was not a transsexual, was disliked by many fans on the grounds that she looked 'too much like a woman… too real' and did not, as other performers did, find ways of indicating that her stage gender was an illusion. Gender crossing here thus seems to be not so much an act of transgression as of reassurance.

The ways in which gay men interpret drag performance thus not only provide a definition of masculinity, but a useful way of avoiding the problematic relationship of homosexuality to masculinity in Canadian culture. Through distancing themselves from drag performance, and through defining drag queens as a separate group who appear to be 'not men', gay men define masculinity as *not* being (like) a drag queen. It is interesting that all of the performers whom I interviewed, when out of their makeup, tended to let their beards grow and dress in clothing which visually emphasised their male attributes. At the same time, gay men must acknowledge the strong presence of drag in their culture, and the fact that it is seen as symbolic of it both by outsiders and by themselves. Consequently, they circumvent addressing the paradox of a feminine and arguably heterosexist performance form symbolising gay male culture by *redefining* drag queens as tough and macho, and thus *redefining gay masculinity* as inherently tough and macho, even if it sometimes hides behind an exterior which some deem effeminate. In this way, gay men are able to define their masculinity in a way which allows them to avoid the problematic politics of admitting a feminine component to gay maleness.

The gay male ambivalence towards drag thus seems to stem from the implication of effeminacy, and possibly also from the implicit assertion in the performance that only someone who looks like a woman can permissibly perform sexual acts with a man. By asserting a macho, enduring quality to drag, they are able to avoid not only this ambivalence, but also the issue of what this ambivalence says about them as gay men. The ways in which gay men interpret drag performance thus provides at once a description of gay male masculinity, and a way of glossing over problematic social issues.

Rocky Horror? Straight men and drag

Because of drag's association with homosexuality, it was often said to be a way of representing gay culture to straight people. To straight audiences, both informants and secondary sources agree that it is safe to say that drag queens 'symbolize homosexuality' (Newton 1979: 3). All the straight people with whom I spoke associated drag with gay culture, without particularly questioning the equation. Many gays and lesbians with whom I spoke felt that the more straight people see drag shows, the more they will come to accept gay culture as normal (Goodwin 1989: 59). One performer had gone into local secondary schools to answer students' questions about drag queens and homosexuals, and to demonstrate, in his words, that 'we're just like everyone else'. Performers who engaged in benefits and charity activities said that they thought these shows introduced the genre to heterosexuals who might not ordinarily see a drag show. People thus spoke of drag performance as a way of representing gay male culture to the straight world.

However, despite the assertion of some performers that drag played an 'ambassadorial role' between the gay and straight worlds, few heterosexuals seemed to draw a positive message from the performance. There were few straight audience members at the bar, or at any rate few who would agree to be interviewed. Some straight women, according to a performer, were so uncomfortable around performers that they preferred to use the male washroom rather than share a washroom with gay men in drag. One retired performer said that 'the drag act in the gay bar is beyond the perception of the average heterosexual'. While he had been retired from the scene for some time at that point, it is worth noting that the straight people who visited the Fifty-Four were mainly of the liberal white middle class, who are reputed to be more gay-positive than most. It is worth noting that publicity material for a benefit drag show which was published in the local mainstream newspapers mentioned only performers best known in straight venues; when the show was advertised in the Fifty-Four, performers better known in the Village were highlighted. There is thus an unspoken divide along drag lines between gay men and the straight world, in which drag is seen as defining the gay man.

Straight men, in particular, seemed to be deliberately excluded. While a handful of straight women attended shows and indeed were among performers' keenest fans, I had a difficult time finding even one straight male informant; when I asked performers and friends to introduce me to one, the people who had previously extolled the ambassadorial role of drag and spoken about the mixed nature of the show's audience responded with variations on 'what, in *here*?!' There is also a degree of significance in the conversation I had with a gay man about the boyfriends of straight women in the show's audience:

> *Gay man*: It takes the boyfriends a while to get used to being in a gay bar, but then they have a good time …
>
> *Interviewer*: Do they come back?
>
> *Gay man*: Yeah, some come back … with their boyfriends!

This suggested that any 'straight' man who came to a drag show was simply a closet gay man. Straight men were thus symbolically excluded from the performance.

Straight men are also in some ways singled out for negative attention by the drag show. As noted, drag shows are a send-up of entertainment aimed at straight men, portraying heterosexuality, in a way reminiscent of Ken Basso's (1979) Apache informants' imitations of 'Whitemen' as a hostile other on whom the oppressed group exact revenge by sending up their peccadilloes in a deadpan way. Newton (1979: 65) speaks of the tradition of straight male hostility towards gay men; one sequence in the film *Priscilla, Queen of the Desert* shows a performer, in drag, deliberately acting to humiliate a group of straight men (Elliott 1994). A gay man said 'if you take any straight woman to a [gay] bar she'll have a good time, 'cause it's a safe environment', linking straight male sexuality with danger. Drag was thus used by gay men as a way of expressing aggression against straight men, whom they portray as hostile outsiders, and also, as illustrated in the gay man's sarcastic comment above, as a way of suggesting that they can be 'brought into the fold' and neutralised through drag.

Straight men, however, even those sympathetic to drag, seemed almost to participate in their own exclusion. Drag was described by Ackroyd, a straight male writer, as evoking 'fears of female … sexuality at the same time as playing upon anxieties about male homosexuality … [it] can be a way of releasing sexual anxieties through laughter'. (1979: 103–104). My sole straight male informant never attended drag shows unless he knew a performer, and seldom without his wife; at the show where I met him, his wife was a personal friend of the MC. Moreover, he was in the arts world, and consequently had a lot of gay friends. Further, my straight male informant was the only one to request a pseudonym in my initial write-up. Outside of the performance sphere, I made some efforts to find out from straight male acquaintances the reason for their avoidance of the genre, and consistently got the response that 'it's not really my sort of thing; I don't find it terribly funny'. My straight male informant spoke of a 'general male phobia of drag'. Straight men thus also play a part in defining drag as a performance form which excludes them.

However, drag does actually include straight men in other ways. All men in my sample, straight or gay, had tried drag (anecdotal evidence subsequently suggested that this is widespread). It is worth noting that for the most part, straight men tried drag normally at 'liminal' times, when 'crossing' is socially allowed, such as Halloween (Douglas 1966). Another good example might be performances of *The Rocky Horror Picture Show* (Sharman 1975), a film which depicts an 'ordinary' heterosexual couple being placed in a liminal environment in which a dragged-up Dionysian figure encourages them to otherwise taboo sexual exploration, and whose audiences customarily include men of all sexual preferences who dress as the transvestite protagonist for the duration of the performance. The fact that straight men practice drag under certain circumstances can also be seen to define drag performance as a liminal act, something which asserts the status quo through allowing its transgression in limited circumstances (Douglas 1966). For straight men, drag expresses masculinity through portraying the not-masculine, and thus they define their masculinity by distancing themselves from it.

As with gay men, then, straight men use drag as a symbol by which to define their masculinity. Rather than reinterpreting the performance to avoid ambivalences about femininity, however, straight men do this by acknowledging the femininity within the performance but relegating the performance and performers to the role of the other; to something permissible only at times of licensed reversal or by sexually liminal groups, thereby defining masculinity by what drag is not.

Passing women: the views of performers

Finally, it is worth considering the words of performers about drag and masculinity. In the first instance, drag is an almost exclusively male art form. Since my fieldwork, male impersonators or 'drag kings', although still a less visible group, have become more of a common sight, while at the time of my study they were rare. One might further add that their performances deliberately parallel those of drag queens, being almost exclusively lesbian and given to impersonating a particular sort of flamboyant, sexually loose man. Furthermore, there seemed to be less agreement on what exactly constituted drag on a woman; when doing a joint interview with a lesbian couple, one member began to say that she had done drag because she had worn male clothing, but her partner promptly interrupted to voice doubt as to whether a female drag artist would be dressed as a man or as an outrageous woman. There was one 'Victor/Victoria' performer in Toronto at the time – this being a woman in exaggerated female costume – who had won an otherwise-male drag competition the year before the study, but she was the only example of this that I know of. Drag is thus, in a sense, a contradiction in terms: an all-male art form which focuses around portraying female characters.

As implied earlier, performers said that they did not see themselves as envying or realistically emulating women:

> I never wanted to 'be' a woman … I'm part of an oppressed minority [gay men], I don't want to join the oppressed majority. I say that I'm sympathetic to feminism, but that I'm not a feminist because I'm a man. I have no real idea of what it's like to be a woman.

Another remarked 'it's obvious that I'm a man in a dress', underlining that her performance was visibly all just an illusion. One of the performers at the show had as her theme tune 'One of the Gals who's One of the Guys', again emphasising the male body under the female dress. Performers were quick to assert the sympathy with women that they felt the performance had lent them, but also distanced themselves from women. Drag performers thus divorce the performance from any sort of reality as it relates to femininity.

Despite their assertions to the contrary and the puncturing of the illusion inherent in the genre, however, performers did take pride in their occasional ability to be actually taken for women. One performer took a certain amount of pleasure in her ability to 'pass' as a woman when in drag, telling with a slight note of pride a story about a man following her home when she was dressed as Anne Murray. However, the punch line of the joke was the horror with which the would-be stalker recoiled when he realised that he had been following a man. There is also an undercurrent of turning the tables: the idea of being followed by a stranger is a familiar fear for many women, but here the 'woman' proved to be more than capable of defending herself. Again, then, there is an unspoken ideal of being able to 'pass' as a woman, which contradicts performers' assertions that drag has nothing to do with real women.

This 'passing' is the source of a seldom-expressed tension between performers and audiences. Several people alluded to the suggestion that drag is somehow intended to show a 'better woman' than a natural woman. All of the women who attended drag shows made some sort of half-joking remark to the general effect that the performers looked better in female dress than they did. A gay male fan whom I interviewed expressed concern about the then-current advertisements for MAC cosmetics which featured American drag performer RuPaul, saying that to use RuPaul as their chief model was 'saying a drag queen's better than a woman'. Performers thus cannot help but be aware that the images of femininity they portray might be seen as an attack on women.

Furthermore, one might consider the type of women portrayed in the show. As well as generally being carefully made-up, bewigged and dressed in ways seldom seen outside of the sort of 1950s fashion magazines pilloried in early feminist writing, the women who were impersonated in the shows were all singers with an exaggerated, even aggressive air, such as Bette Midler, Cher and Barbra Streisand. Joseph P. Goodwin (1989: 40, 42) describes the women impersonated as ones who 'were known as strong, distinctive and quick witted' and who found it 'easier ... to flout conventions than it is for most people'. However, they are also usually ones who exhibit the 'macho' behaviour discussed above: all are known for leading lifestyles which are not typical of the women of their time. As Nanda (1990) notes that the *hijra* of South India look like women but do unfeminine things, so drag performers dress in female clothing, but engage in activities which are at least mildly taboo for women. Consequently, drag may not only be seen as an attempt to portray a 'better woman', but to suggest that this ideal is one who displays unmistakably masculine social behaviour of a sort which real women generally eschew.

It is also interesting that strong female performers who happen to be lesbians, such as Billie Holiday, are seldom impersonated. The one exception might be Dusty Springfield, but her bisexuality did not become known until late in her life, and she has fallen out of favour as a subject for impersonation since her death. Most of my informants seemed to feel that a woman's orientation affected the way she perceived drag: over half of them made some attempt to find out my orientation, however indirectly, and three asked me point-blank, one saying that she 'wanted to know where I stood'. Also performers, when they singled out a female audience member, inevitably quizzed her about her orientation; the closest I saw to this, with a male audience member, was 'are you a sissy boy?' which only implies homosexuality. It seemed to be generally assumed that lesbians would be hostile to drag; when I mentioned writers who had called drag 'misogynous', all the gay men and performers assumed these were lesbians (they were in fact men). Drag queens thus distance themselves from a social group who are seen as female but not 'feminine' in the way that performers are; drag therefore portrays femininity, but only of a particular sort.

Drag thus once again expresses social tensions surrounding masculinity, in this case by portraying figures which are at once idealised women, but also firmly removed from associations with actual women. This performance, as many writers have noted, could therefore be seen as misogynous and asserting masculine superiority. However, this makes it difficult to explain why drag does have a strong minority of female fans (including lesbians), or the fact that the performance focused around exceptional female performers rather than implying, as do other sorts of comedians (e.g. Howard Stern), that they are sending up the feminine norm. The reason would seem to lie in the choice of symbols in the performance; by deliberately being selective in their portrayal of women, and through actively distancing themselves from certain forms of womanhood, drag performers can thus ensure that the show is seen as addressing only a particular model of femininity, and indeed subverting it by making it a model with masculine components. Drag performers thus make use of the symbols of masculinity and femininity in their performances to convey a message about gender which is non-threatening to themselves and, for the most part, to audience members.

In the case of performers, as with the other two cases, drag once again addresses contradictions surrounding masculinity. In this instance, however, performers are unconsciously selecting the symbols used in the show to ensure that the contradiction does not come to the fore, and that drag is ultimately a non-threatening, feel-good sort of entertainment, at any rate for the groups which performers view as their target audience.

Masculinity, sexuality and liminality: discussion and conclusion

I have argued that drag is firmly associated with masculinity; however, the way in which it is associated depends very much on the interpretation of performer and audience. In all three cases – gay men, straight men and performers – drag is a performance which raises tensions with regard to masculinity, but its symbolic nature means that these tensions can be resolved through interpretation. For gay men, the symbolic association of drag with homosexuality very much begs the question of what it is to be a gay man: certain groups, such as leathermen, assert their masculinity by vehemently opposing drag, and others 'reclaim' it by attributing to it a macho ethic. For straight men, the performance was interpreted as something Other, permissible and enjoyable in the context of Saturnalia-type occasions or by such groups as gay men, who are constructed as 'liminal' to the heterosexual social norm. Finally, with regard to performers, manipulation of the symbols in the performance allows them to walk a fine line between portraying women humorously and engaging in a misogynous or, alternatively, 'too real' performance. Drag thus, in all cases, reflects tension with regard to masculinity and provides solutions through being used as a symbol, and therefore subject to interpretation.

The performance also brings in the relation of sexuality to masculinity. It is universally acknowledged to be a 'gay thing' to dress in drag; yet all men, straight and gay, had done it. Furthermore, gay men were ambivalent, enjoying it and acknowledging it as part of the culture, yet also being uneasy about it, all of them emphasising to me that they liked to sleep with men, not men dressed as women. As noted, drag at once celebrates and rejects a heterosexual ideal of sexuality. The ambivalence to drag among gay men thus indicates the relationship of drag to masculinity of all sorts: they both embrace and fear drag because of its suggestion that they themselves, like the performers, are not masculine, and they relate to drag in ways which reassure them that they are in fact masculine rather than feminine. For straight men, it forms part of a symbolic mutual exclusion pact, as it were: they are happy to be excluded from the joke, just as gay men are keen to exclude them, because in this way they can assert that their sexuality is 'normal', and avoid having to address the question of what it is to be masculine, if not to sleep with women. Even for performers, sexuality is involved in defining femininity as well, in their avoidance of lesbian images in favour of other sorts of female toughness. Masculinity is thus conceived of in terms of sexuality throughout.

However, the most important aspect of drag as a symbol of masculinity is that no single group's interpretations and uses of drag can exist without the others' interpretations and uses of these. Gay men's use of drag to avoid addressing issues surrounding masculinity and sexuality, and whether being sexually active with men is a non-masculine act, could not exist without the use of drag as a mutual-exclusion pact with straight men, in which straight male behaviour is sent up aggressively and drag performance is confined to what straight men perceive as socially acceptable contexts for inversion. The performers' actions, similarly, pick up on feedback from audience members and are influenced by the image of performers as 'wanting to be women' as well as by the hostile reaction of audience members to performances which are 'too real'. They also help to define the audience as being primarily gay men and straight women, through tolerating or actively excluding other groups. In a sense, then, drag is a means of collectively defining masculinity; this is not, however, through organised consensus, but through different discourses coexisting around the same art form.

Drag is therefore a means of defining masculinity within Canadian, and indeed North American, society. However, the fact that such a concept is highly complex, with multiple ways of relating to the masculine, means that it is used in diverse ways by diverse groups, ways which coexist within the general symbolic complex surrounding masculinity. The diverse uses of drag by different interest groups thus work together to construct a collective definition of masculinity; this definition must, however, by its very nature include different discourses within itself.

Drag is thus, for its consumers and producers, not so much a site of gender-bending or ritualised denigration of women, as a site of defining masculinity symbolically. The fact that drag is a symbolic performance, and therefore open to interpretation, means that different groups pick up on different aspects of it, and use it to define masculinity and their relation to it in diverse ways. These ways of defining it, with very different origins and agendas, not only operate simultaneously, but in a sense feed off each other; no single use of drag as a symbol of masculinity can exist, or indeed have credibility, without any of the others.

Notes

1. Fieldwork was carried out from November 1996 to March 1997, as part of the requirements for a B.A. Honours degree at the University of Toronto.
2. I would also like to acknowledge the invaluable assistance of Take a Walk on the Wildside, a Toronto-based organisation which caters to drag queens as well as to the transgender and transsexual communities.

References

Ackroyd, P. 1979. *Dressing up: Transvestitism and Drag: The History of an Obsession.* London: Thames and Hudson.

Basso, K. 1979. *Portraits of 'The Whiteman': Linguistic Play and Cultural Symbols among the Western Apache.* New York: Cambridge University Press.

Bullough, V.L. and B. Bullough 1993. *Cross-Dressing, Sex and Gender.* Philadelphia: University of Pennsylvania Press.

Docter, R.F. 1988. *Transvestites and Transsexuals: Towards a Theory of Cross-Gender Behaviour.* New York: Plenum Press.

Douglas, M. 1966. *Purity and Danger.* London: Ark.

Elliott, S. 1994. *The Adventures of Priscilla, Queen of the Desert.* AFFC/PolyGram.

Foote, S. 1989. 'Challenging Gender Symbols'. In *Men and Women: Dressing the Part*, Brush Kidwell, C. and V. Steele (eds), Washington: Smithsonian Institution Press, 144–57.

Garber, M. 1993. *Vested Interests: Cross Dressing and Cultural Anxiety.* New York: Harper Perennial.

Goodwin, J.P. 1989. *More Man Than You'll Ever Be: Gay Folklore and Acculturation in Middle America.* Bloomington: University of Indiana Press.

Livingston, J. 1990. *Paris Is Burning.* Off White Productions Inc.

Lurie, A. 1983. *The Language of Clothes* [second edition]. New York: Vintage Books.

Molinaro, E. 1979. *La Cage aux Folles.* Les Productions Artistes Associés.

Nanda, S. 1990. *Neither Man nor Woman: The Hijras of India.* Belmont: Wadsworth.

Newton, E. 1979. *Mother Camp: Female Impersonators in America.* Chicago: University of Chicago Press.

Sharman, J. 1975. *The Rocky Horror Picture Show.* Twentieth Century Fox.

Showalter, E. 1990. *Sexual Anarchy: Gender and Culture at the Fin de Siècle.* New York: Viking.

Russo, V. 1987. *The Celluloid Closet: Homosexuality in the Movies* [Revised edition]. New York: Harper and Row.

Woodhouse, A. 1989. *Fantastic Women: Sex, Gender and Transvestitism.* Houndmills: Macmillan.

8

MALE DAMES AND FEMALE BOYS: CROSS-DRESSING IN THE ENGLISH PANTOMIME

Shirley Ardener

English vulgar comedy

The English have had a long fascination with the grotesque and the vulgar. Formerly, for example, we found geurning (making ugly faces framed in a horse's halter) a highly comic form of entertainment. More recently, the knobbly knees competitions at holiday camps, and the risqué seaside postcards featuring large fat women and small skinny men, similarly play with exaggerated physicality. On television we had the Benny Hill shows with their 'exaggeratedly built' scantily dressed girls; Eric Morecambe with his risible unfitting clothes and crooked spectacles; and the ludicrous cross dressing of the Two Ronnies, Barker and Corbett – they all raise a laugh. If we were to meet such oddities and inversions on the street, we might pass with a giggle, but most likely would accord them 'civil inattention' from embarrassment or disgust.[1] In a bounded space, such as on stage with a captive audience, the likely responses are nervous titters, or hilarity. Such reactions underpin the success of farce – defined in the *Oxford Companion to the Theatre* as 'an extreme form of comedy in which laughter is raised at the expense of probability ...', and glossed by the great contemporary exponent, Brian Rix, as 'tragedy with its trousers down' (Rix 1995).[2]

This chapter deals with a theatrical discourse involving vulgarity and 'gender bending' in what Cookman (1998:17) considers to be 'one of our only true British art forms: the Christmas pantomime', for which here I commonly use its popular short form, panto. For Michael Coveney (2001: 54–5) 'The whole ritual [of panto] is part of our national character and behaviour, at least since the "Victorian Times"'. As a small contribution to this study of identities, I attempt to look beyond the laughter to the skills and methods of the writers and actors, to various interpretations of audience loyalties, and at panto's changing contexts, themes and expressions over time.

So what is the English pantomime?[3] For Brandreth (1974: 7) it is:

> a phenomenal phenomenon ... a romantically farcical fairy tale set to music, peopled
> with men dressed as women, women dressed as men, humans dressed as animals, and
> packed with spectacle and slapstick, topical jokes and old chestnuts, community
> singing and audience participation ...

A famous actor in the genre, Roy Hudd (1998: 9), suggests the panto is a:

> bewildering mix of comedy, 'drag', audience participation and topical jokes. In the
> Panto, the man dressed as a woman is, of course, known as a Dame, while the young
> woman who dresses like a young man is The Principal Boy.

A notable feature of the pantomime is its popularity in the community, among all
ages and across gender. Tamara Malcolm, when Director of the Theatre at Chipping Norton, noted, also, that 'the beauty of panto is that it cuts across the class
system and is totally dependent on the audience' (2001). It is well known that, as
children, Queen Elizabeth II and her sister Princess Margaret devised and acted
in private pantos for the Court – just as local schoolchildren were performing for
their parents.

Unfortunately, owing to escalating production costs, commercial panto is no
longer found on London's West End stages, but it still flourishes in the London
suburbs, and in many provincial towns. Its popularity in these venues is attested
by the report that 'in 2000, two million people paid more than £20 million to see
27 Pantos, presented by the chief producing organisation, Qdos ...' (Coveney
2001: 54–5). Beyond that there are hundreds, perhaps thousands, of productions
in schools, community halls and in hospitals, in which both amateurs and pro-
fessionals are engaged. For groups in such venues, the earnings from panto help
to finance the rest of their programmes throughout the year, including their aid
to social welfare projects, be they local or overseas.

In one view, 'Pantomime is less likely to be performed at seats of higher learning [than elsewhere] as it is considered to be unworthy of academic notice' (Cookman 1998: 20). I must dispute this, not only because there are numerous
Christmas pantos performed annually by students in English universities,[4] but
because, as a manifestation of popular art, panto is obviously an eminently suitable topic for an anthropologist.

Commercial theatre often refurbishes old scripts and re-uses scenery. But in
the run-up to Christmas new topical scripts are also written, with local and
national allusions. In 1925, Disher (1925: 277) wrote that 'Pantomime was once
the mirror of society', and in many ways it still is. Mothers are still found making
costumes, while uncles are painting scenery. There are numerous how-to-do-it
books to guide them. Arguably, the oldest amateur dramatic group in England is
the St Joseph's Players at Leigh, Lancashire, which is now absorbed in the conur-
bation of Wigan. The group was founded in the 1850s, or earlier, but only began
pantomimes annually after the last World War. Linked to a Catholic church, its

60–70 members now come from all faiths; for example, Doreen Johnson, a leading member since the '60s, is not a Catholic. It competes with five other pantomime stagings in its catchments area, yet in 2005 it sustained eleven panto performances, drawing a total audience of about 3,000, which included the local MP, Bishop and Mayor – and provided useful income to support its other shows.

In Oxfordshire, in 2001, among the local venues for pantos were: The Oxford Playhouse (*Mother Goose*); The Theatre at Chipping Norton (*Babes in the Wood*), which was attended by a party of social anthropologists and their children; The Old Fire Station at Oxford (*Peter Pan*), and at The City of Oxford Guild (two plays by Charles Dickens). As an example of community theatre, the *Oxford Mail* (6 February 2002) recorded that:

> Parents, pupils and people living near Ducklington School in west Oxfordshire are to come together to stage their second pantomime after the success of their debut last year … Director Sara Church said: 'The plan originally was that we would do one every two years because there is so much work involved. It's by public demand that we are doing one again just 12 months later'.

In 2003, the amateur Launton Village Players, who write, score and produce a new panto each year, complete with local allusions and 'special effects', presented *Red Riding Hood*, the male Dame being Countess Hairbrush, while a young woman represented Bramble the Mischievous Elf.

For those who have not seen a Panto, it can be recommended as a true 'ethnic' experience. In a panto audience, hundreds of children and parents will 'cross the fourth wall' of the stage to boo and hiss the villains, and join in repartee with the players on stage. Unlike in other forms of theatre, through information secretly passed to the players before the performance, individuals and groups in the audience may be addressed by name from the stage. Indeed there is a sense of cosy complicity in the suspension of disbelief, between the players and the audience. Deborah Manley (personal communication) was amused when, at Christmas 2000, she was with 'two Dutch visitors, not warned of this tradition, who shushed the audience around them when they called out as the curtain went up on the Oxford Playhouse Panto!'

Despite panto's popularity, when in 2001 I began looking for material on pantos I encountered an interesting fact: despite the popularity of the genre, it is not possible to hire a commercial video of a complete on-stage pantomime. Such videos just do not exist, perhaps because watching without being able to participate negates the point of it. I did find an interesting early (1982) video produced and directed by Elizabeth Wood, compèred by, the then young, Victoria Wood (now a high-profile comedienne), entitled *The Pantomime Dame*. I am indebted to this video for the excellent interviews with performing Dames, some now dead, whose comments I have drawn on. Private videos do exist; Gina Burrows kindly lent me her copy of a pantomime performed at the charming theatre in Chipping Norton. Although the West End theatres and videos shun this genre, each Christmas radio broadcasts and television programmes present entertainments that include in whole or in part seasonal pantomimes. In fact, in 2001, the only video of a panto I might have obtained – by special application – was a TV panto, with the comedian Paul Merton as the star. Indeed, panto makes its mark in many TV and radio scripts which, like some stage shows, rely heavily on references to broadcast programmes and on actors and comedians regularly seen on screen. For example, the 2002 Christmas edition of the soap opera *East Enders*, set in a working-class district of London, had its cast of characters taking part in a panto. The long-running radio saga of rural life, *The Archers*, has its characters involved in a panto most years.

A potted history of pantomime

Writings in the considerable literature on theatre history find many intermingled sources for the modern 'traditional' panto. Most agree that English pantomime owes something to the Greeks and Romans. In a letter, Pliny describes the elderly matriarch of a distinguished and wealthy Italian family – Ummidia Qadratilla – who passed her later years as a fan of 'pantomime'; indeed she is reported to have what might be called a small 'theatre empire'. The soothing of the masses with the enjoyment of pantomime gave her control and thereby access to limited political power (Sick 1999).

But as Brandreth (1973) notes, the Roman 'dumb-shows' were very different from modern panto. More relevant was the fusion of the Italian tradition of *commedia dell' arte*. This very popular Italian entertainment included the Harlequinade, in which the actors assumed the roles of a familiar group of characters – Harlequin, Columbine, Pantaloon, Scaramouche and others – who improvised within a series of stock situations. According to Thelma Niklaus (1956, quoted in Frow 1985:21), in Europe:

> Every actor of experience had … a vast collection of phrases and speeches that could be drawn upon to fit any occasion. According to the type of role he normally played, his *repertorio* would consist of reproaches, boasting, obscene jokes, angry tirades, declarations of love, challenges to mortal combat, protestations of despair, delight, or delirium, streams of wild oaths, soliloquies that were rhetorical, impassioned, or gibberish, all ready to spring to mind when required.

Thus pantomime has always been (and remains) formulaic – full of stock episodes, repetitious old jokes and so on, regardless of the story.

If the dating of 'the first' English panto, like the source of the River Thames, is problematic, despite contenders, the first play to contain the ingredients of a proper English pantomime is said to be William Mountfort's 1685 adaptation of Marlowe's *Doctor Faustus* (Frow 1985). To Marlowe's plot Mountfort (1664–92) added the comic characters of Harlequin and Scaramouche and re-titled the drama *The Life and Death of Doctor Faustus made into a Farce* (Brandreth 1973).

In the theatre of Elizabethan England, as we all know, female roles were taken by boys and young men. This enabled Shakespeare to play many games involving transvestism. During the Commonwealth, public theatres were closed for political and moral reasons, but with the Restoration, when players followed Charles II and his court to London, French fairground entertainment brought continental influence to England. However, even after actresses entered the profession at the Restoration, the convention of a man playing a comic old woman continued (Frow 1985). Indeed, well into the eighteenth century some actresses *preferred* to see their male colleagues playing the unflattering parts of older or ludicrous women commonly found in high comedy and farce.

For a while the pantomime settled down as 'a one-act entertainment, divided into roughly eighteen scenes, which lasted perhaps two hours. The opening, which was always the shorter part of the performance, was usually based on a nursery rhyme or a classical myth, and invariably involved a pair of young lovers having to flee from the girl's disapproving father and unsuitable suitor' (Brandreth 1974: 141). The pantomime ended with a splendid transformation scene, with a happy resolution, especially of all love lives. By the 1860s and 1870s, with its comical Dame and glamorous Boy, with its rhyming couplets and verbal jocularity, with its lavish scenery and token harlequinade, the Victorian panto was a far cry from the pantomime of Regency days.

As for the modern period, the typical pantomime structure, as summed up simply by Cookman (1998: 39), has five main elements:

1. *Hero and Heroine under threat (financial or physical)*
2. *Introduction of further threat*
3. *Introduction of possible saviour*
4. *Battle between the forces of good and evil*
5. *Evil vanquished and hero and heroine united*

Story lines

The origins of some of the stories used as themes for panto, and of the writers who adapt them, are fascinating, but space precludes much detail here.[5] Often the stories are a mixture of fact with fiction – such as in *Dick Whittington* in which the historical Sir William Whittington of Gloucester is linked with a cat. Almost all the more popular English panto subjects have long pedigrees, and many of them reached English shores from alien parts. For example, it is thanks to a seventeenth-century Frenchman, Charles Perrault, that we know the stories of *Cinderella, Sleeping Beauty, Red Riding Hood, Puss in Boots*, and *Bluebeard*, and it is due to *The Arabian Nights* that we were introduced to *Aladdin, Sinbad the Sailor* and *Ali Baba*. According to Gill Davies (1995), of all the panto stories, the two most popular are, and always have been, *Cinderella* and *Aladdin*. *Cinderella* reached the English stage in 1804 as a 'New Grand Allegorical Pantomime Spectacle', but it was not until Boxing Day 1860, that H.J. Byron presented *Cinderella* as 'a Fairy Burlesque Extravaganza'. Over four hundred versions of the Cinderella story have been traced and all of them differ slightly from the tale we have come to expect. The modern English version is very much as Perrault (1697) recounted it in his *Contes de Ma Mere L'Oie*, except that, in the original, Cinderella wore a *fur* slipper not a *glass* one; *en vair* (fur) was mistaken for *en verre* (glass) (Brandreth 1974: 8).

A great deal is owed to John Rich (c.1682–1761), the eighteenth-century Harlequin 'John Lun', who established pantomime in London. Harlequin, along with Columbine, Clown and Pantaloon, became a basic element in the popular theatre until comparatively recently, but he first emerged in sixteenth-century Italy as 'Arlecchino' (Frow 1985: 21). Indeed Arlecchino (as Harlequin) – being the first of the two stock servants, the other being Brighella (Frow 1985) – was to become the most important, most popular, and longest-lived character of the entire genre. In turn mime, acrobat, dancer and actor of many parts, he was a sort of cross between Figaro and Pagliacci in opera. He stood out by his skin-tight spangled costume of multicoloured lozenges and triangles, derived from the coloured patches of his original servant's costume, which was introduced by James Burne in his *Harlequine Sheppard* [6] (Disher 1925: 293). Gilbert (of Gilbert and Sullivan fame), writing in 1868, recalls his childhood:

> To be a Harlequine, or Columbine was [then] the summit of earthly happiness to which a worthy man or woman could aspire, while the condition of Clown or Pantaloon was a fitting purgatory in which to expiate the guilty deeds of the miss-spent. (Gilbert 1868: 51)

In the nineteenth century there was great competition among the impresarios to dazzle the public by spectacular scenery and elaborate props, often supported by intricate mechanisms. The elaborate scene at the end became less extravagant, but nevertheless remains there today as a transformational climax to the evening's entertainment. As the pantomime shrank, the Harlequinade story itself began to disappear, and the panto opening became the panto proper.

Dames

The origins of the stock characters in pantomime who 'bend gender', and of those that have played them, can now be looked at in more detail. Again, authors offer various origins for the roles. The earliest English ancestors of the pantomime Dame are said by one authority, Frow (1985), to be Mrs Noah and Mac the Sheepstealer's Wife in the miracle plays of the Middle Ages. These had comedic elements, as when Mrs Noah flatly refuses to board the newly built Ark because she does not want to leave the 'gossips' who are her friends (Frow 1985). Despite such possible ancestries, it is also said that the now 'traditional' role of the Dame, as we understand it, was not created until the part of the Principal Boy was well established.

Today it is said that:

There's nothing like a dame: pantomime wouldn't be pantomime without her. *Cinderella* minus the Ugly Sisters, *Jack and the Bean-stalk* without Dame Trot (or Trott), *Aladdin* lacking Widow Twankey, would be like Christmas without Santa Claus – a contradiction in terms, and a dreary one at that. (Brandreth 1974: 21)

As a young child I grew up to think that the name of our feared next-door neighbour *really was* Widow Twankey, as she was known in my family! In fact, Widow Twankey, a character in Aladdin, was so-named in 1861 when Twankay was a tea, popular in London, which came from Tuan Kay Province of China (Ellacott and Robbins undated).

Men can get away with things, as women, that they could not as men. Thus, of the Dame role, Douggie Byng says: 'You can be more saucy as a woman than as a man. "What he did to me" is very different from "What I did to her". She's on the *def*ensive. A man's on the *off*ensive' (quoted in Frow 1985: 184). Kwame Sintim Musa (KSM), 'the only man doing stand-up in Ghana', who was trained in the United States, as part of his act has 'donned a dress to become Afia Siriboe, the four-times divorcée with a passion for flirtatious clothes and ruby red lips'. He is quoted as saying 'There are advantages to playing a woman'. For one thing, 'in a dress he can talk candidly about men – particularly their relations outside marriage' (Simpson 2003).

Given the role's long history, there have been too many famous Dames to mention all of them. Grimaldi nevertheless deserves note. He was born in 1778 and retired from the stage in 1828. He played several female roles in various pantomime 'openings' before being 'transformed' into a great, and still remembered, nineteenth-century Clown (Frow 1985). He became a popular hero; an actor with versatile skills he is credited with having made the pantomime a national cult. Also outstanding in the role was Dan Leno (1860–1904) – 'A legend in his own lifetime' (Brandreth 1974: 22), whose house is dignified by a commemorative blue plaque. 'When he died the nation mourned. The three and a half miles of his funeral route were lined with people standing three-deep all the way' (Brandreth 1974: 22). He was adept at conveying what some think of as an essential quality in the portfolio of Dames – pathos. Max Beerbohm wrote:

> I defy anyone not to have loved Dan Leno at first sight. The moment he capered on, with that air of wild determination, squirming in every limb with some deep grievance that must be outpoured, all hearts were his... The face puckered with the cares of the small shopkeeper or the landlady or of the lodger; that face so tragic, with all the tragedy that is writ on the face of a baby monkey, yet ever liable to relax its mouth into a sudden wide grin and to screw up its eyes to vanishing-point over some little triumph wrested from Fate, the tyrant; that poor little battered personage, so 'put upon' yet so plucky, with his squeaking voice and his sweeping gestures; bent but not broken; faint but pursuing; incarnate of the will to live in a world not at all worth living in – surely all hearts went out to Dan Leno with warm corners in them reserved to him for ever and ever. (quoted in Brandreth 1973: 148 and Brandreth 1974: 22)

Leno's appeal to the public's sympathy is paralleled by the fact that, according to tradition, it should only be the Dame, with the occasional exception of the servant Buttons, who may address the audience directly – thus breaking the 'fourth wall' of the stage ('Dame' Stirling Roberts, personal communication, 2003). George Robey (of the expressive bushy eyebrows) became another national institution. Born in 1869, he is described by Ivor Brown (in the *Dictionary of National Biography* as 'bonneted and bridling, at once grotesque and genial, creating out of a termagant's tantrums a fountain of hilarity'; before he died in 1954 he was given a knighthood.

For over a hundred years, Dames were drawn from the variety stage and the music hall, until the impresario Augustus Collins introduced musical comedy stars into the Drury Lane pantomimes (Frow 1985). But in recent years, as noted above, radio and television have also provided a number of notable Dames, including the late Arthur Askey, Cyril Fletcher and Terry Scott. Currently, stalwarts such as John Inman and some would say especially, Roy Hudd, Danny La Rue and the younger Stirling Roberts, are among those Dames who can be seen on the boards at Christmas. The above are all experienced comics; in recent years, various so-called TV celebrities – programme presenters, anchormen, newsreaders and the like – have appeared on screen in pantomimes. Even the London boxer Frank Bruno (World WBC Heavyweight titleholder in 1995, whose family was of West Indian origin) has taken to the pantomime boards, including at the Wolverhampton Grand in 2001.

Although stories and characters are pretty stock, the panto usually manages to reflect everyday culture. Today pantos may include 'soap' characters, and refer to popular concerns of the moment. These days, 'Instead of entering with a large basket on her arm, the Dame is more likely to be seen pushing a supermarket trolley' (Frow 1985: 1). She might well make a topical joke about someone in the news – perhaps (in 2003) Jeffrey Archer languishing in prison, or a disgraced comic star, such as Angus Deyton or Michael Barrymore – whose notoriety will, no doubt, soon be forgotten. Comic Rogues and Bandits have their places, but probably there will be no international terrorists this year, as they would seem too serious and threatening – though the defeated Saddam Hussein and the satirised Osama Bin Laden may prove this wrong!

Victoria Wood (Wood 1982) echoed Laidlaw when he described a Dame as a 'fellow in a frock with truth', when she said 'if comedy isn't true it's not funny'. And, indeed, many stress that Dames are based on real life – on the mother-in-law, the daft maiden aunt (Laidlaw, in Wood 1982), the aunt who has never had sex (Terry Scott, in Wood 1982), but above all they are based on the mother (Wood 1982). Thus, Billy Dainty (1927–1986) claims to have picked up many of his jokes from his mother's unwitting malapropisms ('I have a stimulated mink in my cupboard') (Wood 1982). Jack Tripp would reject lines not life-like, and claimed he got more like his mother as he aged. For Laidlaw 'Dames are mums, and usually elderly. They are The Third Sex …' (in Wood 1982). If Dames are mums, then typically they are neither happily married, nor as well behaved as one would wish

8.1 Dandini and two Ugly Sisters from Cinderella.
(Courtesy St Joseph's Players, Leigh, Lancaster.)

one's mum to be. As a widow she is likely to be depicted as over-eagerly seeking a husband or, if unmarried, as a frustrated spinster.

Some Dames play the roles of the Ugly Sisters in *Cinderella*. Like other characters, the Sisters have changed their names and clothes frequently to keep up with fashion. Originally Clorinda and Thisbe, they have been Daisy and Buttercup (names associated with cows), Hysteria and Hydrophobia (Ellacott and Robbins, undated) and, at the Theatre in Chipping Norton in 2001, Euphoria and Aphasia. But it has occurred to me that, given the age of many actors playing Dames, they must be the mums, not of the *children* in the audience, for whom they more resemble grandmothers, but of the *accompanying parents*. Perhaps that is why pantomimes attract adults as much as children.[7] It is a time to laugh at the older authority figures, just when they are becoming a burden. Nevertheless, although Dames are grotesque and outrageous, they must be gentle and kind, as they must not offend. For Gill Davies, she should be seen as 'a nice man being a nice lady' (Davies 1995: 108). In fact the Dames must be naughty but nice.

Dainty stated, on video, 'I don't play sexy – I play vulgar. I show my knickers'. Thus, the Dame must not be too crude, and although 'she' may be ridiculed, she is not usually subjected to gross violence. At the end of the performance, like the Principal Boy, she usually ends up happily engaged to be married to one of the characters.

Dress and make-up

Make-up is very important. Dames usually put on their own cosmetics. But, except for the glamorous Dames like La Rue, the make-up is usually applied deliberately crudely; lipstick overflows the lips; rouge appears as bright red circles, false hair is piled outlandishly high. Nevertheless, it seems that it is largely the make-up that changes the man into the Dame. George Lacy (1904–1989), claimed 'I begin to smile like a woman' (in Wood 1982). Terry Scott (in Wood 1982) says much the same. He sees the Dame as an extension of himself, reflecting his feminine side: 'How could anyone feel masculine with all this makeup on?'

8.2 Dame Buckle-me-Shoe from Babes in the Wood.
(Courtesy St Joseph's Players, Leigh, Lancaster.)

Traditional Dames wear many layers of outrageous clothes which, as the evening warms up, they discard, sometimes down to their long-johns in a sort of strip-tease, with appropriate music. The preposterous sight of these ugly old Dames behaving sexily brings out the titters. Strip-tease itself is thus mocked. The aged are reminded of their proper place and appropriate behaviour. After many quick changes, Dames usually end up in an over-the-top glamorous outfit, covered in jewels and crowned by feathers – a dress suitable for the grand finale of the pantomime – when they all live happily ever after.

Women, drag and female impersonators

Although most Dames have been played by men, there have been some female Dames. For example, in Covent Garden's 1826 and 1836 versions of Aladdin, the Widow Ching Mustapha was played by women. And one of the greatest of Dames was Nellie Wallace, the music-hall artiste, who also made a robust Principal Boy (see below). Nevertheless, it has been suggested that no woman is ever as convincing as a man is in a Dame part. Indeed, Clinton-Baddeley (Frow 1985) has pointed out that, for a woman to play a Dame is to attempt to make sense out of nonsense.

It follows that, if women do not make good Dames, men who are too successful as imitators may also be thought to fail in the role. In 1982 the late Arthur Askey (who went into pantomime in 1924) believed Dames must be 'butch men ... His trousers must show'. He went on to say 'Recently a little touch of feminacy has been coming in' (in Wood 1982). Askey, who never wore make up but always played himself, with his own voice, regretted when people were not quite sure whether they were watching a man or a woman. It has been said that those whose 'disguise' is so good that you cannot really tell that the wearers are 'not what they seem', would be transsexuals, not actors. The distinction is an important one, pace Germain Greer – who equates the two and even refers to transsexuals as pantomime Dames who should not be allowed to delude women into accepting them as true sisters (Lezard 2000).

Again, according to Brandreth, 'To some panto-enthusiasts, glamorous drag queens don't count as Dames; they are seen more as female impersonators' (1974: 23). Danny La Rue, who performs as a drag entertainer all year round, and who has starred in more than sixteen pantomimes, appeared in December 2002 in *Cinderella* at the Wycombe Swan Theatre, as Countess Voluptua. Such a role suits his normal glamorous stage persona better than were he to take the role of Principal Boy (perhaps difficult to get away with at his present age, anyway) or a preposterously dressed hag-like Dame.

Those who are unfamiliar with the traditions of panto might fail to see the significance of the stage name of Barry Humphries when he plays 'Dame Edna Everage', whose make-up and flamboyant eyeglasses and clothes seem clear referents to the English panto. Like panto Dames (and some other drag [or cross-dressed] entertainers, including Hinge and Brackett[8]), part of his joke is that he is not what he claims to be – and we have to know that. Humphries' act also has implicit, if not explicit, references to the honorific title of Dame (the counterpart today, for a female member of an Order of Chivalry[9]) which the Queen of England bestows on notable worthies – hence, no doubt, his frequent suggestions of intimacy with the Queen. The ambiguous gender identities portrayed by male stage transvestites nevertheless draw our attention, for we are often uncomfortable with uncertainties. When the uncertainties are resolved, we have the pleasure of relief.

Principal Boys

The eighteenth-century practice of having women play young men's parts in opera is a precedent for female Principal Boys. However, possibly in contrast to opera, it is a heresy to suppose that Principal Boys are concerned with male impersonation. They merely assume postures that are meant to be recognised as manly, and are 'not trying to create an illusion of manhood' (Frow 1985: 90).

The role of the Principal Boy has been a star part ever since it was introduced by the actress Peg Woffington early in the nineteenth century (Brandreth 1974). Even though the girl playing the role of Principal Boy may be junior and less well-know than the other stars, she still comes on last, bringing the Principal Girl with her. The Principal Boy should always have the last word, the valedictory couplet which, according to theatrical custom, he must not speak before the first night, for fear of bringing bad luck (Brandreth 1973, Davies 1995).

A notable Boy was Madame Vestris. In 1815, she made her London début (as an opera singer) at the King's Theatre in the Haymarket, when her husband put her on in his own benefit performance. She was a considerable success, and was thus launched upon a stage career.

> Born Lucy Elizabeth Bartolozzi (her grandfather was the eminent engraver Francesco Bartolozzi) into the London of 1797. Her father was a commercially indolent Italian with a passion for music and a talent for the tenor violin; her mother a German, vain and tending to corpulence, who indulged a liking for flowered hats and provided for the family by giving piano lessons. When she was sixteen, Lucy entered into a short-lived marriage to a French dancer, ballet-master and rake named Armand Vestris. (Frow 1985: 90)

Vestris was described as 'remarkable for the symmetry of her limbs'. She had her numerous admirers, one saying 'She is the best bad young man about town, and can stamp a smart leg in white tights with the air of a fellow who has an easy heart and a good tailor' (Frow 1985: 91). The buxom Madame Vestris, 'a highly gifted performer in all manner of parts and a noted singer and impresario', was still playing breeches parts when she was fifty. She is referred to here as 'impresario', as she became the first woman ever to manage a London theatre when she took over the Olympic Theatre in 1830 (Frow 1985).

8.3 Dandini and Prince Charming from Cinderella.
(Courtesy St Joseph's Players, Leigh, Lancaster.)

But many other distinguished ladies of the theatre have cut dashing figures in the role of Principal Boy across the years. James Agate, the dramatic critic of the *Sunday Times* from 1923 to 1943, described the Boys of the Victorian pantomimes as of 'the big-bosomed, broad-buttocked, butcher-thighed race'. He thought them examples of 'walking definitions of what the scientist means by "mass" and the Victorians by the "statuesque"' (quoted in Frow 1985: 183). Augustus Harris who managed Drury Lane Theatre in the 1880s was one of the impresarios of that time who insisted on having Principal Boys with 'opulent curves'. Harriet Vernon, one of his favourites, was 'a magnificent creature of ample figure' (Brandreth 1973: 43). Of course, not everyone cheered the Boys. One critic said that 'This theatrical system of putting the female sex in breeches is barbarous and abominable' (Frow 1985: 91).

There are a number of children's plays performed at Christmas, often, but not always, based on fairy stories, some of which share some features of panto, including of the Principal Boy. J. M. Barrie's (1904) play *Peter Pan*, about a boy who can never grow up, was instantly successful on stage. Savage (1993: 25–6, quoting

Gaber) states that, from the beginning, Peter was played by a young woman, because 'a woman will never grow up to be a man'.

For a period from 1912, the impresario Arthur Collins, who took over Drury Lane Theatre after Harris at the end of the nineteenth century, gave the role of Principal Boy to a man. And in the 1950s and 1960s in particular, the Principal Boy role fell into the hands of male pop stars. It remained for Cilla Black to reclaim Aladdin's breeches at the London Palladium in 1971 (Frow 1985).

An interesting twist is when a 'gay' performer, who habitually dresses on stage in exotic gender-indeterminate clothes, and adopts a high camp manner, takes the role of Principal Boy – as Julian Clary[10] did as Dandini in Cinderella, in Richmond, in December 2000, a role he repeated in 2001 (Coveney 2001).

Commentary

According to Christine Yousseff (undated), in her commentary 'Pantomimic Convention in the plays of Peter Nichols', the cross-dressing in Victorian pantomimes legitimately subverted the principles of Victorian morality. She writes, 'All symbolic inversions define culture's lineaments at the same time as they question the usefulness and absoluteness of its ordering'. For Yousseff, the nineteenth-century pantomime depicted 'the moment of upturning' and 'the world turned upside down'. For her it was a silent protest against oppression, both against the State and its mechanisms. Pantomime, unlike real life, permitted a girl, as Principal Boy, 'to assume a primary role in influencing the other [pantomime] characters' behaviour'. The audience accepted that, for the limited period of the performance, life could be different from reality.

Yet we must ask, 'how realistic is this alternative persona?'. Davies, in advising the amateur girl on how to play the Principal Boy defines him as 'thigh-slapping, jaunty, chivalrous, brave, and in love with the heroine' (1995: 109). Wishful thinking perhaps, as it is a long time since a young man has habitually slapped his thighs – if he ever did – or bears those other fine qualities! No wonder that, in fiction, the young leading male is sometimes referred to as Prince Charming. Perhaps, rather, we meet in this idealised role the interpretation of a former Principal Boy, Dorothy Ward, who saw the Boy as 'an attractive woman's version of how a man behaves in romantic circumstances' (quoted in Frow 1985: 184).

Yousseff, quoting Bakhtin (1968: 7), links pantomime to Carnival where there are no barriers of caste, property, profession, age or sex. Many others, including Simon Trussler (1994: 30), have noted that panto offers space for 'Rabelaisian topsy-turveydom' traditions, commonly found at Christmas or carnival, when authority and class structures are (temporarily) reversed. Examples include when junior clergy swapped places with senior brethren at the Feast of Fools, and when army officers serve Christmas dinners to 'Other Ranks' as they do today.[11] Further, in opera we find maids and mistresses changing places, in fairy stories a prince may (temporarily) transform into a toad or a beast, while the impoverished

Aladdin becomes rich, and downtrodden Cinders becomes a princess. In such an ideal world people were 'reborn for new' (Bakhtin 1968: 7). This renewal and revival can also be seen in the transformation scenes at the end of the pantomime, with the union of the lovers who start a new life.

Sometimes we see an overlap between the stage identities and theatrical devices of pop stars and pantomime characters. Peter Pan (who we know was characteristically played by a girl) has been described by Jon Savage (1993: 25–6) as a 'founding text of the 20th Century pop culture'. One of the attractions of the evergreen Cliff Richard, who, at the age of sixty, apparently defied time, has, perhaps, been his identification as 'the Peter Pan of Pop'. Savage (1993: 25–6) likewise argues that the pop singer Michael Jackson 'enshrines the Peter Pan principle within his own body. In transcending the boundaries of age, race and gender, he epitomises one pop paradigm: the unity of apparent opposites'. Can we see this denial of natural laws of maturation, as with the reordering of gender-bending, as a triumph of man's will over nature? Do these real special cases, and the fictional possibilities, give us pride and the hope that we can change the world, if we will?

I have quoted the views of comics that when in 'drag' they can say things that as men dressed in their normal male attire they could not. Is it also possible that such transvestite comics also fill a gap, by talking on behalf of women about men, when conventions inhibit comediennes from doing so? In England today, women (including Victoria Wood who when young compèred the video I have drawn on) have entered fields of humour, including that involving sex, that they had not heretofore explored. Have such females changed the scripts for drag comics in England? Will KSM be in competition with Ghanaian comediennes one day? If so, will it change his stage material in the future?

The flexibility possible within the panto frame attests to the vitality of the form. In 2001 Stratford Theatre in East London put on *Snow Black & Rose Red; a tale of two babes in the wood*. This 'musical Christmas fable',[12] is described as a magical and intoxicating blend of African, Caribbean and Asian myth and legend. Moreover, it was said that:

> If you go down to the woods this Christmas … in the forest, anything goes. Girls can be boys and boys can be girls. Drink the blood of two young maidens and [the spider] anansi will live forever and be always beautiful. Snow Black and Rose Red are alone in the wood. Trapped in a spider's web. Only with Kali's help can they discover the secret of true love and be free once more …

Another example of innovation was in the version of Cinderella performed by the children of St John's Primary School in Wallingford, near Oxford. It appears that Cinderella 'made it seem that the shoe was too small for her so she didn't have to marry the prince because he wasn't very charming at all' and Prince Charming ended up marrying one of the Ugly Sisters.[13] Another variation in 2001, by the Oxford Youth Theatre, was entitled *The Sanity Clause: a pantomime in disguise*. The title is, of course a variation on Santa Claus. Based on *The Pied Piper of Hamlyn* story, the hand-out ominously said 'the rats are back, and this time they're not alone …'

Nowadays, with the familiarity of drag shows on TV, and since the outrageous costumes and coloured wigs which used to draw a laugh can be seen at night club raves, or even on the street, Dames are wondering where their next laughs will come from. The licence for Dames to use mild innuendo which, it has been assumed, passes to adults over the heads of young children, may have a different reception from them today than formerly. Stirling Roberts reports (verbal communication) that on one occasion when the Principal Boy embraced the Principal Girl, he distinctly heard a young child call out 'Lesbians!'

Savage (1993: 25–6) noted that 'playing with Gender Roles can take many forms. The most common is cross-dressing which, for many people, is a sign of homosexuality (though often not true) and is somewhat shocking…' He goes on: 'after a period when men have been men, and women women, gender-bending is back on the pop scene'. Writing of the pop group The Manic Street Preachers, he notes that, in 1991, 'all heterosexual, they were coming over extremely camp, both as a provocation, and in an implicit understanding of the transformational possibilities inherent in pop'. They transformed themselves by use of women's make-up, and by wearing 'cheap white women's blouses manhandled with stencilled slogans like Death Culture and Generation Terrorists'. Savage (1993: 25–6) suggests that, 'for a long time now, popular culture – whether by pantomime Dames or pop stars like Boy George – has provided a space within our morally restrictive societies for sexuality and gender in all its forms to be discussed, rehearsed, and changed. Within popular culture we can see what we are not, but what we could be'. But, despite his defence of cross-dressing, and his recognition of its roots in English tradition, Savage also recognises it as potentially dangerous. He states 'there is something threatening and disturbing' about it. It is a 'refusal to take the world at face value, a refusal to accept things as they seem' (1993: 25–6).

Danger, in a controlled setting, like a thrilling ride on a roller-coaster, has its attractions for many – even for children. Perhaps it is fear stimulated by danger that compels us all to laugh, as a coping strategy – and the comics know and exploit this. In a long discussion of laughter, Disher (1925: xiii-xiv) noted the strong link between emotion and laughter: 'loss of control over the one is accompanied by outbreaks of the other… in normal emotional disturbances, internal conflict causes grim laughter'. Moreover, for him laughter 'tends to take away fear and anger' (1925: xiv). Disher also claims that 'to know what is ridiculous we must know what is sublime' (1925: xiv). Presumably the reverse is also true: when we laugh at panto's ludicrous distortions of normal life, perhaps we more clearly perceive, and become more contented with, the charms of our daily lives. Fortunately, the panto always ends reassuringly 'happily ever after'. Good triumphs over evil and disaster; villains are outwitted; anxiety is followed by the satisfaction of relief. Following the subversion of conventional life, normality, even be it of a theatrical kind, returns. We can leave the theatre happy.

When beginning research on this topic, I was told by a community theatre manager that pantomime should not be analysed by academics – its ephemeral, transitory nature could not, should not, be captured by them. Disher (1925: xii-xiv) also piles scorn on 'the professors', who analyse humour (in this case the psychologists[14]). For Brian Rix (1995: 43) defining farce, which is a large component of panto, is 'like trying to catch feathers in a gale force wind'. Echoing such sentiments, I agree that there is no easy way for writers to express the meaning panto has for all involved in such a complex and varied, ever evolving, annual event. Panto is multivalent, and has many possible meanings, not necessarily all of which are shared by everyone. I therefore warmly recommend readers, if they have not already done so, to experience the English Christmas Panto for themselves. May the other contributions in this book, as well as this chapter, make that all the more interesting and enjoyable.

Notes

1. This apt phrase I borrow from Hilary Callan when she referred to the attitude of male Oxford Dons towards wives of fellow Dons with whom they supped recently in College (verbal communication; see Ardener 1984).

2. Farce: a dramatic work (usually short) which has for its sole object to excite laughter (OED). The term derives from the action 'to stuff' or interpolate, in this case jokes and impromptu buffoonery.

3. Pantomime's original meaning of dumb show, or voiceless mime, is poorly represented in its modern realisation.

4. For example, at Oxford University, every year since 1923 the first year students at Nuffield College have put on a winter panto, usually based on traditional fairy stories. Their 2002 panto was based on the Harry Potter books, and in 2003 it was a spoof on the Mafia (The College Porter and Rob Forde, personal communication). Wadham College also puts on pantos in the Moser Theatre; their 2003 Panto was put on by the College Medical Society (College Porter, personal communication).

5. An early writer, Aphra Behn who produced some twenty plays, essayed a Harlequin farce called *The Emporor of the Moon* (spelling *sic*) 1686. Mrs Behn (the 'incomparable Astraea'), the first Englishwoman to earn a living from writing, was, even in her own uninhibited day, famous for her robust dialogue and indelicate situations (Frow 1985: 30).

6. A. E. Wilson (1934, 1974) gives Harlequin four colours: yellow (for jealousy), blue (for truth), scarlet (for love) and black (for invisibility). According to Wilson (1974), James Byrne, in the play *Harlequin Amulet* (1800), introduced a much-copied costume of three hundred coloured pieces attached to a silk base, with thousands of metal spangles that sparkled wonderfully. The dress of many coloured lozenges (the motley) still appears on stage occasionally (e.g. in *Salad Days*); it is more often found at Christmas in advertisements, and at children's fancy dress parades (viz. 'Charlotte Bull, who wore a colourful clown's costume', *Oxford Mail*, 18.1.2003)

7. Michael Coveney (2001) suggests that children over eight might prefer other forms of entertainment to panto.

8. Other examples of cross-dressing in popular culture include the play *Charlie's Aunt*, the film *Some Like it Hot*, and the Monty Python television shows. In none of these is the illusion of womanhood meant to be successful; the portrayals are grotesque.

9. Some wives and widows of Baronets and Knights are formally described as Dame in legal documents. Dame may also be the formal address of a nun in her final vows, but this is now uncommon (*Debrett's Correct Form* 1999).
10. Clary is described in the *Cambridge Illustrated History of British Theatre* (Trussler 1994: 371) as 'high-camp but low-intensity', who responded with an outgoing and often outrageous humour to his situation. One is reminded of the Shakespearean 'twist' in As you Like It of having a youth pass himself of as a girl impersonating a youth, who then reveals 'herself' to be a girl.
11. In our less deferential society ritualistic cross-classing is becoming something of an embarrassment, and is dying out. For example, the academic staff of Queen Elizabeth House no longer serve the seated domestic kitchen staff at the (joint) staff Christmas lunch – both now share this task.
12. The text of the handout was in a different font to that given here. The text was by the award-winning writers Valerie Mason and John Aka Queenie.
13. According to the report in the *Oxford Mail*, eighty children between ages seven and eleven made up the choir; Cinderella and the Ugly Sisters were all aged eleven. The infants were given an early performance and 'they all understood the difference from the original story'.
14. William McDougall (1908) is among the psychologists Disher (1925) quotes.

References

Ardener, S.G. 1984. 'Incorporation and Exclusion: Oxford Academics' Wives'. In *The Incorporated Wife*, Callan, H. and S. Ardener (eds). London: Croom Helm, 27–29.

Bakhtin, M. 1968. *Rabelais and his World*. Translated by Helene Iswolsky. Cambridge, Mass: MIT Press.

Blanchard, E.L. 1891. *The Life and Reminiscences of E. L. Blanchard, in Two Volumes*. London: Hutchinson and Co.

Brandreth, G. 1973. *Discovering Pantomime*. Aylesbury: Shire.

———— 1974. *I Scream for Ice Cream*. London: Eyre Methuen

Cookman L. 1998. *Writing a Pantomime*. Plymouth: How To Books.

Coveney, M. 2001. *Daily Mail*. London, 7th December.

Davies, G. 1995. *Staging a Pantomime*. London: Black.

Debrett's Correct Form. 1999. London: Headline.

Disher, M.W. 1925. *Clowns and Pantomimes*. London: Constable.

Ellacott, N. and P. Robbins. Undated. *Its-behind-you* [http://www.its-behind-you.com]

Frow, G. 1985. *Oh Yes It Is!* London: BBC Publications.

Gilbert, W.S. 1868. *Getting Up a Pantomime*. London: London Society.

Hudd, R. 1998. 'Foreword'. In *Writing a Pantomime*, L. Cookman. Plymouth: How To Books.

Lezard, N. 2000. 'Greer Uncut' (Review of G. Greer, *The Whole Woman*, Anchor). *The Guardian*, 26th February.

Malcolm, T. 2001. *Oxford Mail*. 20th March.

McDougall, W. 1908. *An Introduction to Social Psychology*. London: Methuen.

Niklaus, T. 1956. *Harlequin, Phoenix; or the Rise and Fall of a Bergamask Rogue*. London: Bodley Head.

Perrault, C. 1697. *Contes de Ma Mere L'Oie, ou, Histoires ou contes du temps passé: contes en vers*. Strasbourg: Brocéliande.

Rix, B. 1995. *Life in the Farce Lane or Tragedy with its Trousers Down*. London: André Deutsch.

Russell, J. 1889. *Victorian Theatre*. London: Black.

Savage, J. 1993. 'Oh you pretty things'. *The Times*. 3rd April. [www.thisisyesterday.com/int/pretty.html]

Sick, D. 1999. 'Ummidia Quadratilla: Cagey Businesswoman or Lazy Pantomime Watcher'? *Classical Antiquity*, 8, 2, 330–348.

Simpson, S. 2003. *West Africa*, 3rd–9th March, p. 27.

Trussler, S. 1994. *The Cambridge Illustrated History of British Theatre*. Cambridge: Cambridge University Press.

Wilson, A.E. 1934. *The Christmas Pantomime: The Story of an English Institution*. London: Allen & Unwin; Reprinted as *The Story of Pantomime*, 1974, with a foreword by Roy Hudd, Wakefield: E.P. Publishers.

Wood, E. 1982. *The Pantomime Dame*. Video, a Woodfilm Production.

Yousseff, C. Undated. *Pantomimic Conventions in the plays of Peter Nichols*. [http://members.tripod.com/~warlight.christiney.html]

9

CROSS-DRESSING ON THE JAPANESE STAGE

Brian Powell

This chapter considers cross-dressing on the Japanese stage in terms of perform-ance history. Japan can boast of more than six centuries of sophisticated theatre, beginning with the elegant and deeply spiritual genre of *nō* that emerged at the end of the fourteenth century. Since that time many other genres have developed as new audiences, new times and new practitioners have presented themselves. Unlike European theatre traditions, in which a new development has usually dis-placed or superseded what existed before, Japan's new genres have always existed alongside what they have challenged, the old being preserved after the new has developed.[1] The result in present-day Japan has been an unparalleled multiplicity of genres. *Nō* still exists, much as it did in the fourteenth century. *Kabuki*, a prod-uct of the seventeenth-century explosion of popular culture, dominated nine-teenth-century Japanese theatre, and was joined by a number of new genres that grew out of it, and by one which found its raison d'être in rejecting it. The latter was *shingeki* ('new drama'), which set itself to establish a Western-style realism and having done that was itself rejected in the mid-1960s by the so-called *angura* movement (*angura* being a corruption of the English word 'underground'). A list of genres would have to include the *bunraku* puppet theatre, the Takarazuka 'girls opera', and many more.[2]

The primary factor that distinguishes these various genres is their mode of per-formance. Whereas historically there has been much borrowing between genres of plots and even whole plays, they have been marked out from each other princi-pally by the ways in which they have performed their material to their audiences. In some cases this has involved cross-dressing. The focus here will be on two gen-res that represent the extremes of cross-dressed performance in Japan: *kabuki*, per-formed entirely by males and Takarazuka, performed entirely by females. In this chapter, cross-dressing will be considered only as a phenomenon within Japanese performance history. Other approaches may find it difficult to give any positive evaluation of cross-dressing by males in circumstances where females were barred from performing. Theatre history, however, concerns an art form whose development in all cultures has been particularly subject to outside influences and pressures, and in this chapter the effect of force majeure has been accepted as a given.

Cross-dressing on the Western stage has attracted the attention of anthropologists because it can have implications of liminality, in that cross-dressers operate on the margins or just beyond the margins of society and represent a relaxation of social rules which maintain order by normalising certain types of sexual behaviour. Such work as there is on liminality in early Japanese theatre points to the function of players as intermediaries between the gods and the human audiences. Before the fourteenth century when performances evolved into the highly respectable and officially recognised *nō* theatre, they had a dual relationship with Buddhist temples, which both abhorred their possible contact with the other world, and utilised it to empower themselves in the eyes of their parishioners (Marra 1993: 56–61). Women had no place in this world, and this may explain why all actors in the *nō* theatre (and its comic subsidiary, *kyōgen*) are male.

The closeness of developed *nō* to its ritual origins makes the genre unsuitable for the approach to cross-dressing that will be adopted here. There is no specialisation among *nō* actors in cross-dressed roles. Much *nō* 'acting' consists of dances and chants which are relatively indeterminate as to maleness and femaleness. The question of whether a male actor can, or is trying to, become a female character on the stage does not arise in the sense in which it is raised in connection with other genres. In the context of performance, the production of the same *nō* play by an all-female cast as opposed to an all-male one, would not be significantly different or send out to the audiences significantly different messages.

Female actors

During the seventeenth century the rapid urbanisation of Japan, combined with economic changes that brought surplus cash into the towns, provided fertile soil for the development of theatrical entertainment. The origins of what we know as *kabuki* are shadowy. The genre is usually traced back to a figure called Okuni, a female shrine dancer at the great Shinto cathedral at Izumo. In 1603, Okuni danced rather eccentric and offbeat dances in the capital, Kyoto, to raise money for her shrine, and it is quite possible that a new form of theatre evolved from her way-out dances. What she danced was referred to as *kabuki*, from a verb meaning 'to incline to one side' and, by extension, to be somewhat outside accepted norms (Ernst 1956: 10). Little is known of Okuni. The received wisdom, popularised in modern plays and novels, is that she was, or at least became, a dedicated artist who resisted temptation to popularise and vulgarise her art (e.g. Ariyoshi 1994). A near contemporary representation of her, cross-dressed and with a Christian cross hanging round her neck, certainly suggests that she was not afraid of conveying a plurality of messages from the stage, and this aspect of her performances had many imitators (Leupp 1995: 90). While Okuni's modern fans will not abide any suggestion of immorality in her professional life, her female imitators openly combined the selling of sex with their performances. This so-called *yūjo-kabuki* – *yūjo* meaning a 'woman of pleasure' and therefore a sex-worker – was aimed at the city-dwelling merchants and craftsmen, but *samurai* were attracted to their performances and, in 1629, the *samurai* government, fearing disturbance of its carefully contrived social order, banned *kabuki* by women.

At the time, the lack of inhibition over bisexual, purchased sex led theatre entrepreneurs to substitute attractive young males, who also turned the heads of *samurai* in the audiences, and were therefore in their turn banned in 1653.

Male actors

Out of this grew an institution that is still regarded as central to *kabuki*: that of the *onnagata* or the (male) actor who specialises in female roles. Some of the greatest stars of *kabuki* have been *onnagata* and this still holds true today. Far from being restricted by government regulations, *kabuki* developed the art of portraying symbolic femininity to a high degree. Historically, *kabuki* benefited from the appearance of three individuals who established criteria of a high order for their art. They were all actors, and *kabuki* has remained actor-centred up to the present day (Kominz 1997). One of the three was an *onnagata*. Yoshizawa Ayame (1673–1729) worked his way up the theatre hierarchy by dint of great attention to detail and unsparing endeavour until he became the leading *onnagata* of his time. Rejecting the limited ambitions of most of his predecessors simply to reproduce the erotic mien of courtesans, he insisted on studying character-motivation minutely. Through his success Yoshizawa Ayame laid an obligation on all future *onnagata* to combine impersonation with interpretive acting. So conscious was he of the need to minimise the disadvantage of being male in his chosen profession, that he behaved, and expected others like him to behave, as far as possible like a woman in his life outside the theatre (Dunn and Torigoe 1969: 51, 62). Apart from dressing as a woman in public, which other *onnagata* were already doing, he tried to avoid talking about his wife and children. He ate the sort of food that women would choose and he ate it in a demure way. He was deferential towards others as a woman would be, and in many other ways endeavoured to create a base of naturalism on which to build his stylised stage movements.

The historical legacy has presented a great challenge to modern *onnagata*, as extremely high standards were set at an early stage of *kabuki*'s development. Over more than two centuries, playwrights wrote female parts in the knowledge that they would be played by men. One effect of this has been that *kabuki* audiences have long been conditioned to expect that femininity will be portrayed in *kabuki* plays in a certain way. The effort that the *onnagata* has to make to become a woman, before even beginning to interpret his role, when compared to that of an actress who starts from the relaxed attitude of knowing that her movements are naturally feminine, appears to enhance his performance in the eyes of *kabuki* audiences even today.

Two contrasting *onnagata*

While the *kabuki* world of the last two decades of the twentieth century was fortunate in having a large number of highly skilled *onnagata*, two in particular were prominent in the popular consciousness. Bandō Tamasaburō V (1950–) took his present stage name in 1964 at the age of fourteen, and he still keeps it today. This is very unusual in a profession where one is awarded different names, identified as more senior and prestigious, as one moves through a successful career. In 1964 his later fame was not anticipated, but by the late 1970s the name Tamasaburō had become an important part of his identity, as he moved towards being one of the best-known actors in Japan's extensive theatre world. Thus, Tamasaburō, a name which had only previously been used by junior actors, became synonymous with extraordinary artistic achievement as he collected prize after prize (*Engeki-kai* 1985: 147).

By contrast Nakamura Utaemon VI (1917–2001), no less well-known as an *onnagata*, progressed through his long career in a more traditional way. Born the second son of Nakamura Utaemon V, he was granted successively senior names in the family hierarchy until he achieved the honour of the name which, in 1951, marked him as a worthy successor to his father. Utaemon VI was one of the *kabuki* actors who in the 1950s worked hard to re-establish traditional *kabuki* at a time when it was under much pressure. Not only did *kabuki* suffer extensively from occupation censorship in the immediate postwar years, but most of its top actors had died either during the war or soon afterwards. Utaemon was very much a standard-bearer for the *kabuki* classics and his name is particularly associated with famous performances of dances and roles from the eighteenth century (Ōzasa 1986: 195).

Tamasaburō has been something of a phenomenon in post-second World War Japanese theatre. Extraordinarily graceful, with an uncanny female sexuality on stage, he has been able to appear as a woman in plays on television and is versatile enough to move away from *kabuki* from time to time. He has, for example, played Lady Macbeth. His latest non-*kabuki* role is as a young wife in one of Japan's most famous postwar plays. Based on a folktale, this play (Yūzuru [Twilight Crane, 1949] by Kinoshita Junji [Kinoshita 1988]) shows a farmer losing his beautiful wife because of his greed for the money he acquires by selling cloth that, mysteriously, she weaves for him from crane feathers. This part of the crane wife was created for an actress, who played it from 1948 until her death in 1993 (at the age of ninety-one).[3]

Tamasaburō can assume a falsetto voice that is near to a real female voice and this allows him to participate in performances that adhere to some degree of realism. In the seventeenth century, when the style of acting was being developed and when the acting profession was not far from the time when it was secondary to personal sexual services, Yoshizawa Ayame believed transvestism was essential for his art. Tamasaburō, on the other hand, is not a transvestite actor; he has a facility for combining the stylisation of the *onnagata* with a mien and voice that are realistic, but he reserves these mainly for his non-*kabuki* appearances.

Most Westerners seeing *kabuki* for the first time will recognise after only a few minutes that the female characters are played by males, if not from their appearance, at least from their voice. To be sure, the movements are stylised, but so are the movements of most male characters. While the obviously constructed grace and femininity of the *onnagata*'s deportment may only emphasise that *kabuki* is a theatre of stylised movement, the timbre of the vocal delivery of the *onnagata* immediately alerts the audience to the fact that the part is being played by a man. No-one watching Utaemon during the last two decades of the twentieth century would have associated the often cracked quality of his high-pitched delivery with a female voice. Utaemon's art as an actor, like that of all *onnagata* in classical *kabuki* pieces, depended on his selection and performance of sequences of movement (referred to as *kata* – 'patterns' – in the language of *kabuki*) that over the centuries had been created and refined by great actors before him (Leiter 1979: xvi-xxi). *Kata* are accepted by *kabuki* fans as a valid way of physically expressing the varied and, in many cases, extremely intense emotions of the leading female characters. Utaemon was a master of this kind of traditional acting. Such a master would have learnt and polished the *kata* for all the roles that he might be expected to play in classic pieces, and therefore naturally his art developed through the years. Hence, the interpretation by Utaemon of a character biologically fifty or sixty years younger than him had more validity than that of a younger *onnagata*.

The objective of mature *onnagata* such as Utaemon, as famous in his way as Tamasaburō, is to attain the highest expression of their art, but this militates against any attempt to assume a different gender on stage. We should not think of *onnagata* as being female impersonators in the sense that they are trying to become women on the stage. A more accurate image would be of highly trained and skilled actors who historically have done their utmost to act their female parts in a way that has satisfied the expectations of their mixed-sex audiences, but who are not necessarily transvestite or indeed uniform in their sexual preferences.

Takarazuka

Takarazuka, as a theatre company, was part of a trend in the first two decades of the twentieth century, in which live theatre was seen as a commercial business whose management did not necessarily derive from practical experience in the theatre. It evolved as a businessman named Kobayashi Ichizō (1873–1957) made various attempts to raise revenue for a railway, which he had built in 1912, from Osaka to a hot-spring resort called Takarazuka. Developing the resort, which was small, was an obvious option and Kobayashi set about this enterprise with some vigour. Most customers of such hot springs (*onsen*) would have been male, and their need for various kinds of entertainment was satisfied by the many women, some of whom were prostitutes, who were resident in the area. Kobayashi wanted more custom for his railway and was keen to attract whole families to the resort. He tried a heated indoor swimming pool, something very modern for its time, but the technology at his disposal was not equal to the temperature requirements (Ōzasa 1985b: 101).

In the early 1900s exhibitions were very popular. The new department stores, which organised and housed them, found them (and still find them) highly effective as a way to attract families into their buildings (Yoshimi 1995). Kobayashi took the idea from them. This was successful in bringing more family groups to Takarazuka, but something more was needed. Mitsukoshi, at the forefront of these new methods of attracting customers, had early hit upon the idea of organising a band of child musicians, Mitsukoshi Shōnen Ongakutai (the Mitsukoshi Youth Orchestra), which gave regular performances of self-accompanied choral singing at exhibitions and other public events (Yoshimi 1995: 87). Kobayashi says openly that he copied this for his first Takarazuka company (Ōzasa 1985b: 102).

The original group, formed in July 1914, consisted of sixteen girls between the ages of ten and fourteen. They gave their first public performance in April 1914 after Kobayashi had covered over the unsuccessful swimming pool and reconstructed the rest of the building to become an auditorium. Kobayashi himself had something of a talent for composing catchy songs and he wrote much of the early material that his troupe performed. Mindful of his original objective to attract families to Takarazuka he was concerned to create a wholesome atmosphere and was gratified when a leading Osaka newspaper, whom he had been cultivating, wrote up the shows as being entirely suitable even for school parties. Apart from choral singing, the group performed dramatised adaptations of children's tales, folk-dances and other innocuous material. They became a tourist attraction associated with Osaka (Ōzasa 1985b: 104–107).

Kobayashi was ambitious for his troupe and within a few years several librettists and composers were employed to produce material that became technically more demanding. Sentimental plays with romantic plots were now being combined with set-piece dance numbers performed by large numbers of performers. The latter were not referred to in Japanese as 'actors' but as 'pupils', and competition to enter into the training programme was intense. Kobayashi insisted that transferable skills (inevitably this meant those traditional skills expected of women in the marriage market, such as flower arranging and the tea ceremony) formed a prominent part of the curriculum. Out of this finishing school came Japan's first chorus line in 1923, in a lavish show of sixteen scenes and a finale entitled *Mon Paris* (Ōzasa 1985b: 114). This is largely what Takarazuka material still is today, with the addition of all the stage effects that the latest high-tech equipment can provide.

Jennifer Robertson, in her sexual-politics approach to Takarazuka, identifies and emphasises the eroticism which has assumed greater prominence in Takarazuka performances since the Pacific War (Robertson 1998). It is true that now, occasionally, thighs are stroked, but few Japanese mothers would worry about their teenage daughters going unaccompanied to Takarazuka shows. One common pattern is for those daughters to take their mothers to the shows as a treat.

Emergence of the actress in Japanese theatre culture

Takarazuka started in 1914; women had been banned from the *kabuki* stage in 1629 and this situation was still continuing in 1868 when Japan opened itself to the rest of the world. Clearly something happened in Japanese theatre between 1868 and 1914.

One of the things that happened was that in 1888 the ban on women appearing on stage was lifted. By the mid-1890s actresses were regularly playing female parts in full-length plays. But not in *kabuki; kabuki* remained, and remains, an exclusively male performing art. This does not mean that *kabuki* actors playing male parts have never acted with actresses; many of them they have, but outside the *kabuki* framework.[4] In the 1890s, to the large and enthusiastic sexually mixed theatre-going public, theatre meant *kabuki. Kabuki* male actors had a three-century tradition behind them, which included countless revivals of classic plays, long and arduous training for actors and, perhaps most important, a finely honed appreciation of how to manipulate the actor-audience relationship. It was inevitable, therefore, that the earliest actresses in Japan tended to adopt stage mannerisms that would not alienate audiences used to seeing women portrayed on the stage by men. So, for a decade or so around the turn of the twentieth century, women on the Japanese stage were alternatively condemned because they were technically incompetent and had no stage presence, or praised because they had successfully recreated some aspects of *kabuki* acting in their own performance (e.g. Tsubouchi 1911: 6, Poulton 2001: 36).

A book has recently appeared which attempts to locate precisely the point at which actresses came into their own. In an extensive feminist study of two early actresses, Kano Ayako identifies, as the turning point, two productions of Oscar Wilde's *Salome*, held in 1914 with these two actresses alternating in the title role (Kano 2001: 219–30). Salome performs the Dance of the Seven Veils, which is in fact the dance of removing the seven veils one by one. Kano finds in her source materials evidence that, in the case of the performance of one of these actresses (Matsui Sumako 1886–1919), for the first time the actress's female body became a focus of attention, thus achieving a 'new alignment of sex, gender and performance' (Kano 2001: 224), and that from this time on women were taken seriously as performers of female roles in plays.

In terms of Japanese theatre history I would put the date slightly earlier. Matsui Sumako is usually credited with being Japan's first real actress. She did have an ample body, which in the context of Japanese female physique in the 1910s might well have made her Dance of the Seven Veils alluring; she did have a scandalous sex life which undoubtedly also encouraged prurient viewing of her stage performances. She was, however, pre-eminently a dedicated professional actress – far more dedicated to rehearsal and training than the male actors with whom she worked

(Powell 1975: 140). Before her Salome, she was already a sensation as an actress – as Ophelia and as Nora (in Ibsen's *A Doll's House*), two rather unsexy parts.

One can therefore see the development of the art of the actress in Japan much more in terms of her being a product of a theatre culture primarily concerned to find the best people for the parts that needed to be cast. Such decisions were based on the aims of the individual theatre organisation and the audiences they were targeting. They used the acting talent that was available. In the early 1880s the basic premise, for better or for worse, was still that only men could act, and there was a flourishing and powerful type of theatre – *kabuki* – to prove it. The actors assumed a gender on stage as necessary for the part they were playing.

There are many examples to support this view. In the 1890s a genre of theatre emerged called *shimpa* (a literal translation would be 'new school', a name coined in apposition to the *kyūha* – or 'old school' – by which was meant *kabuki*). In performance terms it was inevitably close to *kabuki* and female parts were played by men, but it was not restricted by tradition, and it was looking for new audiences, so it also used actresses for some of the female parts in the plays it performed. Two female characters on the stage together, therefore, could be played either by two men, or two women, or a man and a woman. Such male actors of female parts in *shimpa* were also referred to as *onnagata* (Powell 2002: 11–16).

My second example concerns a 1907 production of *Hamlet* by a group that can claim to have been a pioneer of modern theatre in Japan. The professed aim of the director was to have all female parts played by women, but he found this impossible. In the end he had a male Gertrude and a female Ophelia (Powell 1998). My third example relates to a 1913 production of Maurice Maeterlinck's *Monna Vanna*. This was the opening production of a new company whose leading actress was Matsui Sumako, now already famous for her performance as Ophelia in the former group's more successful second production of *Hamlet* with all female parts played by women. Matsui Sumako had another great success in *Monna Vanna*, but she refused to go on tour with this production, so a man (Akita Ujaku) played the part on tour instead (Ōzasa 1985a: 143). A fourth example, which I often quote, is of Matsui Sumako playing Katusha in an adaptation of Tolstoy's *Resurrection* in 1914, and the same part being played by a man in that same year in the version for film – that most modern of entertainment forms (Anderson and Richie 1959: 36).

Takarazuka did not start out as a theatrical company, in the sense of a group of trained actors that mounted productions of plays, but it developed into one within a few years. The productions of *Salome* that have been identified as crucial by Kano (2001) took place after Takarazuka's founding and before its adoption of the performance style that we know today. Maybe Kano is right to suggest that attitudes to female performers changed after this, or maybe the change that undoubtedly occurred was partly due to *Salome* and partly due, as I would prefer to think, to the maturing stage art of actresses such as Matsui Sumako. Whichever was the case, the battle for women to be accepted as stage performers, as actors, was won by the time that Takarazuka became a fully fledged company. Takarazuka performers became actresses in the same way that *kabuki* and other male performers were actors. Acting in Japan at the time was not gender specific. It was therefore unusual and new to produce plays enacted entirely by actresses, but it was not outrageous and did not necessarily imply that the audiences were to be attracted by an undercurrent of sexual deviance.

Change and changelessness

The performance modes of the nineteenth and early twentieth centuries that have been touched on here still exist largely unchanged today. To explain why, when Western theatre has prided itself on moving on and on developing new ways to put its message across, we need to look at two aspects of traditional Japanese theatre and theatre-going. *Kabuki*, in common with many other arts and crafts, passed its techniques on by requiring its practitioners first to internalise what had been achieved in the past. As each actor was an individual human being, his performances would inevitably have some distinctive features, even if they were the result of long years of watching and learning from those senior to him in experience and age. Learning by watching (in Japanese: *minarai*) has always characterised training in *kabuki* acting, and it is premised on a strong consciousness of hierarchy among groups of actors. When Kobayashi Ichizō founded Takarazuka, he naturally established such hierarchies within the company of performers, as all other theatre organisations did at the time and for the most part still do. There is thus an in-built conservatism, which persists because it is so obvious that it produces very high technical standards, even though both *kabuki* actors, Takarazuka actresses, and most other actors, find life very hard at the beginning of their careers. Secondly, Japanese traditional theatre, in common with much other Asian theatre, builds into the audience/stage relationship a mutual knowledge of conventions that somehow suggest to the audiences that they have a kind of privileged status. They know and recognise these conventions and expect them to be present whenever they patronise the one genre of theatre that they have selected for themselves. The Takarazuka management also, very cleverly, built an extensive range of conventions, covering everything from the theatre buildings themselves to the makeup and hairstyles of the actors, into the company's performances, and the genre's fans apparently wish these to be preserved. On the whole Takarazuka's almost exclusively female fans go to see idealised men, not real men, on their favourite stage.

Cross-dressing in contemporary Japanese and Western theatre is not that uncommon. Ninagawa Yukio, a Japanese director well known in Britain, cast a man in the part of Medea in a production of the play in Japanese that took Edinburgh, not to mention Athens, by storm. Suzuki Tadashi, another Japanese director well-known in the West, but in his case mainly the United States, has directed an all-male *King Lear* and cast a woman as Hamlet. In nineteenth century Britain female Hamlets were not at all uncommon (Edmonds 1992).

In the West, feminist theatre studies have shown some interest in cross-dressing either within the text or as performance. The assumption is usually made that where cross-dressing occurs, a tension is created, either between characters in the play, or between the actors and the text/playwright, or between the actors and their audiences, which would not have been there if cross-dressing were not involved (Howard 1993). Such a tension is sometimes discussed against the background of the prevailing moral climate of the society in which the cross-dressed theatre takes place. It seems fairly clear that, in the examples I have just mentioned, the director has made a conscious decision to vary the expected sex of one of his or her characters. Theories of sexual politics clearly have a role in explaining why such a change might have been made. Such productions may be seen to be subverting received perceptions of the role concerned, subverting theatrical norms in cultures where cross-dressing is the exception, subverting accepted gender relationships based on the male/female dichotomy. There is, however, a marked contrast between cross-dressing in such individual productions, which are by intent *un*conventional, and cross-dressing in *kabuki* and Takarazuka, which are entirely conventional in a theatre culture where traditionally conventions are very powerful.

The question remains as to how such representations of cross-dressing are received in the wider society. Historically, the link between theatrical cross-dressing and general moral standards was frequently made in European societies. Social cross-dressing in Japan in the modern period has been regarded with great suspicion and in 1873 was forbidden in Tokyo by regulation (Pflugfelder 1999: 152). It has been invariably associated with homosexuality, to which attitudes changed radically under Western influence. Male-male sexual activity was no longer something discussed in the same terms as male-female sexual activity, as it had been for the previous two centuries. Rather, it became one of the 'evil customs of the past' to be eliminated from modern Japan, and homosexuals were subject to discrimination and criminalisation in much the same way as in Christian societies of the West in the first half of the twentieth century (McLelland 2000: 245). The Japanese media constantly project an image of same-sex attraction as necessarily involving some aspect of transgenderism, including the desire to appear as the opposite of one's biological sex (McLelland 2000: 9).

Theatre, however, seems largely to be isolated from this. It was exempted from the anti-cross-dressing regulations of the 1870s. Historically, popular discourse had rarely assumed a connection between the *onnagata*'s occupation and his sexual preferences. This changed somewhat in the early twentieth century after the shift in official attitudes towards homosexuality, but, in general, performance still seems to be viewed as a relatively contained area of activity. A contemporary observer of Japan notes that 'when cross-dressing takes place in specific social spaces such as the television, the entertainment world, and entertainment areas... [Japanese people] are reluctant to read this as an expression of sexual identity, preferring to see it as an individual's act or performance' (McLelland 2000: 44). The conventions that obtain in all genres of theatre in modern Japan, but especially in *kabuki* and Takarazuka, are sufficiently numerous and binding to ensure that most spectators principally view performance as performance.

Notes

Names of Japanese people follow their conventions, with the family name first.

1. However, see the continuity and adaptations in the English pantomime described by Ardener in Chapter 8.
2. For *nō* and *bunraku* see Keene 1990; for *kabuki* see Ernst 1956 (1974) and Kominz 1997; for *shingeki, angura* and modern theatre in general see Powell 2002; for Takarazuka see Robertson 1998 and for *shimpa* see Poulton 2001 and Powell 2002.
3. This was Yamamoto Yasue, one of two actresses in the theatre company credited with introducing and developing modern drama in Japan, at the Tsukiji Little Theatre, which opened in 1924.
4. For example, in *shimpa*, in which male-role *kabuki* actors often made guest appearances and played alongside *shimpa* actresses.

References

Anderson, J.L. and D. Richie. 1959. *The Japanese Film, Art and Industry.* Tokyo: Tuttle.

Ariyoshi Sawako. 1994. Translated by J.R. Brandon, *Kabuki Dancer.* Tokyo and London: Kodansha International.

Dunn, C.J. and Bunzō Torigoe. 1969. *The Actors' Analects.* New York: Columbia University Press.

Edmonds, J. 1992. 'Princess Hamlet'. In *The New Woman and her Sisters, Feminism and Theatre 1850–1914,* Gardner, V. and S. Ruthford (eds). Hemel Hempstead: Harvest Wheatsheaf, 59–75.

*Engeki-kai.*1985. XLIII.14, *Rinji Zōkan, Kabuki Haiyū Meikan.*

Ernst, E. 1956 (1974). *The Kabuki Theatre.* Honolulu: University of Hawaii Press.

Howard, J.E. 1993. 'Cross-dressing, the Theatre, and Gender Struggle in Early Modern England'. In *Crossing the Stage, Controversies on Cross-dressing,* Ferris, L. (ed.). London: Routledge, 20–46.

Kano Ayako. 2001. *Acting Like a Woman in Modern Japan, Theatre, Gender, and Nationalism.* New York and Basingstoke: Palgrave.

Keene, D. 1990. *Nō and Bunraku,* New York: Columbia University Press.

Kinoshita Junji. 1988. 'Yūzuru'. *In Kinoshita Junji-shū,* Etō Fumio, Sugai Yukio, Miyagishi Yasuharu, Fuwa Michiko (eds), Volume 1, 1–32. Tokyo: Iwanami Shoten.

Kominz, L. 1997. *The Stars Who Created Kabuki: Their Lives, Loves and Legacy.* New York: Kodansha International.

Leiter, S.L. 1979 . *The Art of Kabuki, Famous Plays in Performance.* Berkeley: University of California Press.

Leupp, G.P. 1995. *Male Colours, the Construction of Homosexuality in Tokugawa Japan.* Berkeley: University of California Press.

Marra, M. 1993. *Representations of Power, the Literary Politics of Medieval Japan.* Hawaii: University of Hawaii Press.

McLelland, M.J. 2000. *Male Homosexuality in Modern Japan, Cultural Myths and Social Realities*. Richmond: Curzon.

Ōzasa Yoshio. 1985a. *Nihon Gendai Engeki-shi, Meiji Taishō-hen*. Tokyo: Hakusui-sha.

Ōzasa Yoshio. 1985b. *Nihon Gendai Engeki-shi, Taishō Shōwa Shoki-hen*. Tokyo: Hakusui-sha.

Ōzasa Yoshio.1986. *Nihon Gendai Engeki-shi, Sengo-hen*. Tokyo: Hakusui-sha.

Pflugfelder, G.M. 1999. *Cartographies of Desire, Male-male Sexuality in Japanese Discourse, 1600–1950*. Berkeley: University of California Press.

Poulton, M.C. 2001. *Spirits of another Sort, the Plays of Izumi Kyōka*. Ann Arbor: The Centre for Japanese Studies, University of Michigan.

Powell, B. 1975. 'Matsui Sumako, Actress and Woman'. In *Modern Japan, Aspects of History, Literature and Society*, Beasley, W.G. (ed.). London: Allen and Unwin, 135–146.

Powell, B. 1998. 'One man's Hamlet in 1911 Japan: the Bungei Kyōkai Production in the Imperial Theatre'. In *Shakespeare and the Japanese Stage*, Sasayama Takashi, J.R. Mulryne and M. Shewring (eds). Cambridge: Cambridge University Press, 38–52.

Powell, B. 2002. *Japan's Modern Theatre, a Century of Continuity and Change*. London: Japan Library, Taylor and Francis (Routledge/Curzon).

Robertson, J. 1998. *Takarazuka, Sexual Politics and Popular Culture in Modern Japan*. Berkeley: University of California Press.

Tsubouchi Shōyō. 1911. 'Teikoku gekijō nite enzuru *Hamlet* ni tsuite', *Waseda Bungaku* LXVI (May 1911).

Yoshimi Shun'ya. 1995. 'The Evolution of Mass Events in Prewar Japan'. In *Japanese Civilization in the Modern World, XI, Amusement*, Umesao Tadao, B. Powell and Kumakura Isao (eds). *Senri Ethnological Studies no 40*, Senri: Kokuritsu Minzokugaku Hakubutsu-kan (National Museum of Ethnology), 85–99.

NOTES ON CONTRIBUTORS

Shirley Ardener is a Senior Associate of Queen Elizabeth House, the University of Oxford's International Development Centre. She was the Founding Director of the Centre for Cross-Cultural Research on Women, also known as the International Gender Studies Centre, whose programme was recognised by her OBE; she remains an active honorary member. She has edited and contributed to many books on gender, including Berg's series, and has worked and written in the field of Cameroon Studies

Marie-Bénédicte Dembour is a Senior Lecturer in the Sussex Law School at the University of Sussex. She is the author of *Recalling the Belgian Congo: Conversations and Interpretation* (Oxford: Berghahn 2000), co-editor of Culture and Rights: Anthropological Perspectives (Cambridge: Cambridge University Press 2001) and currently writing a monograph on the concept of human rights, its critiques and the European Convention.

Mark Johnson is a Senior Lecturer in Social Anthropology in the Department of Comparative and Applied Social Sciences, University of Hull. His publications include *Beauty and Power: transgendering and cultural transformation in the Southern Philippines* (Oxford: Berg 1997).

Roland Littlewood is Professor of Anthropology and Psychiatry at the University College Centre for Medical Anthropology, University College London. His many publications include *Aliens and Alienists: Ethnic Minorities and Psychiatry* (Penguin 1982), *Pathology and Identity* (Cambridge: Cambridge University Press 1993), *The Butterfly and the Serpent* (Free Associations Press 1998), Religion, Agency, Restitution (Oxford: C.U.P. 2002), *Pathologies of the West* (Compendium/Cornell 2003).

Fiona Moore is a Senior Lecturer at Kingston University, and a Research Associate of Queen Elizabeth House (IGS/CCCRW); previously, she was a Research Associate at the Said Business School, Oxford. She is an industrial anthropologist whose research interests include self-presentation and performance, gender and ethnic diversity in organisations, Anglo-German business ventures and the ethnography of multinational corporations. Her monograph *Transnational Busi-*

ness Cultures: Life and Work in a Multinational Corporation was published by Ashgate in 2004.

Brian Powell works on modern Japanese theatre and until 2004 was Lecturer in Japanese History at the University of Oxford. His publications include: *Kabuki in Modern Japan, Mayama Seika and his Plays* (1990) and *Japan's Modern Theatre: A Century of Change and Continuity* (2002).

Alison Shaw is a Senior Research Fellow at the University of Oxford, Department of Public Health. Her research interests include medical anthropology, South Asia, migration, ethnicity, kinship and social aspects of genetics. Her publications include *Kinship and Continuity: Pakistani families in Britain* (Harwood/Routledge 2000); *A Pakistani Community in Britain* (Oxford: Blackwell 1888) and *Get by in Hindi and Urdu* (1989 BBC Books).

Shaun Tougher is Lecturer in Ancient History in the Cardiff School of History and Archaeology at Cardiff University. He specialises in late Roman and Byzantine history, and has written several articles on subjects such as eunuchs, Julian the Apostate and Leo VI. He is the author of The Reign of Leo VI (886–912) (Brill, 1997) and the editor of *Eunuchs in Antiquity and Beyond* (Duckworth and The Classical Press of Wales, 2002). He is currently preparing a monograph on Byzantine eunuchs.

Antonia Young is an Honorary Research Fellow in South East European Studies at Bradford University (UK) and Research Associate at Colgate University in New York State. She has a long-term specialist interest in Albania. Her publications include *Women who become Men: Albanian Sworn Virgins* (Oxford: Berg 2000), and, as co-editor, *Black Lambs and Grey Falcons: women travellers in the Balkans* (2000).

INDEX